Emp. Lit.
7.50

9

THREE MEDIEVAL CENTURIES
OF LITERATURE IN ENGLAND
1100–1400

THREE MEDIEVAL CENTURIES OF LITERATURE IN ENGLAND
1100–1400

By
CHARLES SEARS BALDWIN

PHAETON PRESS
New York
1968

Originally Published 1932

Reprinted 1968

Library of Congress Catalog Card Number: 68-58890

Published by PHAETON PRESS

PREFACE

This book is written to guide and help those who wish to study the medieval literature of England for themselves. Such study, whether in a college course, or in a public library, or among a few books at home, is the only valid study of literature. To approach, explore, and ponder significant works is often an adventure and always an experience. Merely to learn the correct things to say about them is not only a barren substitute; it may be a hindrance in education. The aim of this book, then, is to lead into the English middle age, to indicate the most significant books and literary habits, to exhibit tried methods of study, and to suggest further experiences.

Materials for such study have increased so rapidly in our century that there is need of a compact guidebook. This is provided, first, by the order and arrangement of the text itself to emphasize the most significant works and trends; secondly, in the Appendix, by providing a concise and tested initiation into Middle English, the standard literary language of the fourteenth century, as it was used by Chaucer; thirdly, in a brief section of notes, by indicating useful editions and works of reference or appreciation and otherwise suggesting further study. The sign *n* indicates that a note will be found in this section bearing the page number of the text.

Since for an increasing majority of students linguistic is a means, not an end, the emphasis is on literary criticism; and this has been widened by suggestions from the other medieval fine arts. Both text and notes are included in a single index. Guidance to details of information is thus both made convenient for reference and kept from interrupting guidance in the course of literary history. Though Anglo-Saxon literature is surveyed briefly to show the earlier, epic habit, and the fifteenth century to conclude romance and contrast the ways of ballad and of medieval drama, the focus is on the high middle age, the twelfth, thirteenth, and fourteenth centuries.

The book supersedes my Introduction to English Medieval Literature, published in 1914 and now out of print. Though it contains, of course, many items in that work, and even some pages, it both omits and adds far more and recasts the whole treatment. It is not a revision; it is a new book. Medieval studies and the apparatus for pursuing them have increased so rapidly in the interim that I have readjusted my guide-book to the present situation and outlook.

C. S. B.

BARNARD COLLEGE
COLUMBIA UNIVERSITY
October, 1931

CONTENTS

	PREFACE	v
I	THE MIDDLE AGE	3
	1. *The Middle Age as a Period*	3
	2. *The Medieval Language and the Medieval Languages*	7
	3. *Other Approaches*	8
II	THE EPIC CENTURIES: ANGLO-SAXON LITERATURE	16
	1. *Beowulf*	18
	(a) EPIC HEROES	18
	(b) EPIC COMPOSITION	25
	(c) EPIC DICTION AND VERSE	29
	2. *Bede*	32
	3. *The Caedmonic Poems and Cynewulf*	42
	4. *The End of the Anglo-Saxon Period*	48
III	MEDIEVAL ROMANCE: LITERARY MOTIVES	51
	1. *The Spread of Romance*	60
	(a) GEOFFREY OF MONMOUTH'S HISTORY	66
	(b) CYCLES OF ROMANCE	69
	(c) THE GRAIL LEGEND	72

CONTENTS

IV MEDIEVAL ROMANCE: LITERARY FORMS   75
1. *Lay and Tale*   77
2. *Exemplum*   78
3. *Saint's Legend*   80
4. *Unified Short Story*   81
5. *Chrétien de Troyes*   83
6. *Anti-Romance*   88
   (a) BEAST TALE   89
   (b) FABLIAU   91

V MIDDLE-ENGLISH ROMANCES, DISTINCTIVE AND CONVENTIONAL   92
1. *Popularized Romances*   94
   (a) KING HORN   94
   (b) HAVELOK THE DANE   98
   (c) SIR TRISTREM   106
   (d) SIR PERCEVAL OF GALLES   107
2. *Conventional Romances*   108
   (a) LIBEAUS DESCONUS   108
   (b) SIR BEVIS OF HAMPTON   109
   (c) GUY OF WARWICK   112
3. *Romancing of Recent History*   113

VI MIDDLE-ENGLISH ARTHURIAN ROMANCES   118
1. *The Stanzaic Morte d'Arthur*   118
2. *The Alliterative Morte Arthure*   121
3. *Gawain and the Green Knight*   127
4. *Malory's Morte d'Arthur*   133

CONTENTS ix

| VII | MEDIEVAL LYRIC | 142 |

VIII	MEDIEVAL SYMBOLISM	157
	1. *Moral Allegory, Piers Plowman*	158
	2. *Mystical Allegory, Pearl*	170
	3. *Symbolism as a Medieval Habit*	173

IX	MIDDLE-ENGLISH POPULAR COMPOSITION	177
	1. *Ballads*	177
	2. *Miracle Plays*	188
	3. *Prose*	195

X	CHAUCER	203
	1. *Biography*	203
	2. *Development of Verse Narrative*	207
	3. *Troilus and Criseyde*	215
	4. *The Scheme of the Canterbury Tales*	219
	(a) GOWER'S CONFESSIO AMANTIS	220
	(b) THE DECAMERON	221
	(c) THE SEVEN SAGES	222
	(d) CHAUCER'S PILGRIMAGE SETTING	224

APPENDIX: INTRODUCTION TO MIDDLE-ENGLISH GRAMMAR   227

NOTES   245

INDEX   269

THREE MEDIEVAL CENTURIES
OF LITERATURE IN ENGLAND
1100–1400

CHAPTER I

THE MIDDLE AGE

1. *The Middle Age as a Period*

THE term *middle ages* or, as other languages say, *middle age* has been in common use so long that it has lost its strangeness. Otherwise *middle* would imply a period between, an age without marked character of its own. So, perhaps, it was originally meant. Critics of the sixteenth[n] and seventeenth centuries, sure that the highest literary ideals were embodied in classical antiquity, and that these had been recovered and renewed by their own time, impatiently passed over the centuries between as merely middle. This scornful attitude, common in the eighteenth century, lingered into the nineteenth. Today the occasional use of *medieval* or *middle age* in such disparagement is a sign of ignorance. No scholar would risk his reputation by slurring the middle age. Study first of the other medieval arts, then of medieval literature, then of political and social history, has meanwhile been so active that the middle age has been widely recovered. Thus it can be viewed both largely in its significances for the course of history, and intensively in those characteristic habits of thought and life which make it evidently a distinct period.

What were the habits of conception and of action that gave the middle age characteristic coherence throughout western Europe? The most conspicuous medieval artistic achievement is Gothic architecture, a structural system meeting in beautiful forms the medieval demand for light in great churches, and for height. But this system of thrusts and counter-thrusts, with its soaring towers and roofs and its wide windows of colored story, was not pervasive. Italy cultivated it little. England, adopting it late and not always consistently, turned it rather to picturesqueness. Gothic in its great thirteenth century and in its architectural harmony is French. The art that preoccupied all western Europe throughout the middle age is narrative, especially verse romance. Narrative was the pervasive medieval art.

The ancient habit of statute law, widely learned in Italy and in France, gained less hold in the north. The rising Germanic peoples were tenacious of their own habits of customary law. England conspicuously depended on that body of traditions still known as common law. The Roman Law, then, though it was indeed a bond, was limited geographically. More widespread was the habit of feudalism, a system of tenure binding each man to his overlord. In political theory this centered in the king. Socially it fostered the virtue of loyalty. The English word *truth* in the middle age usually meant loyalty. But here again the binding force was limited by the fact that feudalism in practical operation was local. Nations in the modern sense being not yet born, feudalism was not politically sufficient to draw the western world together. It is, indeed, medieval historically. The middle age developed it and died with it. But it did not achieve a large reach of unity.

The great medieval social bond was the Church. The Church was pervasive as an institution and unifying as the single cult. Men and women of the middle age, whether Germans, Spaniards, or English, had common religious habits. Differing as individuals and as peoples, they yet had everywhere a common fund of observance, of thought, and of imagery. What that meant for social unity must be imagined by contrast with modern diversity. What it meant for artistic unity appears in the pervasive habit of symbolism. The sculptured porch of Bourges is French only in detail, as the *Divina Commedia* is Italian. Both are essentially medieval. So we may confidently speak of medieval literature as we cannot speak of modern literature, because in their most fundamental concerns and their highest aspirations men had ideas and images in common. The greater artists in stone, in glass, in verse, revealed new aspects, stimulated to more vivid realization; but they relied on communal emotions. The formulation of the corresponding conceptions in a system of thought was centered in theology. The view and the method of the characteristic medieval philosophy, scholasticism, received final form in the *Summa Theologica* of St. Thomas Aquinas. The Church gave the middle age a common outlook on life.

Most directly operative to this end was the Church as the center of education. Throughout the English middle age the word *clerk*, which of course originally meant cleric, meant any man of education. The missionaries of education in its widest sense, especially during the eighth, ninth, and tenth centuries, had been the monks. Burgundy, for example, may without much exaggeration be said to have been civilized by its monasteries. Through the following centuries the monasteries were centers not only of ordinary schooling, but of publishing, of illumination, and often of verse, sculpture, architecture, or painting[n]; and cathedral schools increased their range. The medium of all learning was Latin. Every student, therefore, much more every man of letters or science, commanded at least two languages: his native English, Norman, or Tuscan, and Latin. The survival in Paris of the name "Latin Quarter" recalls the thirteenth-century community of students at the University. Though housed sometimes by "nations", they heard in lectures and used in disputations the international language. Latin was not a field to be cultivated in certain courses or for a certain number of years. Often the medium of literature, it was always the tool of a lifetime. Since every educated man thus had it at least for his second language, if not for his main medium of expression, medieval Latin was a living language. The Renaissance, trying to recall its ancient usage, confined it to specialists. Even so it was not a "dead language" till long after the vernaculars had won first literary place. Throughout the middle age it was vividly alive.

2. *The Medieval Language and the Medieval Languages*

Wide and precise study, then, of any medieval literature demands at least two languages: the pervasive Latin, and the vernacular English or French or German. Medieval Latin is not so different from classical Latin as to impose special study at the outset. Any one who can really read classical Latin can begin it at once, and by systematic attention can build up increasing command.[n] The labor is worth while. Not only text-books, treatises, and histories were written in Latin throughout the middle age and throughout the western world, but also poems and stories. No medieval lyrics are more interesting or more important than the Latin hymns. But though every student of the middle age should thus use whatever Latin he commands, no reading of Latin texts is presupposed in this volume.

Anglo-Saxon,[n] the vernacular of England during the centuries before the Norman Conquest, though very useful to the study of English literature in the centuries following, is not prerequisite. But Middle English, a literary language in the thirteenth century and the language of Chaucer in the fourteenth, should be the first field of study. It should not be reserved to the few whose interest is linguistic. Those many others whose immediate interest is literary can begin to read Middle English at once, and gain a fair command quickly, by using the initiation provided in the Appendix. Certain earlier Middle English texts, of the period before the language was fully recognized as literary, are quoted either in translation or with footnote glossaries. Middle English spelling is so variable that reading aloud, which is always the better way of reading poetry, is useful here even for language.

Translation can give so much to the study of any literature that it is used freely throughout this volume. It shows the whole sequence of a history, a drama, even a story. Where it often falls short, or deviates, is in rendering the style. Though even style can be communicated by translation at its best, it should be pursued as often as possible in the original. To read Walter Map's Latin stories in translation will suffice for readers concerned not with his style, but with his material; and such readers are the great majority. To read the hymn *Dies irae* in translation, though some of the versions are highly literary, is to miss the best use of one's knowledge of Latin. To read Chaucer in modern versions is not only to be absurdly timid; it is to miss the flexible verse and the suggestive diction of one of the greatest English poets. Though a survey of English medieval literature may profit by translations, no student can begin it more surely than by spending a few weeks on the language of its great period.

3. *Other Approaches*

No less important than the approach to literature through language is the study of literary form, of the plan and movement of a story, of its artistic shaping, or composition. No other approach is more directly and rapidly instructive. It not only fixes a work in memory; it shows on the one hand the habit and convention of the time, on the other the progress and achievement of the individual artist. Generally the surest guide to literary history, it is the more widely available here because the successive forms of many medieval stories invite comparison.

Biography of authors, a common approach today, is in the middle age restricted. Much of medieval literature is even anonymous; of much more the authorship is uncertain. Who wrote *Pearl?* Thomas of Celano probably wrote *Dies irae.* Adam of St. Victor wrote great hymns — *which* hymns we are not always sure. Even where he is known, a medieval author rarely has what we now call a biography. Walter Map was Archdeacon of Hereford in the late twelfth century. More may be pieced out, in his case and in others, from the history of the time, but not often much of literary significance. We are left guessing even for greater authors: Chrétien de Troyes, Snorri Sturlasson, Chaucer, even Dante. Of Chaucer's life we know principally what he did when he was not writing. The middle age was not curious about the lives of poets. After all, the dearth of recorded event may be no more serious a hindrance than our present superabundance of news. A poet, medieval or modern, is learned far better through his reading. That is often mentioned by medieval authors; and we know fairly well their common medieval literary fund. Seeing thus how the art of Vergil furthered the art of Dante, or how Boccaccio was absorbed and transmuted by Chaucer, we supplement biography by literary history.

The books usually available to a medieval author were few. The change wrought in this respect by the printing press is too great to be realized without an effort of imagination. In the middle age a book was a precious possession. Chaucer expresses his Clerk's devotion to learning by saying:

> For him was lever have at his beddes heed
> Twenty bokes, clad in blak or reed,
> Of Aristotle and his philosophye
> Than robes riche, or fithele, or gay sautrye.
> Prologue to the Canterbury Tales,
> 293–296.

In our time to say that a student had rather have twenty books than their value in clothes or musical instruments does not suggest extraordinary expenditure on either; but in Chaucer's time twenty books were a considerable collection, such as would not often be seen outside of the monastic and cathedral libraries. Richard de Bury, Bishop of Durham, author of the *Philobiblon*[n] (i.e., *Booklover*, 1344), had probably the largest private collection of this time. "He collected," says Adam Murimuth, "an infinite number of books, as well through gifts as through exchange of favors with various monasteries and through purchase." And the bishop himself devotes a chapter to enlarging upon his unusual opportunities for collecting, through his offices at court, his embassies to Rome and to Paris, his learned friends, the traveling friars, and finally through his own staff of "binders, correctors, illuminators, and generally of all who could usefully labor in the service of books."[n] Yet this "infinite number" of books was somewhat more than five cartloads,[n] hardly enough to be called a large private library today. Nor were even the libraries of cathedrals and monasteries either large or accessible according to our modern habits. Adding to the situation the slowness and difficulty of travel, one begins to realize that in the middle age wide reading was easy in only a few centers, and that even in these a man must sometimes have studied not so much what he wanted as what he could get. The medieval formula of citation is "my author says", or "the book says."

Thus compends, or digests of knowledge, such as Florus's epitome of Roman history, or Orosius's of universal history, were used widely. *Cursor Mundi*,[n] a huge fourteenth-century English compend, versified history for English readers in seven divisions: (1) from the Creation to Noah, (2) from the Flood to the Confusion of Tongues, (3) from Abraham to the death of Saul, (4) from David to the Captivity, (5) from the Parentage of the Virgin to the Baptist, (6) from the Baptism of Christ to the "Invention" of the Cross, (7) Doomsday and after. Some of the sources of this compend are themselves compends, especially the *Historia Scholastica* of Petrus Comestor (twelfth century). The fourteenth-century *Polychronicon*[n] of Ralph Higden wove with sacred history secular history, even some geography, and brought all down to the writer's own time. The most ambitious of the medieval compends was the *Speculum Majus sive Bibliotheca Mundi* of Vincent of Beauvais [n] (thirteenth century), "The Greater Mirror, or Library of the World." It is divided into: I. *Speculum Naturale*, The Mirror of Nature; II. *Doctrinale*, of Teaching; III. *Historiale*, of History. A cyclopedia in scope, this vast digest is in method rather more like what is now called a survey. Limitations on individual study and reference were largely offset by the coöperation within communities, both monasteries and universities. Not only did the middle age establish universities, developing an organization of studies that lasted into modern times; it also thus provided habitual interchange of knowledge and of ideas.

Of the Latin classics the most widely current, perhaps, was Ovid. Vergil, though studied in school and universally admired, was sometimes used at second hand. Livy and Tacitus were less known than Lucan and Statius; the greater works of Cicero than his youthful rhetoric *De inventione* and the *Somnium Scipionis*, a part of his *De republica* commented by the fifth-century grammarian Macrobius. The late-Latin Ausonius, Claudian, and Sidonius received more attention than is approved by their modern fame; but one of the widest of medieval influences spread from an even later author, whose greatness is now clearer than ever, Boethius.[n]

Philosopher and poet in the classical tradition,

Boethius also mediated to the middle age much of what it knew of Aristotle. Though something was added through Latin versions of texts preserved among the Arabs of Spain, the translations and interpretations of Boethius were a main medium for the general dominance of Aristotle over medieval thought. Plato was known far less, in Latin translations of a few works and indirectly through philosophies derived from his. Instead of Homer's *Iliad* and *Odyssey*, medieval readers had the barren histories of Troy compiled under the names of Dares and Dictys. The great Greek historians and dramatists could be read only by a rare scholar here and there. Through most of the middle age there was no general knowledge of Greek.

The copying of books by hand made an author dependent on scribes. Chaucer addresses a humorous protest to his *scriveyn*.

> Adam scriveyn, if ever it thee bifalle
> Boece or Troilus to wryten newe,
> Under thy lokkes thou most have the scalle,
> But after my making thou wryte trewe.
> So ofte a daye I mot thy werke renewe,
> Hit to correcte and eek to rubbe and scrape;
> And al is through thy negligence and rape.

Not only the original scribe might be inaccurate, but any of the successive scribes. Thus books that circulated in many copies show variations of text, many of them accidental, some of them due to glosses first written by way of caption or explanation and afterward drawn into the text. One of the essential tasks of scholarship is the restoration of original texts by the comparison of various manuscripts.

The social history of the middle age, though it has gained more from literature than it has given to literary history, has nevertheless enabled us better to understand and to imagine the environment not only of an author, but of his audience. So are brightened for us the Irish or Norse hero tales, the courtly love of Erec or Troilus. Two cardinal instances of this value are: (1) pilgrimages, as furnishing the actual audiences of the *chansons de geste* [n] and the dramatic setting of the *Canterbury Tales;* and (2) guilds, as the practical promoters of the miracle plays. Not only social habits, but sculpture, the illumination of manuscripts, the storied glass of church windows — in a word, other forms of art, may supplement study of literary forms.

The most remote approach to literature in any period is from political history. Nevertheless a modern reader needs to understand both the scheme of feudalism and the habitual interrelations of Church and State. The great medieval example of an author who was also a statesman is John of Salisbury, secretary to two archbishops of Canterbury, well known at Rome, and in his last years Bishop of Chartres. His marvelous letters cannot be understood without some knowledge of the Roman Curia and of the policy of Henry II in the bitter struggle between Church and State. But though these letters, with some others of the age when ceremonious letter-writing was a fine art,[n] are highly literary, they are hardly necessary to our grasp of medieval literature. Their eminence is special, much as is that of the written opinions of Chief Justice Marshall in our own country. John of Salisbury was, indeed, an Englishman; but his contribution was rather to medieval thought than to English literature. The widest bearing, perhaps, of politics on literature was in the union of England with an increasingly large part of France, and in that subsequent separation which gave higher vogue to English as a literary language.

The relative importance of these approaches, (1) language, style, and verse, (2) literary form and progress, (3) biography and social habits, (4) political habits, varies not only from author to author, but from student to student. No one can study literature well without studying it for himself. Whatever excites his special attention thereby invites all four approaches. But the first two, as the most important for all students, are most used in this volume.

CHAPTER II

THE EPIC CENTURIES:
ANGLO-SAXON LITERATURE

MEDIEVAL literature is largely story. Drama was in abeyance until it began afresh in mystery and miracle plays. Lyric, as in other ages, expressed less the character of the time than the emotions of every time. The typical poetry of the middle age is narrative; and so is much of its prose. History was usually conceived and composed as story. Even preaching made more use than has been common since of illustrative anecdote and narrative method.[n] Most of the great legendary stories of Europe are medieval: Tristram and Iseult, the fated lovers; Roland, gallant unto death; Arthur and his Round Table; Galahad, pure to behold the Grail. Heroes of ancient Troy, reappearing in medieval guise, performed new feats; and Alexander the Great passed from history into romance. As Vergil had shaped old legends to the glory of his Rome, so medieval story-tellers sought to glorify their own new peoples. Charlemagne, Frankish king of a new Rome, was celebrated with his paladins in stories of patriotic pride and aspiration. Meantime heroes of elder days had been sung in Germanic epic. The

THE EPIC CENTURIES 17

tales of the Nibelungs and Volsungs, as the epics of Greece, preserve an older mythology. Many even of the later medieval stories are legendary; they keep echoes of folklore, wonder, and a certain youthful zest for adventure. The Celtic legends of Arthur, spreading over Britain and Brittany into Italy and Spain, grew into a great cycle.

But there is a clear difference between the stories of the earlier and those of the later middle age. New habits of story-telling emerge in the twelfth century. The general characteristics of earlier medieval stories may be summed up in the word *epic*, those of the later stories in the word *romance;* and the imaginary line between them may be drawn about 1100. The history of English literature divides thus sharply at the Norman Conquest in 1066. The Anglo-Saxon period is the epic period. Elsewhere the chronological separation is less definite. The Norse in the seclusion of Iceland kept an epic habit in their sagas[n] long after other peoples had turned to romance. On the contrary, the French *chansons de geste*[n] won literary vogue only after romance had already made headway. Nevertheless, in a broad view of medieval literature as a whole, the earlier habit is epic; the later, romance.

Medieval epic is called primary because it is more like the *Iliad* than like the *Aeneid*. In primary epic an unknown poet has made a continuous story out of evidently older hero-stories, which may have been sung separately, and which he has been more careful to follow than to fuse. In secondary epic, on the other hand, a very well-known poet, using old stories indeed, has shaped them according to his own ideas into a well-rounded artistic whole. For the history of literature primary epic is full of significance as the earliest art of extended poetic narrative.

1. *Beowulf*[n]

(a) Epic Heroes

The Anglo-Saxon *Beowulf*, the longest Germanic epic (3183 lines) and the earliest extended vernacular poem of the middle age, shows most amply the northern poetic spirit, scope, and method. "We have heard," it begins, "the glory of the Spear-Danes' folk-kings in days of yore." Thus it takes us back of English history, back of England itself, to lands where the English folk was bred from Germanic stock. Its prelude echoes a yet older tradition, the burial of Scyld, founder of the Danish house, in the great deep.

> Then departed Scyld at his appointed hour,
> Glorious to go unto God's keeping.
> Together they bore him to breaking surges,
> Bosom companions, as he bade himself
> While he wielded words, warden of Scyldings,
> Loved land-ruler, long their master.
> At the roadstead bode his ringéd bow,
> Icy, eager, atheling's ship.
> They laid him there, beloved chieftain,
> Bringer of booty, on the breast of the ship,
> Mighty by the mast. There were many treasures
> From long voyages laden beside him.

> Ne'er heard I that comelier keel provided
> Hacking weapons and harness warlike,
> Brands and byrnies. On his bosom lay
> Store unstinted that must start with him
> On the flood's realm to float outward.
> Nowise did they leave him less riches,
> Tribal treasures, than those gave him
> Who at his first hour forth sent him
> Alone over ocean, only a baby.
> Yet more, they set him a standard golden
> Above his body, let the brine take him,
> Had him to high sea. There was heavy spirit,
> Mourning their mood. No man is able,
> Hero under heaven, hall-counsellor,
> To say in sooth who received that burden.
> *Beowulf*, 26–52.[n]

As Scyld was a seafarer in death, so are his epic descendants in life; and so were the preservers of his story, those Anglo-Saxons who beached their prows on Roman Britain and made it England. With them they brought their Germanic hero-songs; and in England, early in the eighth century, some of these were used in the *Beowulf*. Hrothgar's famous hall Heorot, it tells, was nightly devastated by a monster from the fens, one Grendel. Beowulf, a thane of the chieftain Hygelac, brought his band over sea, killed Grendel in single combat, and afterwards despatched Grendel's avenging mother. Returning home laden with gifts, he became a great chieftain in his own land, and finally died, at a ripe age, from a fight with a third monster. All this is told with epic vividness of detail.

> Straightway they went. The warship waited still;
> Bode near the beach the broad-stretched bark,
> Safe at anchor. Shone the boar-images
> Over their cheek-guards, chiseled in gold;
> Fair and fire-hard, fended them from foes.
> Warlike went they; warriors, they hasted,
> Kept their company till they might catch glimpses
> Of the royal roof-tree all rich with gilding.
> . . . .
> Shone with stones the street leading them,
> Good men together. Glittered their mail;
> Hard, hand-woven hammered rings
> Sang in the steel as they strode to Heorot.
>
> (301–323.)

After formal announcement Beowulf speaks for himself with straightforward epic brag: "Thou Hrothgar, hail! I am Hygelac's friend and follower. I have won many praises in battle from boyhood. . . . There (in my own land) five I bound, caught the kin of giants, and killed in the water nickers by night. . . . I have also remembered that (your) monster (Grendel) in his recklessness cares not for weapons. I therefore scorn . . . to bear sword or broad shield, yellow-rimmed, to the fight; but with my grip I will grapple with the fiend and fight for life, foe with foe" (407–440). Every hero of early epic says: "Each of us all must abide the end of earthly life. Win he who may fame ere he fall" (1386). And Ulysses might have said as naturally as Beowulf: "Far countries are seemliest sought by a man sure of himself" (1838). But "win he who may fame ere he fall" meant in Germanic thought that since every one's death-day was foredoomed, and could be neither hastened nor retarded, a man's part was to fear nothing. The goddess of fate would take him neither sooner nor later. "Ever goes Wyrd as she must." Therefore, said the Germanic hero, I will never shun death, but fill my lifetime with manful deeds in the face of danger. Otherwise he neither hoped nor wished for long life. The joy of old age was that of Beowulf before his last fight: "Many are the battles I abode in my youth, hours of fighting; I have all in mind" (2426).

The epic hero was always, of course, a strong man, a fighter with his own two hands; but with his "might" he had "mood", and, besides courage, his people wished in him skill and foresight. His rashness was not recklessness. A shrewd man of his time, he was glad both of the fight itself and of its gains. He fought generously, without base greed; but then afterwards he rejoiced in winning both the victory and the treasure. Quite simply Beowulf, after despatching Grendel, "trod the turf, of his treasure proud, glad of his gettings" (1880). Though fighting was good sport for itself, and the greater the danger the greater the glory, still the epic hero fought also for other gain. He sought something more reasonable than adventure for its own sake. He liked also to carry off booty or to win rewards.

So the epic lord is "the defence of heroes." Giving shelter in his hall, and good cheer, he gives also good gifts. His virtues are hospitality and liberality.

See Hrothgar in his hall after Beowulf's victory over the monster Grendel:

> Then was time and hour
> That to hall should go Healfdene's son;
> Himself the king would sit at meat.
> Never heard I that a greater host of people
> Around their prize-giver proudly gathered.
> Bent them to benches blithe followers,
> Fain of the feasting. Fairly uplifted
> Beakers of beer their brothers mighty,
> Drank hail to them deep in the hall,
> Hrothgar and Hrothulf. Heorot within was
> Filled with friends. Any foulness then
> The Scylding people scorned to perpetrate.
> Then the son of Healfdene handed to Beowulf
> A golden standard, guerdon of his victory,
> Hand-wrought hilted banner, helm and byrnie.
> From the hoard a huge sword beheld full many
> Before him borne at bidding. Beowulf drank
> A flagon before them. Never with these fee-gifts
> Among warriors need he wince for shame.
> Never found I friendlier four treasures,
> Garnished with gold, given by heroes
> On the ale-bench over to others.
> A wreath around the roof of the helmet,
> Wound with wires, its ward held outward;
> So that filéd weapon might find it doughty,
> Shock-hard sword, when the shield-bearer
> Before foes must fare to battle.
> Had then the earl's hope eight horses,
> Bridled with gold, brought to hall
> Within the barriers. On one was set
> A saddle sewn with gems, splendid with trappings.

It was fighting-seat fit for the king,
When the sport of the sword the son of Healfdene
Longed to enjoy. Never lagged at the onset
His far-famed force when fell the chosen.
And then to Beowulf both the twain
The lord of the Ingwines delivered in full,
Horses and harness; bade him hold them well.
So, manlike, the mighty chieftain,
Hoard-ward, heroes' hardships well repaid
With steeds and store, so that still he is praised
By whoever will say the sooth aright.
                                        (1008–1049.)

After the song is sung, Wealhtheow, the queen, bears a cup to her lord, and then to Beowulf:

A cup was borne to him, and friendly greeting offered, and twisted gold graciously presented him: two armlets, rings, and armor, and the goodliest of collars I have ever heard of upon earth. Never heard I of a fairer among the treasured jewels of heroes beneath the sky, ne'er since Hama bore away to the bright city the collar of the Brisings, the fair gem and its casket; he fled the cunning snares of Eormanric, and chose everlasting gain. This ring had Hygelac, grandson of Swerting, on his last raid, when 'neath his banner, he defended his treasure and guarded the plunder of battle. Wyrd took him away, when he, foolhardy, suffered woe in feud with the Frisians; for that mighty chieftain bore the jewel with its precious stones over the arching sea; and he fell beneath his shield. Then the body of the king came into the possession of the Franks, his breast-mail, and the jewel, too; meaner warriors stripped the body after the slaughter of battle; the corpses of the Geats were strewed upon the field.

The hall resounded. Wealhtheow spoke before the host

and said: "Receive with joy this collar, dear Beowulf, beloved youth, and use this armour, — treasures of our people, — and prosper well."

(1192–1218.)[n]

These gifts are not mere hire. The value of saddle or collar is not merely its use, nor its weight in gold, but its beauty and its history. As the history of the shield of Achilles or the staff of Agamemnon was sung in the *Iliad*, so the sword of Waldere or this collar of the Brisings and Wiglaf's "old giant sword that Onela gave him" (2616). When Beowulf himself came to die, "the great-hearted king took from his neck the ring of gold, gave to his thane, the youthful warrior, his helmet gold-adorned, his ring and his byrnie, bade him enjoy them well" (2809–2812). The simple relation of lord and thane was recognized on the one hand in rewards, on the other hand in loyalty. "So ought a youth," adds the prologue, "to win favor by giving gifts unto his father's friends, that afterwards willing companions may attend him in his age, and the people serve him in time of war."

Beowulf ennobles fighting without making it unreal. True, the epic praise and boast tend to make of the hero a demigod. Beowulf, as Achilles, has more than the might of a man, and his victory is over a mythical monster; but he wins by his hand-grip. So in general epic fighting sounds real; and the fighters appeal even to modern readers as men of flesh and blood. They are in touch with actual material things: good tools, good craft, good meat and drink. They not only strive mightily, but also eat and drink, laugh and cry, as friends. With their common steadfastness, boasting, and revenge they show some individuality. They are ideal to their people as representative individuals.

The outlook upon nature is northern. The sound of the sea, which echoes throughout English poetry, is heard here again and again. But though there is close knowledge of the sea, admiration, and a fierce joy in daunting it, there is no other fondness. Anglo-Saxons loved the sea only as they loved a strong foe; it was dark, cold, forbidding. So, indeed, seems all their world, a place to fight in and to fight against. Merriment and all comfort were withindoors, in the hall. Without were trouble and struggle. The *Iliad*, knowing a warmer sea and a kinder, brighter world, is full of sunlight and the joy of the earth. In its first book Greeks, pulling up their boats, even feast and sleep upon the strand. Anglo-Saxons made straight for the hall.

(b) Epic Composition

The *Beowulf* shows Hrothgar's gleeman awakening joy in hall along the mead-bench by songs of heroes, and inserts here and there several of these songs. The one about Finn[n] we know in another version. After pausing to give the gleeman's, the *Beowulf* resumes its own tale. The likeness between such passages and a famous scene in the *Odyssey* suggests how primary epic used legendary material.

But after they had put from them the desire of meat and drink, the muse stirred the minstrel to sing the songs of famous men, even that lay whereof the fame had then reached the wide heaven, namely, the quarrel between Odysseus and Achilles, son of Peleus. . . .

Then Odysseus of many counsels spake to Demodocus, saying:

Demodocus, I praise thee far above all mortal men, whether it be the Muse, the daughter of Zeus, that taught thee, or even Apollo, for right duly dost thou chant the faring of the Achæans, even all that they wrought and suffered, and all their travail, as if, methinks, thou hadst been present, or heard the tale from another. Come now, change thy strain, and sing of the fashioning of the horse of wood, which Epeius made by the aid of Athene, even the guileful thing that goodly Odysseus led up into the citadel, when he had laden it with the men who wasted Ilios. If thou wilt indeed rehearse me this aright, so will I be thy witness among all men, how the god of his grace hath given thee the gift of wondrous song.

So spake he, and the minstrel, being stirred by the god, began and showed forth his minstrelsy. He took up the tale where it tells how the Argives of the one part set fire to their huts, and went aboard their decked ships and sailed away, while those others, the fellowship of renowned Odysseus, were now seated in the assembly-place of the Trojans, all hidden in the horse, for the Trojans themselves had dragged him to the citadel. . . . And he sang how the sons of the Achæans poured forth from the horse, and left the hollow lair, and sacked the burg. And he sang how and where each man wasted the town, and of Odysseus, how he went like Ares to the house of Deiphobus with godlike Menelaus. It was there, he said, that Odysseus adventured the most grievous battle, and in the end prevailed, by grace of great-hearted Athene.

This was the song that the famous minstrel sang.

Odyssey viii, 62–75 and 486–521, Butcher and Lang's prose translation.

Of the heroes thus sung by the Greek minstrel, one is present before him; and the song is adapted to him. So an epic poet weaves legends familiar to his audience into his own story. The *Beowulf* also brings in that hero of most Germanic peoples, Sigmund. The legend of his dragon-killing is adapted to the festivities celebrating Beowulf's killing of Grendel.

At times one of the King's thanes, whose memory was full of songs laden with vaunting rhymes, who knew old tales without number, invented a new story closely bound up with fact. The man deftly narrated the adventure of Beowulf, and cunningly composed other skilful lays with interwoven words.   (867–874.)

After thus telling the Sigmund story, the poet adds a contrast.

Beowulf . . . was more gracious to all the children of men and to his friends. Sorrow befell Heremod.

In some such way as he imagines the adaptation of an old Sigmund story to his hero, the poet of the *Beowulf* may be thought of as recalling old Beowulf stories in his epic.

In another way epic poetry carries out the spirit of earlier popular song. The earliest poems were chanted before they were written and after. Some of them, doubtless, were never written at all. The minstrel in the hall of Hrothgar, or in the hall of Homer's Alcinous, hardly had a manuscript. He chanted the songs that he had learned by ear and knew by heart. The legend of Homer as a blind singer, whatever may have been the facts about the unknown actual Homer, suggests the older habit. Epic poetry keeps this trait of its source and inspiration, that it was composed not to be merely read, but to be heard.

So long as it remains merely oral, narrative is fluid. An old hero-song like that of Sigmund may be found still in several different forms. It was sung as Hrothgar's gleeman sang it; and in the singing it might be adapted to some like deed of might. When an epic poet carried it out for itself, as in the *Beowulf*, achieved some artistic sequence, and committed it to writing, it tended to become fixed in that form. Thus primary epic preserves hero poetry in forms fixed by writing and single by their predominant merit of composition. The form in which each has come down to us is the work of a single poet. But reading it in print as we read modern poems, we need to remember that an epic poet, less a writer for himself than a modern poet, was more the spokesman of a people.

The unknown poet who thus wrote the *Beowulf* had less shaping skill than the poet of the *Iliad*. Greek epic art is larger and more sustained. In mere bulk the *Beowulf* is only about one fifth of the *Iliad;* and it lacks Homer's orderly development of parts in one large plan. The *Beowulf* seems less transformed than the *Iliad* from the older songs. But in all this it is superior to the other Germanic epics. For

Germanic skill in composing a large whole we must await the Old Norse prose sagas.

(c) Epic Diction and Verse

Groping sometimes in the composition of the story, the art of the Beowulf is sure in style and verse. To begin with what it has in common with all other epic, it is vividly concrete. "The street was stone-set. Glittered their mail. Hard, hand-locked, the hammered rings sang in the steel." When Beowulf seizes Grendel, we see him in action. "Uplong he stood and gripped him fast. His fingers cracked." So Homer describes the blinding of Polyphemus.

"When that bar of olive wood was just about to catch fire in the flame, green though it was, and began to glow terribly . . . they thrust it into his eye, while I from my place aloft turned it about, as when a man bores a ship's beam with a drill while his fellows below spin it with a strap."

Odyssey ix, 378, Butcher and Lang's translation.

Compare with any passage of the *Beowulf* this typical selection from the *Anglo-Saxon Chronicle*.[n]

An. DCCCXXXVII. In this year the alderman Wulfheard fought at Southampton against the crews of thirty-three ships, and there made great slaughter, and gained the victory. And in the same year Wulfheard died. And in the same year the alderman Aethelhelm fought against a Danish army at Port with the Dorset men, and for a good while put the army to flight; but the Danes held possession of the battle place, and slew the alderman.

Anglo-Saxon Chronicle, translated by Benjamin Thorpe, Rolls Series, volume ii, page 55.

This is the barest of prose. Poetry begins wherever words of sensation — of sound, movement, smell, light, color — are used to call up images.

Even in this common epic habit of concreteness there are differences of race. Where Greek poets or Anglo-Saxon give the details of light and shade, the gleam of sun on water or armor, the shadows of the hills, Celtic and Latin poets give also details of color. The Irish and Welsh bards call a thing specifically red or blue or purple; the Greeks and Anglo-Saxons of the epic time use color terms more rarely and more vaguely. In another way Anglo-Saxon epic diction differs from Greek. The *Beowulf* is often satisfied with specific mention of details, or with such simple descriptive compounds as *gannet's bath* for the sea; but the *Odyssey* carries out an image by comparisons like that of the shipwright in the quotation above. Greek epic is full of such similes, and some of them are carried out to great length. Similes are a regular poetic method with the Greeks and Latins. Anglo-Saxon epic has hardly anything of the sort. This one habit accounts for much of the descriptive amplitude of Greek epic, and dilates some later imitations in Latin and in Italian. The absence of it leaves Anglo-Saxon epic no less strong, indeed, but comparatively bare. Instead of supplying the hearer's imagination fully, the *Beowulf* suggests by a few sharp nouns and verbs. More direct, more reserved, it is sometimes abrupt. It leaves more to the hearer.

Anglo-Saxon epic verse has short lines composed

in two parts, called staves. What binds the two staves into one line is alliteration, that iteration of an initial letter which is seen in all the older Germanic poetry. Any vowel may alliterate with any other; but usually the alliteration is upon a single consonant. Instead of a correspondence in end-sounds, as in rime, there is correspondence at the beginnings, a kind of initial rime. Initial letters of stressed syllables in the first stave point to the same initial in a stressed syllable of the second. Used by later poets as an addition, a reinforcement of the verse pattern, alliteration is in epic the main correspondence, the pattern itself. Anglo-Saxon verse, being Germanic, is accentual, a pattern of stresses, or beats. Like medieval Latin verse in this, it is freer with the number of syllables. Any stave may begin either with a stressed or with an unstressed syllable, with two unstressed syllables, or in rare cases even with three. The rhythm is thought of as beginning with the first stress. Within the line also there might be either one unstressed syllable or two between beats. This traditional freedom of variation distinguishes modern English verse from modern French. The rhythm does not depend on the number of syllables. Again, the sense, instead of concluding with the line, often runs on into the next, concluding there with the first stave. Such run-on lines have been freely used in English poetry to save the verse from monotony. The rhythm of Anglo-Saxon verse is none the less regular. The pattern was kept by the fixed number of stresses, and the staves were combined in types clearly marked and strictly observed; but the regularity did not preclude variety in the number of unstressed syllables and in the adaptation of the sentence to the rhythm. These are the traditional English ways of freedom within the rhythmical pattern.

The narrative sentences of epic are not called upon to express nice relations of thought; nor has Anglo-Saxon developed the syntax of subordination. *Hrothgar's hall was so famous that its light shone over many lands.* The epic poet put that into three simple sentences. "That was foremost for folk of earth / of houses under heaven. In it Hrothgar bode. / Lightened its light over lands full many" (309–311). The sentences of Homer are in much the same way simpler and looser than those of later Greek poets. But the syntax of Anglo-Saxon is even less developed. It has its own strength of directness and swiftness; but it is sometimes abrupt.

2. Bede[n]

The man that composed the *Beowulf*, as well as the man that wrote it down, may have been a monk. Certainly he was a Christian. Though he keeps Wyrd (Fate) and other conceptions originally pagan as susceptible of Christian interpretation, he omits the old gods of nature-worship. For between the old songs and the *Beowulf* there had intervened the conversion of England to Christianity; and the centering of all education and learning in the Church was at once opening a wider civilization and giving a lead to Latin. The degree to which the development of native literature was thus checked differed from people to people. Gothic literature has left few remains; Norse and Anglo-Saxon not only survived, but grew. But in greater part or in less the literature of every people during the earlier middle age was written in Latin.

The missionaries sent by Pope Gregory from Rome found the Anglo-Saxons in 597 already Christianized in part by the missionaries of the conquered British Celts. The Church in Ireland, Scotland, and Wales had long been a harbor of religion and learning during the fierce storms of heathen invasion. With so noble a tradition it might well feel little need of help. Yet its yielding to direction from Rome as to the proper date of Easter typifies the union of the civilizing force of England with the civilizing force of the whole western world.

The story of this progress is recorded in Bede's *Historia Ecclesiastica Gentis Anglorum*, Church History of the English People. Faithful exposition, this is also vivid description; it illuminates the whole period. Rude old village ways lingered in 642.

While they gave themselves over-long to eating and drinking, with a great fire kindled in the midst, it happened, as the sparks flew up, that the roof, which was wattled and covered with thatch, was suddenly all in flames. *Historia Ecclesiastica*, III. x.

Formal acceptance of the new faith did not prevent some reversions to heathendom. The three sons of Sabert, Christian King of the East Saxons, after his death:

soon began openly to follow idolatry, which in his lifetime they seemed somewhat to have left off, and gave free license to their subjects to worship idols. And when they saw the bishop, at solemn Mass in church, give the Eucharist to the people, they would say to him, as the story goes, puffed up with barbarian folly: "Why do you not offer the white bread to us also, as you used to give it to our father . . . and as you still cease not to give it to the people in church?" He replied: "If you will be washed at the font of salvation where your father was washed, you also may be partakers of that holy bread of which he partook; but if you despise the laver of life, you are no wise worthy to partake of the bread of life." But they said: "We will not approach that font, because we do not know that we have need of it; but nevertheless we will be fed with that bread." And when diligently and often they had been admonished by him that in no wise any one without the most holy cleansing might have the communion of the most holy sacrifice, moved at last to fury, they cried: "If you will not yield to us in so easy a thing as we ask, you shall not remain longer in our province." And they drove him forth, and bade him and his to leave their kingdom. (II. v.)

On the other hand, since heathen temples and heathen religious festivals were fixed by the habit of generations as centers of worship, the Church, instead of destroying them, turned them to Christian use. Pope Gregory wrote to the abbot Mellitus:

The temples of idols in that nation ought by no means to be destroyed; but let the idols themselves which are

THE EPIC CENTURIES 35

in them be destroyed, holy water made and sprinkled in those temples, altars built, relics placed. For if those temples are well built, it is plain that they ought to be converted from the worship of devils to the service of the true God; so that the nation itself, so long as it sees the same temples not destroyed, may put away error from its heart and, knowing and adoring the true God, may the more familiarly resort to the places of its old wont. (I. xxx.)

So our names for the days of the week, and even for the greatest of Christian feasts, Easter, have remained pagan.

Bede's account of the conversion of Edwin, King of Northumbria, reveals both the practical and the poetical attitude of Anglo-Saxons toward the new faith.

[Edwin] in council with his wise men, inquired of each singly how this doctrine hitherto unheard-of, and the new worship of deity which was preached, seemed to him. Coifi, chief of his own [heathen] priests, straightway replied: "See thou, O King, what manner of thing this may be which now is preached to us. For I verily declare to thee from my own certain knowledge, that the religion which we have hitherto held has no virtue at all, nor any use. For no one of thy people has given himself more zealously than I to the worship of our gods; and yet there are many who receive from thee greater favors and greater honors, and who have better prospects in everything that is to be done or had. Now if the gods were worth anything, they would rather help me, since I have been at more pains to serve them. It remains, therefore, that if after examination thou shalt perceive those new things which now are preached to us to be better and stronger, we hasten to receive them without any delay." Another of the King's chief men, assenting to Coifi's argument and good sense, straightway added: "Thus, O King, seems to me the present life of man on earth in comparison with that time of which we have no certain knowledge. As thou sittest at meat with thy leaders and thanes in winter, with a fire kindled in the midst and the hall made warm, while everywhere without rage whirlwinds of wintry rain or snow, a sparrow coming in flits most swiftly through the house, in by one door and soon out by the other. While it is within, indeed, it is not touched by winter's storm; but nevertheless, its tiny space of calm run through in a moment, it slips away from thine eyes, forthwith from winter going back to winter. So this life of men for a little is seen; but of what may follow, or of what may have preceded, we are utterly ignorant. Therefore, if this new doctrine has brought us aught more certain, it seems justly to claim our following. (II. xiii.)[n]

The old gods, as they ceased to avail for the conduct of life, ceased also to suffice for the inspiration of poetry.

Bede's History, his Lives of the Abbots, and his own life show how monasteries, from being missionary centers, became also centers of literature. On the community framework of the "seven hours" of prayer and praise was based a distribution of assignments to individuals. Some had charge of the daily alms to the neighboring poor, others of the care of the chapel, others of the library, others of the field and garden, and so on through a manifold group of industries. A life of regularity and industry for all and for each was thus based upon the maxim, *Ora et labora*, "Pray and work." Fresh air and sunlight were to be found also in the cloister, or open corridor, which usually ran about the monastery court or yard. Here the monks might read, or walk at recreation time, or in fair seasons write or teach. Active physical exercise was provided by the raising of daily food in field and garden; for in the simpler olden time this work might engage each monk some part of each day. Otherwise he would be set at that work for which he seemed fittest. He might teach, or copy manuscripts; he might be sent to preach to remoter hamlets; he might practise some manual craft; he might receive time to exercise his artistic talent in writing or painting.

Such was a monastery seen from within. Seen from without, it was first a little state within the state, preparing its own food and clothing, independent of outside intercourse, sufficient to itself. Secondly, it might be the church for the surrounding country. The choir, or place where the brethren sang their hours, was, indeed, separated by a roodscreen from the nave, or place for the congregation; but at Mass on Sundays and holy days, the nave might be filled with a congregation from all the countryside; and at other times it was always open to individual worshippers. The comparatively large size of the choir in some old English churches is due to their having been originally "abbey" churches, *i.e.* churches attached to a monastery, and thus needing a choir large enough to contain the whole religious household. Through many centuries these abbey churches were among the finest of England in architecture and decoration; for the monks, spending nothing upon their own persons, were lavish in adorning their church with carving of stone and wood, and with paintings on walls or glass. Thus the abbey church, while it might be the religious center of the district, might be at the same time the center of art.

Thirdly, the monastery was a school, both for its own members in the days when reading and writing were rare accomplishments, and also, in later times, for outsiders. And finally it was, in a small way, a library and publishing house. Books were rare enough to be treasures. They were possessed only by kings and queens, great nobles, cathedrals, and monasteries. The monasteries not only had books, but copied them. In the centuries before the printing-press every single copy of a book had to be written out by hand. This transcribing of books became a regular monastic occupation, and often showed great skill and beauty of clear characters and of titles and capitals ornamented in gold and colors. The copyists were called scribes (Latin *scribere*, to write), and the book-room was called the *scriptorium*. Naturally, most of the books were religious. Indeed, it was no small part of the scribes' task to keep their monastery supplied with service-books and with music for chanting. Besides transcribing the books of other people, the monks often kept a chronicle; and some of them wrote books of their own.

From the point of view of the outside world, then,

a monastery was a refuge, a church, a school, and a library. Besides being properly a community of those devoted to a special religious life, it was incidentally a refuge for those who wished to withdraw from the storm and stress of the time. It was the church, first of the community itself, and secondarily, when churches were few, of the surrounding district. It was often the most beautiful church, rivalled only by the cathedrals of the larger towns. It was a school, first for its own members, since most men entering "religion" needed instruction also in reading and writing, and secondarily for such others as wished to learn. It was a library, or place of books and writing, the only place outside of cathedrals and kings' courts, where books could be seen. All these functions it exercised for centuries.

Eloquently suggestive of the civilizing force of the monasteries is Bede's life of the great pioneer abbot Benedict Biscop.

Within the space of a year after the founding of the monastery, Benedict, crossing the ocean to Gaul, sought, secured, and brought back with him masons to build him a stone church after the Roman manner of which he was always fond. . . . Moreover, as the work drew near to completion, he sent messengers to Gaul to bring over glass-makers, or rather glass-workers, hitherto unknown in Britain, that they might set glass with lead frames in the windows of the church, the cloisters, and the refectory. This was done; they came. Nor did they merely fulfil the work demanded of them, but also made the English people thereby know and learn this sort of craft — a craft, indeed, not ill suited either for protecting a church lamp or for various applications to vessels. Besides, his pious care extended to the buying of everything proper for the service of the altar and the church, whether sacred vessels or vestments, because he could not obtain them at home.

And that he might further bestow upon his church such ornaments or furnishings (from Rome) as were not to be obtained even in Gaul, the untiring benefactor, making another journey, the fourth since his monastery had been established according to his rule, returned laden with more various store than before of spiritual merchandise. First, he brought a countless supply of books of every sort; secondly, he bore hither of the relics of Christ's blessed apostles and martyrs what was to be grace abounding to many churches of the English; thirdly, he established as a precedent in his monastery the order of singing, chanting, and serving in church according to the mode of the Roman rite. For Pope Agatho gave him at his request John, archchanter of the church of St. Peter the Apostle and Abbot of the monastery of St. Martin, to go to Britain as the Roman teacher of the English in his monastery. This John chanter on his arrival, not only imparted the traditions of the church to his pupils by word of mouth as he taught at Rome, but also left in writing not a few instructions which still keep his memory in the library of this monastery. . . . Fifth, he brought pictures of sacred figures to adorn the church of St. Peter the Apostle which he had built: namely, a figure of the blessed mother of God, Mary ever Virgin, and also of the twelve apostles . . . figures of the gospel history, to decorate the south wall of the nave; and figures of St. John's visions in the Revelation equally to adorn the north wall; so that all who entered the church, even those who could not read, wherever they looked might contemplate, though but in figure, the lovable countenances of Christ and his saints,

or might harvest the grace of our Lord's incarnation with more alert mind, or, having as it were before their eyes the judgment of the last examination, might the more strictly remember to examine themselves.
Vita Beatorum Abbatum.

Bede's own brief and modest postscript concerning himself shows how in his time religion and letters might be part of one life:

Born in the territory of this monastery (the twin monasteries of Jarrow and Wearmouth), I was given by my family for education to the most reverend abbot Benedict, and then to Ceolfrid. From then on, spending my whole time in the life of the same monastery, I gave all zeal to meditating on the scriptures; and, amid the observance of the monastic discipline and the daily duty of singing in church, I always found pleasure in learning, or teaching, or writing. . . . From the time when I received the priesthood up to my fifty-ninth year, I have undertaken to jot down briefly for my own use and that of my brethren, or to expand as to meaning and interpretation, the following books upon holy scripture from the works of the venerable fathers.

And he adds a list of thirty-seven volumes. Though most of these are strictly religious, three, from which quotations are made above, are histories or biographies; one is an essay in philosophy, one in grammar, and one in rhetoric; and Bede kept the fine tradition of the earlier medieval Church in several Latin hymns.

Bede's life was exceptional only in individual talent. For the organization of the English Church under its first archbishop, Theodore (669), had provided at once for religious and for secular education.

Since both (Theodore and Hadrian) were abundantly versed, as we have said, at once in sacred and in secular literature, streams of salutary knowledge daily flowed to water the hearts of a throng of pupils; so that they gave their hearers, amid wealth of sacred letters, training also in the art of verse and in ecclesiastical astronomy and arithmetic. The proof is that there are living even today pupils of theirs who know Latin and Greek as well as they know English.
Historia Ecclesiastica, IV. ii.

From the school of York, which had one of the most important libraries of western Europe, Charlemagne called Alcuin to direct the education of the Franks.

3. *The Cædmonic Poems[n] and Cynewulf*

The direction of later Anglo-Saxon poetry may be followed first in a beautiful legend reported by Bede, the story of Cædmon, then in the *Genesis* and *Exodus*, and finally in the poems of Cynewulf. Of Cædmon Bede says:

In the monastery (Streaneshalh) of this abbess (Hild, or Hilda) was a certain brother especially distinguished by divine grace in that he was wont to make songs suited to religion and devotion. For when he had learned anything out of sacred literature by interpreters, he would in a little while set it forth in poetic phrase composed with the utmost sweetness and sympathy in his own tongue, that is, in English. Often by his songs the minds of many were

THE EPIC CENTURIES 43

kindled to despise the world and desire the heavenly life. And though after him others too of our English nation used to try to compose religious poems, yet no one has been able to equal him. For he did not learn the art of singing from men, nor was he taught of man; he received the gift of song as one freely inspired from heaven. Therefore he could never make anything trivial or idle in his poems; only such things as pertain to religion suited his religious tongue.

Although fixed in the secular habit up to a rather advanced age, he had never learned any songs. Therefore when at a feast it was sometimes decreed for the sake of mirth that all must sing in turn, so soon as he saw the harp coming his way he used to rush from the midst of the feast and flee homeward. Once when he had done this and, after leaving the house of the feast, had gone out to the stable where he had charge of the horses that night, and had betimes gone to sleep there, in a dream one stood by him greeting him and calling him by name. "Cædmon," said the vision, "sing me something." "I cannot sing," replied he; "for but now I withdrew hither from the feast because I could not sing." Again spoke the vision with whom he was talking, "Yet to me you have somewhat to sing." "What," said he, "am I to sing?" "Sing," was the reply, "the beginning of created beings." Accepting this charge, straightway he began to sing to the praise of God the Creator verses which he had never heard, whose purport is this: "Now we are to praise the Author of the heavenly kingdom, the might of the Creator and his counsel, the deeds of the Father of glory; how he, since he is God eternal, became the author of all miracles. Omnipotent guardian of the human race, he created first heaven to be a roof-tree for the sons of men, and then earth." This is the sense, but not the same order of words as he sang in his sleep. For songs, though their composition be of the best, cannot be translated word by word out of one tongue into another without impairing their beauty and nobility.

Now when he awoke he remembered all that he had sung in his sleep, and soon added in the same manner other words of a song worthy to praise God. Coming in the morning to the steward, his superior, he showed what a gift he had received, and, now being brought before the abbess, was bidden to show his dream and repeat his song in the presence of many learned men, that by the judgment of all might be proved what it was that he related, and whence. And it seemed to all that heavenly grace had been granted to him by God. They explained to him some passage of sacred story or doctrine, instructing him if he could to translate this into the rhythm of verse. He went away with the task and, returning in the morning, rendered it, as they bade, composed in admirable verse. Thereupon the abbess, embracing the grace of God in the man, instructed him to give up the secular habit and take upon him the monastic rule; and when he had been received into the monastery she joined him to the company of her brethren, and bade that he be taught the order of sacred story. And he, by rehearsing with himself everything that he could learn from hearing, and as it were chewing the cud like a clean beast, would turn it into sweetest song and by the charm of his echo make his teachers in turn his hearers.

For he sang of the creation of the world, the origin of the human race, and all the story of Genesis, of the exodus of Israel out of Egypt and their entering into the land of promise, of many other stories of Holy Scripture, of the incarnation of our Lord, his passion, resurrection, and ascension into heaven, of the coming of the Holy Ghost

and the doctrine of the apostles. Besides he made many
songs of the terror of judgment to come, the horror of hell
pains, and the delight of the kingdom of heaven, as well
as many more of divine gifts and judgments, in all which
his study was to draw men away from the love of evil and
arouse them toward delight in the truth and quickness in
good deeds.
Historia Ecclesiastica, IV. xxiv.

The legend guides us not to particular poems,
but to a typical situation. Native poetry survives
in spite of Latin; it is led to Christian subjects;
it finds its place within the monastery as a work
of God. Nor is it merely versified doctrine; it is
also the rendering of sacred story as epic. *Exodus*,
one of the poems that legend ascribed to Cædmon,
thus carries forward the old manner.

> Straightway they saw from southward
> The force of Pharaoh fare against them,
> The spear-grove stir, soldiers glitter,
> Flags come forth, the folk in order.
> Lances steadied; the line shifted.
> Shone their shield-covers; shrilled their trumpets.
> A-wheel whooped the harrier ravens,
> Greedy of battle, . . .
> Dewy-feathered, over dead warriors,
> Swart slain-choosers.   Sang the wolves
> Evil evensong, eager for feeding;
> Desperate beasts, deadly boded
> The folk-might's fall, fierce on the trail.
> Howled these march-wardens at midnight.
> Fled fated souls; the folk was hedged.
> <div style="text-align:right"><i>Exodus,</i> 155–169.</div>

The pursuit at the Red Sea is conceived as a narrative situation and described epically. So Satan sallies from hell.

> Launched himself upward,
> Hasted through hell-gates, had a heart undaunted,
> Wavered in the wind, woe-plotting mind,
> Swinged the fire in two by fiendish craft.
> *Genesis*, 446–449.

Storm in the *Andreas* gathers and culminates.

> Then was troubled,
> Upheaved the whale-mere. The horn-fish played in it,
> Glided through ground swells; and the gray sea-mew
> Woe-wisher, wheeled. The weather-candle dimmed,
> Winds were waxing, waves were grinding,
> Stirred the streams and the stays were creaking,
> Wet with the welter. Water-horror stood,
> Mighty in battle.
> *Andreas*, 369–376.

The verse, sometimes looser than the traditional staves, is more various. The change is most obvious in the stretching of the epic line.

> But bear we now bane in hell, that is blackness and heat,
> Grim, unsounded. Hath God himself
> Swept us to these swart mists. So he may not assert as our sin
> That against him we wrought a wrong in this country.
> Yet hath he bereft us of light.
> *Genesis*, 389–392.

Cynewulf,[n] one of the few definite names in Anglo-Saxon poetry, wove his *Christ* upon the

Advent antiphons, the special invocations at vespers on seven days preceding Christmas. Though this poetic scheme offers no compelling sequence, the realization in detail touches the heights of Anglo-Saxon poetry.

> Dins the deep creation, and direst well-fire
> Walks before the Lord o'er the wide abyss;
> Roars the raging flame; rent are the heavens;
> The flashing firmament falls into ruin.
> Then is turned the sun itself to darkness,
> To bloody hue, which so brightly shone
> At the world's dawn to warm its children.
> Moon, which has nightly for earth's multitudes
> Beamed, itself now bends from its station;
> And stars besides forthwith scatter from heaven,
> Through blasts of might beaten by surges.
> Lo! the Almighty with his many angels,
> King of lords, to his council will come straightway,
> Throned in glory. Of his thanes are there besides
> Heroes in a host. Holy souls
> Move with their Master. Then man's Defence
> With throes of awe throngs of nations
> Visits unveiled. Throughout the vast abyss
> High the hail of heaven's trumpets rings,
> And to seven quarters shrill the winds;
> Blow they breaking of breaches greatest,
> Wake and wither the world with their tempest;
> Fill they with fear all flesh of the earth.
> Then the hurtling crash, hard, unmeasured,
> Grim and grievous, greatest din of sounds,
> Awful uproar, to all is manifest.
> Christ, 930–955.

The tumult of fire and wind moves in clear contrast to the stately approach of the Lord to judgment. English poetry has advanced in the adaptation of sound to feeling.

4. *The End of the Anglo-Saxon Period*

Even in the tenth century the fervor of battle epic glows in two fine poems. The first, included in the *Anglo-Saxon Chronicle* under the year 937, sings the victory of Athelstan and his brother Edmund over Constantine, King of the Scots, and his son-in-law Anlaf Sitricson (or Olaf Cuaran) in the battle of *Brunanburh*[n] with vivid description, and glad epic boasting. The second tells the heroic death of Byrhtnoth in the battle of Maldon[n] (991) against the invading Danes under Olaf Tryggvason. The very spirit of epic fills Byrhtnoth's answer to the demand of the invaders for tribute.

> Hear thou, sea-goer, what this folk sayeth:
> They will give you tribute of trusty weapons,
> Poisoned point and provèd sword,
> This wealth of war-gear, of little worth to you!
> Spokesman of sailors, say yet again,
> Tell thou to thy host a more hateful tale
> That here stands an honest earl with his company,
> Who means to guard this goodly country —
> Aethelred's earth, ever my chieftain —
> Place and people.   (45–54.)

Both poems show the vigorous survival of the epic manner in the last years of the Anglo-Saxon period. For any wide development of native prose Anglo-

Saxon history was hardly long enough. But though prose normally meant Latin, the translations of Alfred, King of the West Saxons (849–901), revealed the capacity of the mother tongue. A century later the abbot Aelfric was exploring this further for the rhythms and correspondences that he practised in Latin.

But the development of native literature, in poetry and in prose alike, was interrupted by two successive foreign invasions. The first, checked for a time by Alfred, was invasion from Scandinavia. The harrying of the Norsemen and Danes, from raids of plunder terrifying the coast, grew into a conquest. Knut, or Canute, became king of England in 1016. The effects of this conquest on the language and on the literature were quite diverse. The Norsemen and Danes were Germanic peoples so nearly akin to the Anglo-Saxons that the two races merged without marked change of language. Certain words in our language today we know to have been derived from Norse or Danish; of certain others we cannot tell whether they come from Scandinavian or from Anglo-Saxon, the two are so nearly alike. On language, then, the effect was slight. But on literature it was as great as it was destructive. For these Scandinavians were still heathen, and had been touched but slightly by Christian civilization. What this meant for literature was written in the sack and ruin of the monasteries. Not only did fighting leave little time for writing, though it brought forth at least the hero-songs of *Brunanburh* and *Maldon;* but much of what had been written was burned by the invaders. In a few years the work of centuries was undone.

The effect of the first invasion on literature was to interrupt; the effect of the second was to supplant. The Norsemen who invaded England also invaded northern France. But there, while they ruled the French, they adopted the French language, as the Franks had before them. True, they modified it by their own Germanic speech; but, as they became Christianized and civilized, they became French. Their northern force was turned into the channels of French literature. Norman French, though it was never standard French, has its place in French literature. A Norseman was a heathen of Germanic stock from Scandinavia; a Norman was a Christian of Germanic stock from France, half French by early intermarriage and wholly French in language and literature. And England, after being conquered by the Norsemen, was straightway conquered by the Normans. The Norman dukes brought in the French language; their successors, as kings of both countries, kept England in touch with all the French literature of the time. When the great Norman duke, William the Conqueror, won England at the battle of Hastings (1066), his minstrel Taillefer had ridden into battle singing a song of Roland, the epic hero of France. The Norman Conquest put the language and literature of England temporarily under the language and literature of France.

CHAPTER III

MEDIEVAL ROMANCE:
LITERARY MOTIVES

THE earliest form of romance and the most permanent is fairy story. Often a remote source of modern romance, fairy story is no less often a direct and immediate source of medieval romance. Folklore was still active in the twelfth century, and was much sought by poets for their stories. The legend of the fairy mistress, for instance, the woman of unearthly power to bless the man of her choice, appears in many stories. There are several forms of it even within the single collection of Walter Map.[n] Sometimes the fairy is seized in a moonlight dance, held through transformations into various beasts, and possessed securely so long as the man refrains from saying the fatal word. In two tales she is not a midnight, but a midday fairy. Of these the following is evidently nearer to the folklore original.

Henno cum Dentibus, so called from the size of his teeth, found the fairest of maidens in a shady grove by the Norman coast at midday. She was sitting alone, clad in silken robes befitting a princess, and weeping piteously without sound of lament, so beautiful that even her tears became her. The youth caught fire at once. He marveled to see so precious a treasure unguarded, as it were a star fallen from heaven bewailing contact with earth. He looked about, for he feared some ambush in the covert; but, finding none, he knelt to her and thus reverently addressed his supplication: "Sweetest and brightest ornament of the whole world, whether the benignity of a face that so awakens desire be of our mortal lot or whether some divinity, wreathed with these flowers, robed in this light, has vouchsafed herself to the sight of her worshippers on earth, I rejoice, and thou mayest well rejoice, that it befalls thee to alight in my power. Ah me! My thought bodes that I am foreordained to thy service (glory to thee!); that thou hast turned to the place of all places where thou art received with most desire." She replied so innocently and dovelike that it might have been an angel saying what would seduce any angel to her prayers: "Amiable flower of youths, and desirable light of men, no plan of mine has brought me here, but chance has carried me against my will. The ship which bore me, with my father, to my marriage with the King of France was driven on this coast by the force of the storm; and when I had escaped with this single companion who is here beside you — and lo! her maid was there beside him — a fair wind succeeding to the tempest, the sailors made off with my father under full canvas. I know indeed, that when they miss me they will return hither with tears. Nevertheless, lest wolves devour me or wicked men attack, if thou wilt promise me my honor, as for thee and thine, I will abide with thee for the time; for it is more to my safety and health that I commend me to thee till the return of the ship." Henno, no dull listener to her prayers, grants forthwith whatever is asked, and brings back his treasure-trove with greatest glee of heart, urging as much joy as may be for them both. He brings home that noble pest and marries her, commits her to the care of his mother, and has by her most beautiful offspring.

The mother was assiduous at church, the daughter more assiduous; she gladdened the hearts of orphans and widows and all in need of bread, that she might the better keep within desired bounds all envy in the sight of men; except that she always shunned sprinkling of holy water and was careful to slip away from Mass before the consummation of the holy sacrifice, covering her absence by the crowd or by some household affairs. Henno's mother noticed this and, fearing everything in the anxiety of her just suspicion, applied herself with strictest care to discover why. She knew that the wife went into church on Sundays after the giving of holy water and came out before the consecration. That she might know the cause, she secretly made a little hole in the bedroom wall and lay in wait. Thereupon, at the first peep of dawn on Sunday, when Henno was gone out to church, she saw her go into her bath and from a most beautiful woman turn into a dragon, and, after a little, springing from the bath upon a new mantle which her maid had spread for her, and tearing it into shreds with her teeth, turn again into her proper shape, which when she had resumed, she served her servant forthwith at every point to the same end. The mother told the son what she had seen. Summoning a priest, they seized them without warning and sprinkled them with holy water. With a sudden bound the demons passed through the roof and with a great shriek left their long-cherished abode. Nor marvel ye if God ascends corporeally, since he has granted this power to the worst of his creatures, who must even be dragged down against their will. Many children of this demon-woman are still alive.

WALTER MAP, *De nugis curialium*, IV. ix.

In undeveloped form this tale has two of the motives that distinguish the later medieval stories from the earlier. Love and adventure appear in aspects, unfamiliar to epic, which were to become habitual in romance. By romantic love we still mean passion and idealizing devotion, wooing and worship. Much as our modern expression differs from the medieval, the motives themselves got their first literary vogue in the middle age. The story of Tristram and Iseult in the hands of Swinburne or Wagner receives modern direction and emphasis; but it remains essentially the romance of fatal passion. In the middle age that story was new; for in the presentation of love romance differs from epic. Epic women appear oftenest as Andromache and Penelope, as honored wives and mothers. They take their place in heroic society and in epic poetry usually after marriage. Of wooing epic says much less than romance. Indeed, epic has echoes of that earlier time when wives were won suddenly with the sword. We can hardly imagine Achilles or Beowulf saying: "Ah me! my thought bodes that I am foreordained to thy service."

Wooing and woman-worship in medieval romance are in great measure a literary code. Influences from Vergil's Dido and from the women of Ovid had been transformed by the courtly poets of the Provence. The love poetry of the troubadours elaborated wooing into ceremonious observance. This Provençal courtly love[n] passed into general literary habit through France, and at the same time was brought into England directly. Eleanor of Poitou, who in 1152 married Prince Henry and thus later became Queen of England, had at her court the famous Provençal love-poet Bernard de Ventadour. The literary change brought about by these influences appears in the romantic convention exalting women as worthy of all devotion.

As love receives in romance a new interpretation and a new emphasis, so adventure. Adventure, of course, is also a motive of epic; but in romance it is more extolled for itself, is less related to the character of the hero, and passes more readily into fairyland. Epic accepts and intensifies reality; romance protests against it. Because real life for most of us is humdrum, romance tells us that behind the closed door, or over the edge of the horizon, is mystery. Fancy, says romance, if on the strand beyond the next point should sit the fairest of damsels! In childhood we frankly play out these fancies and are not ashamed to love fairy-tales. And even when we are grown we keep a world of imagination, more or less hidden according to our temperaments, and more or less based on the real world of facts. Above the real world which we daily touch is an ideal world in which men are brave and generous without calculation, in which women are beautiful, in which, above all, something happens as we should like to see it happen, and turns out in just the right way. This ideal world is the world of fancy; and its expression in literature is romance.

Epic demands fewer fancies because it appeals

more to our interest in the facts of life and in character. Though it has its dragons, too, and its zest for strange feats, its persons are usually both reasonable and distinctly realized. The persons of romance may be strange in action or shadowy in character. But a hero of romance, though often he is not such a man as we meet in actual life, is such a man as many of us wish to meet; and his adventures, far as they may be from what happens to us, are not so far removed from what we wish to happen. Modern romances give us persons and scenes less remote, indeed, than those of the twelfth century from what we conceive to be possible, but still remote from what we actually experience, still belonging less to our actual world than to the world of our dreams. For in every age romance is true not so much to the facts of that age as to its ideals and aspirations. The heroes of epic, more like the real men that we know, are more distinct one from another, Achilles from Ulysses, Beowulf from Hrothgar. The heroes of romance, somewhat indifferently endowed with all manly virtues, are often very much alike. A tale of one is often shifted to another. In medieval romance the character of the hero rarely determines the course of the story. Rather each hero in turn reflects a common romantic ideal of manhood.

Making light of the normal motives of men and the normal course of events, the hero of romance seeks adventure for its own sake. For this he turns aside at any time; and often his main object, if he have one, is not realm or wife or treasure, but that shadowy or fanciful achievement summed up in the word *quest*. Thus a typical scene of medieval romance presents an exciting situation without much regard to the reality of the persons involved or the motives of their actions. One day as Sir Gawain rode with Sir Ywain and Sir Marhaus, they found three damsels sitting by a fountain. The first was threescore, and had a garland of gold upon her white hair. The second was thirty, and wore a golden circlet. The third was fifteen, and wore a garland of flowers. "Why sit ye here?" cried the knights. "To show errant knights strange adventures," they replied.

Each one of you must choose one of us. And when ye have done so we will lead you unto three highways, and there each of you shall choose a way, and his damsel with him. And this day twelve-month ye must meet here again, and God send you your lives; and thereto ye must plight your troth.

"This is well said," said Sir Marhaus. "Now shall each of us choose a damsel." "I shall tell you," said Sir Ywain, "I am the youngest and most weakest of you both; therefore I will have the eldest damsel; for she hath seen much and can best help me when I have need." "Now," said Sir Marhaus, "I will have the damsel of thirty winter age; for she falleth best to me." "Well," said Sir Gawain, "I thank you; for ye have left me the youngest and the fairest."

MALORY's *Morte d'Arthur*, IV. xix–xx (modernized).

These two literary interests, the epic and the romantic, have both remained permanent in literature down to our own day; for both spring from permanent impulses of human nature, the impulse to realize and the impulse to idealize. But one or the other is sure to predominate in a particular reader or a particular period. Those who prefer Scott to Thackeray, Stevenson to Kipling, are romantic. As with individuals, so with periods. Though both the epic interest and the romantic interest can be discovered in the literature of any period, one or the other is sure to have the upper hand, to be the fashion of the time. Down the history of any literature they rise and fall in turn. From 1100 on, the literary fashion was romance. The epic interest was dimmed by the wide kindling of the romantic interest. Old epic stories were retold in the new romantic fashion; and hundreds of new stories appear as pure romance. The middle age is the first great period of romance. Even today when we think of romance, we are apt to think of knights in armor and ladies in long sleeves, of castles and tournaments and hermitages — in a word, of the middle age.

Combined with these motives, but distinct for itself, is chivalry. The hero of a romance is typically a knight; and the adventures are usually single combats, whether in the lists where knights assemble to prove their prowess, or in the forests where they ride "errant." The code of *"noblesse oblige"* means that knightly duty is made by birth and rank. Whereas the combats of the *Beowulf* are stand-fights, the combats of romance are on horseback. The very word *chivalry* has the same root as *cavalry* and *cavalier*.

But *knight* is an English word, and meant originally, as it still means in German, a servant. Nor is this original meaning incompatible with the later. Rather it shows chivalry in another aspect. Though the knight was on horseback, above mean men by birth and conduct, his ideal was service. This was the work of the Church for an age of war, the tempering of war by religion. For knighthood was not merely the result of rank; it was a service undertaken religiously and blessed by the Church. A noble youth was bred to noble manners; but his breeding taught him to serve his elders and all ladies. And when, after serving as a squire in hall and on the field, he was deemed fit in age and strength, he received knighthood by a solemn rite. All night before the altar he kept vigil over his armor. In the morning, after Mass, he vowed to serve God and his lady, to protect all women, to succor the distressed. Only then was he smitten by some knight with the flat of the sword and heard the words, "I dub thee knight,"[n] which admitted him to an order whose professed ideal was service.

Romantic love is typically the service of a knight to his lady, romantic adventures happen usually as the knight rides to succor some damsel distressed. The knight's deeds for her and his conduct toward her and toward his fellows in the order of knighthood are regulated by courtesy. That word comes to us from the age of romance; it recurs constantly in all medieval romances; no word is more characteristic. High-bred, devoted to a high calling, the hero of romance must fulfill at every point of speech and manner the chivalrous ideal of conduct. The actual conduct of the actual medieval man may often have lapsed from this ideal; but romance does not bind itself to the actual. Medieval romance as a whole is tinged with chivalry and keeps the code of courtesy. Its informing spirit is generous devotion. Its love is chivalrous love; its adventures are chivalrous adventures; and its aim is to uphold a chivalrous ideal.

1. *The Spread of Romance*

In England the change of literary habit was hastened by the Norman Conquest. For the Conquest meant more than the domination of English people by French people; it meant the eclipse of English language by French language and of English literature by French literature. The English court of the twelfth century was in literary interests French. Writing in England during that century and the following belongs primarily to the history of French literature. Prose, of course, was still written commonly in Latin; verse was now written commonly in French; and, whether prose or verse, the literature of the island conformed much more rapidly to those general, Continental habits which are seen at their earliest in French literature. What English literature must have turned to slowly, in the gradual inward progress of ideas, was precipitated by French intervention.

For romance became, more widely than epic, international. The medieval romances have so little distinction of nationality that they were current in the middle age throughout Europe. What we find in French literature that sprang up in the twelfth century we find later in medieval German literature and Italian. France usually gives the earliest examples of what came soon to be written in every country where men wrote. Whether through the common vehicle of Latin or through translation, a story that gained success in one country was more than likely to travel to all others.

The *Beowulf* and the *Song of Roland* keep something of an older communal appeal. There is no such appeal in the tale of Henno or the tale of Percival. The former was written at a French court in England; but it shows nothing distinctively French or English. Similar stories may be found in the medieval literature of every European nation. The heroes of romance, Tristram, Lancelot, Ywain, quickly lost any original trait of race. Taken over from French tales into German, Italian, or Spanish, they appear in each language much the same. The scenes of their exploits are often in some vague, shadowy no-man's land. The names of places in the story often have no definite local meaning, and are freely changed and shifted by each new teller of the tale. True, by painful comparison of a dozen medieval forms of a story it is possible to guess its original locality; but the habit of romance is to blur rapidly in transmission the original associations of any story with any particular place. The Arthurian romances quickly lost all local identity in their general currency over Europe.[n]

The romantic habit also widened the range of literary material. Such was the zest for adventures that there was an eager seizing on new ones. The two sources most used were, first, unwritten popular traditions of fairies, demons, and witches; and, second, oriental tales coming into western literature often through Greek versions. The first was most abundant among the Celtic peoples, and was first used by their Norman neighbors in France and England. Many of the romances popular throughout Europe may be traced back to the fairy folklore of the Celts. The oriental source is clear in medieval versions of stories older than history. The Bible story of the temptation of Joseph by Potiphar's wife (Genesis xxxix) appears in medieval romances in various forms. The story of the werewolf, or manwolf, which has been retold a hundred times down to our own day,[n] though it seems in some cases to have been taken from local folklore, is found also in ancient oriental forms. The Crusades must have contributed to bring about the common use of oriental personages. Saracens they are called, or Paynims; and, in addition to the romances in which they are main figures, are many others in which they appear incidentally, side by side with Christian knights. Old as was the oriental source and even the Celtic, the tales were new to European literature.

This eager use of all available material for stories, whether it were old or new, native or foreign, discovered or rediscovered, shows a great stir of literary activity, and may be exhibited both by a modern parallel and by an actual medieval instance. A modern illustration of the ways of romance is the work of Walter Scott. A born romancer, he first turned to account in verse the traditions of the people among whom he lived. *The Lay of the Last Minstrel, The Lady of the Lake,* and his other verse-romances use history indeed, but use it with romantic coloring of fairy folk-lore, and with predominance of the romantic motives of chivalrous love and adventure. As he went on in prose to widen the field of his material, he turned, as the medieval romancers before him, to the mysterious East. He found romantic material and gorgeous romantic color in the Crusades. He gave us, not only *Ivanhoe,* but also the *Talisman.* But to the medieval romancer much of this material was freshly new. Thus Walter Map's Latin book *De nugis curialium,* besides the tale of Henno (page 51), has many other Celtic folk-tales of witch-wives, of ghosts that call the living to death, of men who, as Rip Van Winkle, stayed too long in fairy-land; and these tales he may have got, not from written records overlaid by the centuries, but fresh from the mouths of the Welsh peasantry about Hereford. History too he uses, but history that he heard from the actors or their immediate descendants and chose for its romantic possibilities. Whether he works a tale out or leaves it in mere outline — for much of his book consists of notes — he is always evidently on the lookout for romantic material. And this material he found, not only in folk-lore and traditional history, but also in old tales of the East. Keen for stories, he takes them from everywhere; he casts them now in this form, now in that, but always romantically. He is a type of the great romantic movement of the twelfth century. Walter Map in the twelfth century and Walter Scott in the nineteenth alike reveal the character of romance, its constant motives of love and adventure and its world-wide search for material.

The period of romance, then, as we see it best exemplified in French literature of the twelfth century, is the period of great world-stories. There is hardly one of these medieval stories which had any literary promise but was caught up and carried everywhere. And as they passed over the civilized world, so they have passed down through the centuries even to us. In every civilized country of the world today some one is reading somewhere, in some form old or new, the immortal romances that were made for knights and ladies seven hundred years ago. Tennyson's *Idylls of the King* is the direct descendant of a long and famous line. He got the tales mainly from an English prose version of the fifteenth century. That version was derived from French versions, which in turn were derived from — but the ultimate source is often shadowy, so far back reaches the pedigree of the stories of Arthur. Walter Map himself may have had a hand in shaping them;

and behind him lie lost unwritten Celtic legends of his Welsh marches. Now all this is thoroughly characteristic of romance. Not one of the great romances has ever died; not one but has been changed again and again down the centuries to suit the sympathies of each writer's age. The *Idylls of the King* are conceived very differently from their twelfth-century French originals, very differently even from their fifteenth-century English ones, partly because romance lives by perpetual change.

At the grand opera in Berlin, Paris, and New York the well-to-do listen every year to Wagner's dramatic version of the romance of *Lohengrin*. Meantime the poor in Italy and in the Italian quarters of North and South America never tire of seeing the romances of Charlemagne represented on the little stage of the marionettes. The operator pulling his wires behind the scenes knows the tales by heart; and any of his audience with the will and the skill to read may find the book wherever Italian books are sold.[n]

In their legendary origin the Arthur stories had a certain advantage over the stories of Charlemagne. Charlemagne, even in the romances, remains the historical king of an historical territory. Of course the *Chanson de Roland*, though tinged with romance, is essentially epic; but even the later Charlemagne stories, more romantically rehandled, show some obligation to historical fact. Arthur, on the other hand, though there was indeed a real Celtic chieftain of that name, is almost from the beginning legendary and soon becomes in literature the ideal king of a vague realm. Thus *matière de France*, to use the old title of the Charlemagne stories, offered less freedom than *matière de Bretagne*, matter concerning Britain or Brittany. "Many a marvel hath come to pass in Brittany." Epic obligations might be left behind by one who set out for the frontiers of fairyland. The Celtic strain in French literature is first heard in the Norman-Celtic stories of the middle age, and first made pure romance.

(a) GEOFFREY OF MONMOUTH'S HISTORY (about 1140)

An early Arthur story of some length and consistency is Geoffrey of Monmouth's *Historia Regum Britanniae*.[n] The title *historia* did not connote in the twelfth century that distinction between fact and legend which is now suggested by our word *history*. Geoffrey's *historia*, like others of its time, is largely legendary.

Oftentimes in turning over in mine own mind the many themes that might be the subject-matter of a book, my thoughts would fall upon the plan of writing a history of the Kings of Britain, and in my musings thereupon meseemed it a marvel that, beyond such mention as Gildas and Bede have made of them in their luminous tractates, nought could I find as concerning the kings that had dwelt in Britain before the Incarnation of Christ, nor nought even as concerning Arthur and the many others that did succeed him after the Incarnation, albeit that their deeds be worthy of praise everlasting and be as pleasantly rehearsed from memory by word of mouth in the traditions of many peoples as though they had been written down. Now, whilst I was thus thinking upon such

MEDIEVAL ROMANCE: LITERARY MOTIVES 67

matters, Walter, Archdeacon of Oxford, a man learned not only in the art of eloquence, but in the histories of foreign lands, offered me a certain most ancient book in the British language that did set forth the doings of them all in due succession and order from Brute, the first King of the Britons, onward to Cadwallader, the son of Cadwallo, all told in stories of exceeding beauty. At his request, therefore, . . . have I been at the pains to translate this volume into the Latin tongue.
History of the Kings of Britain, dedicatory epistle.

Whatever his immediate sources, Geoffrey used, among others, Celtic legendary material "all told in stories"; and that material has been shaped, whether by a previous writer or by Geoffrey himself, into consistency and continuity.

Brute, or Brutus, great-grandson of Trojan Æneas, was guided by a response of Diana from Italy through France to Albion. Landing at Totnes, he called the island Britain and his people Britons. Of his three sons, Locrine inherited the middle part (Loegria); Albanact, Scotland; and Camber, Wales (Cambria). Slurring the historical conquest of the island by the Romans, Geoffrey tells how Britain was converted, how the wizard Merlin foretold its greatness, and how it was deceived and harried, but never quite conquered, by the Saxons. By Merlin's enchantment Igerne, wife of Gorlois, Duke of Cornwall, receiving in her lord's stead King Uther Pendragon, became the mother of Arthur and, on the instant death of Gorlois, Uther's queen. Arthur, succeeding to the kingdom, defeated the Saxons and all his other enemies in the island, subdued Iceland, Gothland, and the Orkneys, set his brother-in-law Lot on the throne of Norway, married

Guenevere, a noble Roman lady, and finally held at Caerleon a glorious coronation feast, to which came many princes his subjects and allies. Lucius, Emperor of Rome, demanding tribute, Arthur left his kingdom and his queen in charge of his nephew Mordred, and led a great host of allies to the Continent. He slew single-handed the giant of St. Michael's Mount, and defeated Lucius in a series of battles. As he was marching over the Alps to invade Rome, he heard that Mordred had seized both kingdom and queen for his own. He returned forthwith and defeated Mordred in desperate conflict, but being wounded to the death, he was borne to the isle of Avalon for healing, and gave up his crown to Constantine. Guenevere meantime retired to a nunnery. Thereafter the Saxons conquered, and the kingdom decayed.

For ten books of his twelve Geoffrey's narrative is fairly full. He dwells especially on the exploits of Arthur, and culminates with lively detail on the coronation and the war with Rome. At that point he suddenly lapses into summary. "Hereof will Geoffrey of Monmouth say nought." Perhaps his main idea was to make out of Celtic legends a consecutive heroic story for the composite people, English-French-Celtic, which in twelfth-century England was gaining a pride of common nationality. At any rate, he succeeded in establishing Arthur as a national hero of romance.

Here, moreover, is many another familiar name: Lear, Ferrex and Porrex, Cymbeline, revived in Elizabethan drama; and, of the Arthurian group, Merlin, Uther and Igraine, Lot, Cador, Howell, Mordred, Bedivere, Kay, and especially the gallant

Gawain. Only there is no Lancelot and no Holy Grail. Arthur has the shield Priwen, "Caliburn, best of swords, that was forged within the Isle of Avalon", and the lance Ron. Nor is there lack elsewhere of Celtic fairy marvels. But the fighting has more tactics and stratagem than in the later romances. It reads as if Geoffrey had seen real war, or as if he had in mind those classical authors from whom he may have borrowed the idea of the speeches that he puts into the mouths of his characters on important occasions. The *Historia Regum Britanniae* is not a romance; but it is largely romantic, and it was a wondrous begetter of romances.

(b) CYCLES OF ROMANCE

In another sense Geoffrey's work is like the romances. It shows the tendency of medieval writers to group separate stories into a larger composition about one central figure. A set of stories, derived very indirectly from classical antiquity, was grouped about the siege of Troy. One of its members is the tale of Troilus and Cressida, a story unused by Vergil, but included by medieval writers in a large Trojan cycle, and then detached again later for separate treatment by Boccaccio, Chaucer, and Shakespeare. The most conspicuous instance of this habit is the grouping of some of the best separate romances about the central figure of King Arthur. Some of the stories in Malory's *Morte d'Arthur* and in Tennyson's *Idylls of the King* have little connection with King Arthur. Though

Tristram and Iseult had been connected by the Welsh, it is not integrated by Malory. But the medieval French romancers whom Malory followed liked to give their work large scope, and to further its popularity, by connecting separate stories with some single popular romantic hero. Thus arose an Arthurian cycle which included in one composition many of the most popular medieval romances.

This process of grouping had already been at work before the formation of the great cycles of Charlemagne, Troy, Alexander,[n] and Arthur. Not only were the cycles composed of tales originally separate; but these component tales themselves often consisted of groups of separate smaller tales. A capital instance of this is the romance of Lancelot.[n] It forms part of the Arthurian cycle; but it is a cycle within itself. It is composed of many separate adventures, some of which had originally nothing to do with Lancelot, and were ascribed to him by some French romancer in order to expand the composition and to take advantage of the interest in a popular hero. One of the best remembered of Lancelot's adventures, as told by Malory and again by Tennyson, is the three days' tournament. Lancelot appears as an unknown knight, first in red arms, then in white, then in green, wins the prize each time, and finally declares his identity. Not only is the adventure told of other knights in other romances, but it forms by itself a separate romance, as in the tale of Ipomedon. If we search still farther, we find that it is a wide-spread folk tale, and still farther back

MEDIEVAL ROMANCE: LITERARY MOTIVES 71

a fairy story. Some medieval rewriter, finding the adventure of the three days' tournament good literary material, added it to his version of the Lancelot story, and there it stayed. In like manner the Lancelot story was enriched by adventures formerly ascribed to Gawain. And such was the popularity of Lancelot as a hero that the winning of the Grail, which had very early been added to the story, was eventually taken away to be given to Lancelot's son Galahad.

This sounds like confusion worse confounded; but it is the way in which many medieval cycles were compiled. Confusing it is indeed to those who wish to discover in any case the original form; but it is not confusing to any one reading a romance for literary enjoyment. Who the hero is, after all, makes very little difference. Be he Tristram, Gawain, or Lancelot, he is very much the same. The interest is not so much in his individual character as in his adventures. The more adventures, the better, thought the middle age. So it came about that many popular medieval romances are groups of groups, wheels within wheels, made up by selecting and adapting adventures from various sources. And the preëminence of the Arthurian group is due, not only to the purely romantic character of its material, but also to its having combined a very large number of popular stories. *Arthurian* has come to sum up in English, as in other languages, the literary habits that made cycles of romance.

(c) The Grail Legend[n]

But the most popular of all romantic legends and the one which added most, perhaps, to the vitality of the Arthurian cycle, is the legend of the Holy Grail. As every knight had his quest, and every quest was based upon the knightly ideal of constant and devoted service, so there was one supreme quest, the quest of the Grail. He who should win this quest must be, not only without fear, but also without reproach. As the story grew, it even demanded that he should be without sin. For the Holy Grail story set up beyond the attainment of earthly love the realization of heavenly love, the vision of heaven, a glimpse on earth of the beatific vision of the saints in light. Beyond all earthly and material quests was set up this spiritual quest. Except the *Divina Commedia*, the Grail story is the supreme literary effort of medieval religion. Instead of the unseen things of fairies, magicians, or witches, it offers the unseen things of God, those "unseen things] which are eternal." Its vitality is the vitality of spiritual aspiration.

When Christ was crucified, so the story grew to tell, the wounding lance and a cup that received the blood and water from the wounded side were preserved by Joseph of Arimathea. These relics of Christ's passion were handed down to successive guardians, and the cup became known as the Grail. The Grail was guarded in a mysterious castle, now here, now there, in various early forms of the legend, but always remote, and usually located, as other mysteries of romance, in Britain. No man could even find this castle if he cherished his sins; no man could make his way past the lions at the entrance until he had made himself "clean of his life." The few who were finally found worthy were rewarded by a glimpse of the mystic chalice, by echoes of the music of heaven, and by a taste of the food of angels. The story of the Grail is the romance of spiritual struggle and spiritual reward.

Thus it became a parable of the Mass, the central rite of the Church in the symbols of a story. Repentance, absolution, the long struggle of self-mastery, the sustaining grace of the great sacrament, the reward of heavenly vision, are expressed in terms of knighthood, are brought home in the romance of a quest. What the *Pilgrim's Progress* centuries afterward did for Protestantism, the *Holy Grail* did for medieval Catholicism. It put religion into a story of aspiration, struggle, and attainment. As all romance is ideal, so this romance is most ideal of all; and as the idealism of romance is its most vital quality, so this highest ideal of romance has lived through all the centuries and won all Christian peoples.

Beginning crudely in glimmering half-realizations, it was quickly defined and heightened as it seized the imaginations of successive romancers, and won the admiration of eager readers. Early found congenial to the stories of Percival, the boy reared apart from men by his mother in the wild wood, it made him the Grail hero, the pure knight who alone was found worthy of the heavenly vision. The increasing popularity of the Lancelot stories led some romancer, not to attach the Grail quest to him, for he was a sinner, but to invent for him a son Galahad pure enough to rise so high. In spite of this, the Grail story remained in the popular imagination attached to Percival. The literary attempt to give the honor to another hero shows two things. First, even the overshadowing popularity of Lancelot was not sufficient to permit any violation of the sacred character of the Grail story. No romancer dared to say that the Grail was won by a sinner. Secondly, the popularity of the Grail story is evident. Popularity was the reason for the attempt to combine it with other popular stories. And this popularity it has kept down to our own day. Tennyson and Wagner, utterly unlike otherwise, alike testify to the vitality of the Holy Grail.

CHAPTER IV

MEDIEVAL ROMANCE: LITERARY FORMS

NARRATIVE art was stimulated by the wide diffusion of tales and sometimes by comparison of versions. The very habit of retelling instead of inventing put the teller on his mettle as an artist. He might, indeed, merely rehearse the expected incidents of Tristram, Iseult, and King Mark with the expected descriptions at the expected points. The middle age had its conventions. But evidently there were both experiment and appreciation of achievement. The exquisite *Aucassin et Nicolete*, as most medieval romances, is anonymous. More than one admirable narrative has been ascribed to the wrong author. But though we know little of medieval artists, we may know much of their art. Marie de France was working with the *lai*. Walter Map, besides collecting material from folklore, was evidently experimenting with narrative forms, and has worked out two prose tales in firm sequence and brilliant dialogue. Chrétien de Troyes explored the manners and motives of high society. Wolfram von Eschenbach achieved within manageable limits a coherent Grail story. Chaucer deliberately rejected certain conventions of romance, carried recomposition to re-creation, and set far beyond his age the art of characterization.

The medieval development of narrative art was generally in the shorter romances, because these might be selective. The longer romances often had so much aggregation as to be unwieldy. The leisurely readers of the time liked to hear all — the hero's parentage, his birth and breeding, his early promise, his knighting, his friends, his falling in love, and the more adventures the better. Thus romances became long by covering many years and many adventures. Sometimes also they were made long by descanting on love. The feelings of the lover and his lady might be described in great detail and with great relish. The courtliness and constancy of the knight were regarded as important enough to be exhibited many times. But typically a romance was long because it was collective.

The larger art of conducting an extensive poetic sequence is nowhere more eminent than in the *Divina Commedia*.[n] But this, though it is characteristically medieval in thought and feeling, is solitary in the range of its art. Nor is it essentially narrative. The medieval development, then, of narrative art was not in the collective romances, but in such separate books as Malory's *Balin* or *Gareth*, and still more in certain stories not attached to cycles, such as *Gawain and the Green Knight*.

MEDIEVAL ROMANCE: LITERARY FORMS 77

1. *Lay and Tale*

The Lays (1165) of Marie de France[n] recall a stage in which legend was both story and song.

> Thise olde gentil Britons in hir dayes
> Of diverse aventures maden layes,
> Rymeyed in hir firste Briton tonge,
> Which layes with hir instruments they songe,
> Or elles redden hem for hir plesaunce.
> CHAUCER, Prologue to the *Tale of the Franklin*.

Lai may have meant at first a lyric expressing the emotion of some sharp moment of the story and sung to the rote, or small Celtic harp. French poets rehandling the Celtic material called their whole stories *lais*. Marie's charming *Honeysuckle* is merely an episode in the Tristram story. Iseult, finding a peeled wand by her way through the wood, knew that Tristram was near. This is not unfinished; it is not material, as are most of the plots in Walter Map's collection; but as a story it is undeveloped.

Generally Marie seems more concerned to render than to recompose. Her *lais* are charming and suggestive without narrative force. *Yonec*, for instance, remains in form a fairy-tale. Many medieval stories are thus told in rapid summary of the whole action without choosing significant situations for salience. The prevailing model for such tales was Ovid. An admirable later example of its scope and its limitations is the anonymous *Sir Orfeo*.[n]

2. *Exemplum*

Perennial also is the illustrative anecdote, called in the middle age by its Latin name *exemplum*. The medieval *exemplum* books,[n] compiled for the use of preachers, show not only the current and the typical, but also variety enough to suggest a considerable range in oral narrative. The following story, for instance, though Walter Map sets it down merely as an *exemplum*, might be made thrilling.

But for other men the monastic life turns out otherwise. Far more pitiable was the fate of a noble and eloquent man who, likewise a monk of the same community, was in the same case recalled to arms. Enduring many reverses of battle with a noble fortitude, he was always reanimated by defeat to fight again, and, inflamed as it were with new ardor, would fly at the enemy the more fiercely, and whether they fled or held their ground, would indefatigably stick to them like glue. When his enemies thought to crush him by the size of their company, they found that victory goes to bravery, not to numbers. Burning with wrath, therefore, and increasing their force many fold, they surprised him in a valley hemmed between two cliffs, and had him almost trapped. No hope, for he was caught; no issue, for he was held; they went to work the more leisurely because the more securely. But he, bursting into their midst like a tempest, scatters them like dust in a whirlwind, and so stupefies them by his daring that they see nothing to do but run. Promptly he hangs on their rear with his band, small enough in comparison with theirs; and the throng of the enemy, in the effort to save their lords from him, becomes the prize of a single monk.

But one leader, escaping, makes a detour ahead and, mingling unrecognized with the monk's men, works back steadily, risking his own life to take his. The monk, almost stifled with toil and sun, calls his page, enters a vineyard, doffs his armor, and, while his band passes on, stretches himself half-stripped to the air under the shade of a tall vine. Then the skulker, leaving the line of march and slipping up stealthily step by step, pierces the monk with a deadly dart and escapes. The monk, knowing himself near death, confesses his sins to the page, the only person within reach, bidding him impose penance. He, being a layman, swears he knows not how. But the monk, extreme in his penitence as in everything, says: "Impose upon me by the mercy of God, dearest son, that in the name of Jesus Christ my soul may be in hell doing penance up to the day of judgment; so that then the Lord may have mercy upon me, lest with the wicked I behold the countenance of his wrath and anger." Then replies the boy with tears, "My lord, I impose upon thee for penance that which here before the Lord thy lips have uttered." And he, accepting with word and look, devoutly received the penance and died.

Here let us remember the words of mercy: in whatsoever hour a sinner shall repent, he shall be saved. Wherein he might have repented and did not, whether he omitted anything possible, we may discuss; and God have mercy on his soul. *De nugis curialium*, I. xiv.

That *would make* a good story. Striking as it is, we recognize it not as narrative form, but as narrative material. Walter's *De nugis curialium* is largely a note-book. This note of the warrior monk's tragedy is sketched as if for larger development than mere illustrative anecdote in a sermon;

but it is only sketched. The difference is clear when we place such notes beside those few tales which Walter worked out in narrative sequence for intensity. Typically, as in the *Gesta Romanorum*,[n] an *exemplum* is a sketch or summary suggestive for written or oral shaping. It gives rather the plot than the story. How moving it might become in oral narrative we may see in Chaucer's tale of the Pardoner.

3. *Saint's Legend*

Saints, again, though not medieval, have more relations to literature than in modern times by being more familiar. They are patrons of guilds, objects of pilgrimage, assistants in prayer, not more perhaps in theory, but more in habit. The saints seem more recognized as part of medieval society. So their lives,[n] though like other *exempla* in edification, are realized sometimes with touching homeliness, sometimes with poignant vividness. "They endured as seeing that which is invisible." Summing up the life of any saint, this motive tends to make them all alike. Modern readers preoccupied with individuality are impatient with patient Griselda. Medieval readers were not; nor were they surprised to find also among the Canterbury Tales the trials of saintly Constance and the legend of St. Hugh. They were more accustomed to story focused on idealization.

Thus the characterization of a saint was not for a medieval writer a contradiction in terms. Saint

MEDIEVAL ROMANCE: LITERARY FORMS 81

Mary Magdalen, one of the most popular saints in the middle age, was brought into personal prominence by the antiphonal sequences at Easter. Having been anonymous in the early hymns among the women at the Cross, she emerges in these responses, and becomes personally distinct in the hymns for her own feast. Prose story works out her life in detail; and finally miracle plays make the great penitent, devoted to her Lord's human body, a familiar figure. In composition a saint's legend was likely to remain a tale.

4. *Unified Short Story*

Lay, tale, *exemplum*, story of a saint, any of these might be short without distinction of art, short because undeveloped or summarized; but the middle age knew also the art of focusing a story for intensity.

A mountebank converted and retired to a monastery was confused and ashamed at his ignorance of holy ways. Yearning to express his devotion, he went secretly to the Lady Chapel in the crypt and there performed his best gymnastic feats. Before the brethren could reprove him, the Blessed Mother inclined her statue and touched his head in blessing.

This famous medieval story, the *Tombeor de Notre Dame*,[n] shows even in so bald a summary a distinct narrative form. It has been unified for intensity. Renouncing a series of events, the teller has compressed the past into the present; he suggests a whole life by a single situation. Such limitation of

82   MEDIEVAL ROMANCE: LITERARY FORMS

time and place, giving room for more vivid description, enhances a single dominant significance. Much the same in method, though covering a longer time, is the thirteenth-century *Chastelaine de Vergi*[n] (956 verses).

The Chatelaine of Vergi was ardently loved by a knight, and gave him her love in turn on condition that he keep it an inviolable secret. The Duchess, wife of his lord, seeking his love and finding him cold to her advances, in revenge accused him to the Duke. Declaring his innocence in vain, the knight incautiously took oath to tell the Duke the whole truth, and was thus driven to betray his love of the Chatelaine. The Duke, though he swore secrecy, was so harassed by the jealous Duchess that he in turn betrayed the secret to her. The Chatelaine, on being taunted by the Duchess, died for shame and grief. The knight, finding her dead, killed himself at her feet; and the Duke in his wrath killed the Duchess.

This narrative art of unity for intensity, though exceptional in the middle age, is already grasped in Walter Map's Latin prose *Sadius and Galo* and *Sceva and Ollo*. It is approached in Marie's lays of *Lanval* and *Eliduc*. There is the superiority of her *Lanval* to the anonymous *Graalent* which tells the same story. Whether she merely had the discernment to choose a version already thus told, or herself reshaped the story, is not easy to determine. The unknown author of *Aucassin et Nicolete*[n] gave his exquisite *cante-fable* (story with songs) more focus and continuity than was sought by the usual tale. Discarding the epilogue of subsequent adventures, which was probably added later, we see that its workmanship is not only in style, but also in composition. Walter Map was so evidently experimenting with several narrative forms that we must suppose him to have planned his two strongest tales with this intention. Not until modern times did this terser and more intense narrative form win wide popular recognition; but it was practised by some of the best story-tellers of the very prime of romance.

5. *Chrétien de Troyes*

More amply, but still selectively, Chrétien de Troyes[n] (latter half of the twelfth century) presented individual conduct within the romantic social frame of courtly love. Carrying a romance to five or six thousand lines, he does something more than add adventure to adventure. He keeps a dominant interest in the personal effects of chivalry. With more room for development than is offered by a single situation such as that of the *Chastelaine de Vergi*, he advances the art of characterization.

Chrétien's *Erec* tells a tale which Lady Charlotte Guest translated in her *Mabinogion*[n] as *Geraint the Son of Erbin* from a later Welsh version, and which Tennyson rewrote from her translation for his *Idylls of the King* as *Geraint and Enid*. The Welsh version keeps the Celtic tradition of fondness for details of color. Thus enters the hero:

The rider was a fair-haired youth, bare-legged, and of princely mien; and a golden-hilted sword was at his side, and a robe and a surcoat of satin were upon him, and two low shoes of leather upon his feet; and around him was a scarf of blue purple, at each corner of which was a golden apple. And his horse stepped stately and swift and proud.

>   Lady Charlotte Guest, *The Mabinogion, Geraint the Son of Erbin.*

Enid is stricken with shame that Geraint's love of her should run to ignoble fondness. Her lament, overheard and mistaken by Geraint, rouses his jealous pride to prove her long and cruelly. This moment the Welsh writer sees in its setting:

> And one morning in the summer time they were upon their couch, and Geraint lay upon the edge of it. And Enid was without sleep in the apartment, which had windows of glass. And the sun shone upon the couch. And the clothes had slipped from off his arms and his breast, and he was asleep. Then she gazed upon the marvellous beauty of his appearance, and she said, "Alas! and am I the cause that these arms and this breast have lost their glory and the warlike fame which they once so richly enjoyed?" And as she said this, the tears dropped from her eyes, and they fell upon his breast.
>
>   *Ibid.*

In such a place the Welsh writer's abundance of description is not merely pretty; it is fitting. What he thus dwells upon until we must feel it because we can see it, is an important moment of the story. But in general the Welshman blurs his story by spending equal elaboration on what is quite subordinate, or even irrelevant. The entrance of Arthur's forester is marked by quite as much detail as that of Geraint;

and the preparations for the hunting of the white stag are given in spite of the fact that Geraint did not go. The incidents claim attention equally in succession; Chrétien's are lengthened or shortened with a sense of narrative values. For Chrétien, using descriptive detail less for itself, uses it more to realize the social setting, to bring out character, or to heighten important moments of the story. What is passed over rapidly would not add to our main interest in the proving of Enid, or enhance our sympathetic appreciation of her character; what is dwelt upon in detail serves just this purpose of focusing attention on the conquest of the proud, selfish devotion of the husband by the nobler devotion of the wife. At the end Chrétien impresses the significance of the whole course of adventures, the meaning of the story as a whole.

The same focusing of adventures on one main impression appears in Chrétien's *Chevalier au Lion*, called also from the name of its hero *Yvain*. Here again there are three versions; but all three are medieval. The Welsh version, translated by Lady Charlotte Guest as *The Lady of the Fountain*, stands in the same relation to Chrétien's *Chevalier au Lion* as *Geraint the Son of Erbin* to his *Erec;* i.e., in each case we seem to have not a translation, but a parallel version from a common source. At any rate, the differences of treatment are typically the same. The Welsh version in each case has more color and less focus.

But the Middle English *Ywain and Gawain*[n] (first

part of the fourteenth century) is a translation and in several ways a very good one. Keeping not only every incident of the *Chevalier au Lion*, but the narrative plan and transitions, it reduces the scale by one third, telling in 4032 lines what Chrétien tells in 6802 of about the same length. What is compressed, modified, or even omitted is the detail. Since Chrétien's detail is not merely added for richness, but spent to bring out setting, character, or mood, a change here is a change in the total effect, a shifting of interest from the persons to the events. Thus to Chretien the central situation is this. A widow forced to marry again, as medieval widows were if they had property, accepts the slayer of her husband. How would she feel? Might she not, from making a virtue of necessity, come to love her second husband if he were young and brave? If, tiring of her riches and ease, he would be off to his wars again, would she forgive him for breaking his promise to return on a day? And might he not then, learning from the loss of her to value her truly, devote himself to winning her back by proving his better manhood? The situation is almost the reverse of that in *Erec*. Such questions of character and feeling lead Chrétien to dwell upon the scenes between Ywain and Alundyne, and even to comment satirically now and then on their mental attitudes. Most of this the English translator omits.

Nor is the omission stupid. The translator threw the emphasis where he felt his own interest — in the movement of the story.

Now is the lion outbroken.
His master shall full soon be wroken.
With full fell rush the twain he sought.
To pray for peace availed them naught.
One savage straight he leaped upon,
And to the earth he bare him down.
Then was there none about that place
That was not fain of that fair chase.
The maiden had great joy in soul.
They said, "He shall never again be whole."
His fellow hasted with might and main
To raise him smartly up again;
And right so, as he stooped to lift,
Sir Ywain with his brand was swift
And struck his neck-bone right asunder.
Thereof had all the people wonder.
The head went trundling upon the sand.
Thus had Ywain the higher hand.
(3243-3260 — modernized.)

What makes a story quick and strong he understands so well that he even quickens and varies Chrétien's pace by throwing some of the indirect discourse into direct dialogue. Here and there, as in the passage above, he adds a touch of his own. Ywain bade his lion, says Chrétien, go back from the combat and lie quiet; and the lion did so in his way (*a sa devise*). The Englishman renders:

> He bad his lyoun go to rest;
> And he laid him sone onane
> Doun byfore þam everilkane.
> Bitwene his legges he layd his tail,
> And so biheld to þe batayl.   (2592-2596.)

"What are thou that mournest here," says a damsel to Ywain during his wandering in the wild wood; and the eloquent first words of the reply are not in the original: "A man, he sayd, sum tyme I was." At the end of the poem, when Alundyne discovers that the knight whom she has promised to accord with his wife is Ywain, her own repentant husband, Chrétien says simply that she started (*la dame tresaut*). The Englishman says:

> Then went the lady far aback,
> And long she stood ere that she spake. (3983–3984.)

Such touches, few though they are, show that the English translator could not have been insensible to Chrétien's use of detail for the suggestion of character or mood. He translated with unusual intelligence and spirit, not literally, but with substantial accuracy. His omissions must have been deliberate. Nevertheless they help us to see better Chrétien's delicacy of art. Chrétien is superior, not only in verse and style, but in clear fulness of personal detail and in finer touches of characterization. The translator keeps the whole value of the plan and transitions which hold the tale together; he does not keep the whole value of the situation. His work is like a strong black-and-white copy of a painting.

6. *Anti-Romance*

Romance has always provoked satire. In the sixteenth century "Cervantes smiled Spain's chivalry away." While the early nineteenth century was devouring the wild romances of Mrs. Ann Radcliffe,

Jane Austen made quiet fun of both the books and their readers in her *Northanger Abbey*. Scott wrote *Ivanhoe;* Thackeray wrote *Rebecca and Rowena*. So in the fourteenth century courtly love and chivalrous adventure were parodied by Chaucer in Sir Thopas. Medieval satire was aimed less often against romance in general than against the romantic idealizing of women. Women, said the satires, are so far from deserving chivalrous devotion as to be creatures of impulse, basely passionate, fickle because essentially untrue. The coarseness of many such attacks has been ascribed to the celibacy of some authors; but it should be ascribed rather to the actual defects of feudal society. Neither the chivalric ideal nor the lapse from it presents by itself the whole truth; but perhaps we may estimate the age as a whole more fairly by its ideals than by its failures.

(a) Beast Tale

The ape showed his apelet to the lion and asked him what he thought of it. "Like father, like son," replied the lion; "no joy of the one, no use in the other." The ape went off in a huff, came to the bear and asked him what he thought of the child. "Ah!" said the bear, "is this the beautiful baby I have heard so much of?" "Yes," replied the ape, "the very same." "Let me kiss him," said the bear. "I have been longing to see him." "You are my friend indeed," said the ape; "you take an interest in me." And the bear took the little ape and ate him. "Ah!" cried the ape, "shame on fair speech from a foul heart!"[n]

Nicolas Bozon in G. Paris and E. Langlois, *Chrestomathie du Moyen Age*, Paris, 1897, page 163.

Every one recognizes this as a fable. It so clearly has its type in the fables of Æsop that medieval collections were called *isopets*.[n] The cunning fox, the fierce and stupid wolf, the vain cock, come from far away and long ago. In the doings of beasts who act and talk as men fables present the folly or shrewdness of mankind. In typical actions they exhibit common sense and worldly wisdom. They oppose to romance the practical conduct of real life.

In more extended narrative medieval beast stories often have the form, and generally the effect, of satire. Some of the best verse tales of the sort are grouped about a central figure, the world-famous Reynard the Fox.[n] With their clear types of human nature, their witty dialogue, their criticism of manners, they were popular for centuries in every country of Europe. Every one knew the shifty Reynard, Noble the lion, Bruin the bear, Tibbet the cat, Chanticleer the cock, and all the rest, laughed over them, quoted them, learned from them common sense. Without attacking romance these satires confront romantic idealism with the selfish shrewdness of real life.

In the nineteenth century Joel Chandler Harris's *Nights with Uncle Remus*, expanding the dialogue dramatically and sometimes carrying out the story, kept the essentials of the ancient type. Mr. Kipling's *Jungle Books* embody in animals a scheme of natural education. Rostand's *Chantecler* even tries to capture the beast tale for romance. Five hundred years before him Chaucer had used the same motive to turn the old satire of the cock and the fox to a new story of the cock and the hen. Centuries have shown the capacity of the beast tale to translate human life into figures that we can contemplate dispassionately, or deride through bitter satire, or understand through sympathetic humor.

(b) FABLIAU

The short verse-tale called *fableau* or *fabliau*[n] had a twofold popularity: it ranged beyond knights and ladies among tradespeople and students; and its comedy was broad enough to be usually inclined toward farce. Though the *fabliaux* are often satirical, their object is not ridicule for the sake of correction, but laughter and excitement for their own sake, and especially amusement at some clever trick. They are such humorous tales as in all ages some men have permitted themselves after dining too well. Though they are thus trivial and often base in substance, they are skilful in narrative form. An amusing intrigue is made to hold attention by a narrative movement more rapid than is to be found in any other contemporary form. That focusing on a single situation which is seen in certain short romances is often carried in the *fabliaux* to the extent of compressing within twenty-four hours on a single scene and filling this little space with uninterrupted action. Rapidity is achieved by dialogue and by ingenious complication and solution. The *fabliaux* prevail by sheer skill of plot. More than satire, they break the spell of romance. They not only strip love of its dream; they turn it to brutal jest.

CHAPTER V

MIDDLE-ENGLISH ROMANCES DISTINCTIVE AND CONVENTIONAL

FOR the Norman and the Angevin kings of England the Channel was hardly a boundary. The French part of their realm being larger than the English, they naturally kept their French sympathies. But as the French possessions slipped away from them, while at the same time Englishmen and Frenchmen on the island were successfully united under a strong central government, there grew up a new English nation and a new English national feeling. Like the new nation, the new language was composite; but it kept its Germanic framework. Change would have come even without the Conquest; during the same two centuries (1100-1300) French too had changed; but in English the change was more rapid for two reasons. Treated as an inferior speech, and without sufficient use in literature to maintain a standard of correctness, English was more subject to oral change. Spoken language is always freer than written language. Since the written standard was uncertain, the inevitable changes of language were hastened. The conspicuous result was a blurring of case-endings and tense-endings, so that finally modern English, when set beside modern German, which grew from the same stock, seems to have hardly any inflections at all.

The second cause for change in the language was that Frenchmen, in learning to speak English, as they did more and more every decade, naturally introduced a great many French words. This always happens in like cases. In attempting to speak French, when one is at a loss for a French word he puts an English one into the French sentence. And in England during the twelfth and thirteenth centuries, when a French lord had to converse with his English tenants without any dictionary by to help him, this was done, of course, much more widely. Meantime Englishmen were borrowing from French as from a more elegant language. Besides, for many French words there were no English equivalents. In introducing the feudal system and chivalry, for instance, the French introduced such words as *fief*, *vassal*, *homage*, and *chivalry* itself. The new words came in with the new things; and the habit thus begun has continued in English down to our own day. When we imported motor-cars from France, we imported into our language the words *automobile*, *chauffeur* and *garage*.

But the sentence habit, the way of putting words together, was changed very little. One of the first things that any one has to learn in a foreign tongue is the habitual order of words, the sentence habit. When he has fairly mastered this, he has a practical command of the language, even though he may know comparatively few words. Now the French sentence habit, the French order of words, is quite different from the English; and this which is true as between modern French and modern English, is more marked as between medieval French and medieval English. Thus it is plain that the Conquest, great as its effect was in bringing in French words, had no such effect toward bringing in French constructions. Thirteenth-century English, though freely mixed with French words, kept its native syntax.[n]

1. *Popularized Romances*

When English literature came again to its own, it showed more epic tendencies than survived in French. Among the earliest romances in English *Horn* and *Havelok*, though already told in French, are epic in the English slant of the telling.

(a) KING HORN[n] (about 1250)

Alle be hie blithe	Be they all blithe
That to my songe lythe.	That listen to my song.
A song ich schall you singe	A song I shall sing you
Of Murry the kinge.	Of Murry the king.
King he was biweste	King he was to westward
So longe so hit laste.	As far as it went.
Godhild het his quen;	Godhild hight his queen;
Fairer ne mihte non ben.	Fairer might none be.
Hie hadde a son that het Horn;	They had a son hight Horn;
Fairer ne mihte non be born.	Fairer might none be born.

The rude verse seeks the effect of the common French short line; but the rime is often bungled and the rhythm often rough. As story, however, the 1530 lines are lively and interesting.

Blithe be all that listen to my song! Murry, King of Suddene, and his fair queen Godhild had a fair son named Horn. He was bright as the glass, white as a flower, with cheeks red as roses. Twelve companions he had, all fair and noble; but most he loved two, Athulf and Fikenild. One day, as King Murry rode by the strand, the paynims arrived in fifteen ships, killed the king, destroyed churches, and spared none who would not forsake Christ's law. Queen Godhild fled to a cave, where in solitude she served God and prayed for her son. The paynim chief, struck by Horn's great beauty and yet unwilling to risk his growing up to avenge his father, set him adrift with his twelve comrades in a ship. After a day and a night on the deep, the ship beached upon the shore of Westerness. Ailmar, king of that land, took Horn as his foster-child and bade his steward Athelbrus teach him the lore of wood and river, of harping, and of serving as a squire in hall. Horn was beloved by all, but most by the king's daughter Rimenhild. When she could no longer abide, she sent for Horn to her bower. Athelbrus, fearing the king, tried in vain to put her off. "Horn," said she, when at last the hero came, "have me to wife, and plight me thy troth." "Nay," said Horn. "I am born too low. Help me first to knighthood at the king's hand." When this was done, and Horn in turn had knighted his twelve fellows, he rode on a white steed to Rimenhild. "Let me now prove my knighthood," he said; and Rimenhild gave him a magic ring. "The stones are of such grace," she told him, "that if thou look thereon and think of me, thou shalt fear no strokes." Forthwith Horn rode out on a coal-black steed, slew a band of paynim marauders, and brought their leader's head to King Ailmar. But the traitor Fikenild, declaring that Horn meant to kill the king and reign as Rimenhild's husband, as a proof showed the lovers together in secret. Now Rimenhild had dreamed that she caught in her net a great fish, who thereupon broke the net and escaped. "This is thy dream," said Horn, when the king in wrath had banished him. "I am the fish that broke from thy net. For now I must away to unknown lands. If in seven years I return not to claim thee, thou mayst wed another. Take me now in thine arms and kiss me long." Then, when Rimenhild swooned in his arms, he committed her to Athulf, rode to the sea, and took ship to Ireland. There, under the name of Cutberd, he rid the country of paynims and won the same honor and love as in Westerness. Indeed, King Thurston offered his daughter Reynild in marriage; but Horn declared he must serve seven years. When the seven years were almost over, a messenger from Rimenhild brought word that she was to be wed in her despite to King Modi of Reynes. "Bid her mourn no longer," cried Horn; "for I shall be there betimes." Then telling King Thurston his whole story, he asked and obtained a band of Irishmen. Arrived in Westerness, he left his men in a wood by the shore and went to the wedding feast disguised as a palmer. The faithful Athulf was scanning the sea from a tower, and singing "Horn, thou art long. Rimenhild, whom thou gavest to my care, I have kept till now. Come now or never. I cannot keep her longer." Now as Rimenhild bore the cup to the palmer on the beggar's bench, Horn dropped into it the ring. "No beggar am I," said he, "but a fisher come from far eastward to fish at thy feast. My net hath lain on the strand full seven years." And when a maiden brought him to her bower, he told her Horn had died on

the voyage to Westerness. "Break now my heart,"
cried Rimenhild, and reached for the knife that she had
hidden to slay herself with and King Modi, if it came to
that. But Horn threw off his disguise, wiped the black
from his face, and took her in his arms. With his Irish
followers and Athulf he overcame all resistance and married
Rimenhild. Then said Horn to King Ailmar, "Rimenhild
shall be a king's wife; for I will recover my father's
kingdom of Suddene." So with Athulf and his Irish
fellows, he sailed off once more, won his native land, and
brought his mother from the wild wood. Meantime the
traitor Fikenild had Rimenhild away by his power to a
strong castle surrounded by the sea. But Horn, seeing
in a dream his love shipwrecked and beaten from the
shore by Fikenild, cried "Athulf! to ship!" and before
sunrise was under Fikenild's tower with his band. Disguised as harpers, they made their way in, killed Fikenild,
and brought all Horn's pains to an end. For Rimenhild he
took back as his queen to Suddene, Athelbrus he made king
of Modi's realm, and Athulf he wedded to King Thurston's
daughter Reynild.

> Here endeth the tale of Horn,
> That fair was and nothing worn.
> Let us be gladder ever among;
> For thus is ended Horn's song.
> Jesus that is of heaven king
> Give us all his sweet blessing. *Amen.*

Here is that old story of exile and return which
has been repeated in many forms through many
centuries. Its furnishing is romantic. The ship
that brought the twelve to land, the love of the
princess, the magic ring, the arrival in the nick of

time — all these are marvels of romance. But the interest is no more in them than in such courage as underlies epic. The love of Horn and Rimenhild, though strongly suggested, is not dwelt upon. The magic ring is used only as memento and inspiration; it does not do Horn's fighting for him. Horn's self-control in putting love aside for honor is more distinctly characterized than is usual in romance. In all this the English version may follow some lost Norse saga of Horn. But the companion French romance, *Horn et Rimenhild*, shows no such character. Drawn in the preceding century from the same source as the English version, it is five times as long and much more courtly and elaborate.

(b) HAVELOK THE DANE (about 1300)

The same theme of exile and return is even more strongly epic in *Havelok the Dane*.[n] The story may have been told originally as a Norse saga of Olaf Sihtricson; one of its early versions was probably Welsh, and it is still called a *lay;* but, whatever was the original, the English *Lay of Havelok the Dane* (3000 lines) is not a paraphrase from the French *Lai d'Havelok* (1106 lines). The French tells the tale briefly and without much modification of the conventional romantic manner; the English, keeping the framework of romance and the interest of adventure and love, expands the tale by vivid descriptions. The persons of the French romance are all gentle-folk very much alike; the persons of the English romance are strongly marked men and women, some of them rude common people, and all standing out very clearly because of the abundance of concrete descriptive detail, as is the way of epic. The true prince, treacherously put out of the way, lives to come into his own — that is the old story; and with it is woven a parallel story of a wronged princess.

Athelwold, King of England, at his death left his little daughter Goldeboro, his only child, in the care of Earl Goodrich, after taking oaths from him and all the other barons to seat her on the throne when she came of age. But Goodrich used his control toward establishing his own son. Meantime Birkabeyn, King of Denmark, lodged a like trust at his death in his favorite Earl Godard; and even more outrageously Godard abused it. For he cut the throats of both the little princesses and gave the boy Havelok to be drowned by a fisherman named Grim. When Grim came to the foul work at night, lo! a light shone from the boy's mouth, and on his shoulder was uncovered the royal kinmark. Then Grim, taking Havelok with all his own family, fled to England and established himself on the coast of Lincolnshire, where is a town called Grimsby to this day. The boy grew up among his foster-brothers and -sisters, ignorant of his origin, big and strong, a huge eater. When famine pressed as he came to manhood, he went into the city of Lincoln to seek his fortune, and by his huge strength won a position as porter to Earl Goodrich's cook. Soon he became renowned as the tallest and strongest man of that country. The princess Goldeboro, who had been kept under close guard, was now of age and of great beauty. To do her shame and put her out of the way of his son's advancement, Earl Goodrich forced her to marry Havelok. "I promised," he said derisively, "to give her to the highest man, the fairest, the strongest. Where shall I find a man higher, fairer, or stronger than this churl's son in my kitchen?" At night Goldeboro knew by the light from Havelok's mouth and by the red cross on his shoulder that he was of high lineage. With her and with Grim's sons Robert the Red, William Wendout, and Hugh Raven, Havelok sailed to Denmark, gained the favor of Earl Ubbe, overthrew Godard, and won his father's kingdom. Then leading his Danish army into England, he vindicated Goldeboro's right in a great battle against Earl Goodrich, and made himself King of England also.

> Now have ye heard the gest all through
> Of Havelok and of Goldeboro:
> How they were born and how fed,
> And how they were with wrong led
> In their youth with treachery,
> With treason and with felony;
> And how the villains had by might
> Reft them that which was their right;
> And how they got revenge most fit,
> Have I told you every whit.

All these events are in the French *Lai d'Havelok*, but none of the English distinctness and picturesqueness.

> Herkneth to me, gode [1] men,
> Wives, maydnes, and alle men,
> Of a tale ich you wil telle,
> Hwo-so it wile here, and therto duelle.
> The tale of Havelok is i-maked.
> Hwil he was litel he yede [2] ful naked. (1–6.)

[1] *-e* and *-es* are sounded as separate syllables.   [2] went.

No translation is necessary. Read aloud, these opening lines, though somewhat rude, are far more regular and effective as verse than *King Horn*. Sometimes, indeed, *The Lay of Havelok* approaches poetic quality.

> It was a king bi are [1] dawes
> That in his time were gode lawes [2]
> He dide maken and ful wel holde.
> Him lovede yung, him loveden olde,
> Erl and barun, dreng and thayn,
> Kniht and bondeman and swain.   (27–32.)

But its force is mainly in the epic fulness of detail which makes us realize every situation by specific images. Grim, once settled in his English home, throve as a fisherman. The poem tells us, as the *Iliad* or the *Beowulf* would tell, just what fish he caught — sturgeon, turbot, salmon, cod, mackerel, and so on.

> Gode paniers dide he make
> On til him, and other thrinne [3]
> Til hise sones, to bere fish inne,
> Up o-londe [4] to sell and fonge [5]
> Forbar he neyther tun [6] ne gronge,
> That he ne [7] to-yede with his ware.
> Cam he nevere hom hand-bare,[8]
> That he ne brouhte [9] bred and sowl [10]
> In his shirte or in his cowl,
> In his poke [11] benes and corn.   (760–769.)

[1] former. [4] inland. [7] that he did not go with his wares.
[2] laws. [5] take. [8] empty-handed.
[3] three. [6] farmstead nor grange. [9] without bringing.
　　　　　　[10] relish.　　　　　[11] bag.

It is in such homely details of real life that the poem is most rich. "I eat more," cries the shame-faced lad Havelok, "than Grim and his children five. It may not be thus long." So, after helping Grim mightily by carrying huge panniers of fish, he resolves, in a time of scarcity, to seek his fortune in Lincoln. "But woe is me!" says Grim, "thou art so naked!"

> Of mi sayl I wolde were maked
> A cloth thou mihtest inne gonge,[1]
> Sone, no cold that thou ne fonge.[2]
> He took the sheres of [3] the nayl,
> And made him a cowl of the sayl,
> And Havelok dide it sone on.
> Hadde he neyther hosen ne shon.[4] (853–860.)

So Havelok went to Lincoln; and so we can see him go. In his eagerness to get work as a porter, he toppled a whole row of his competitors over into the fen. He put the stone twelve feet beyond the best champion. Strong and fair, he was also pure. "Of body was he maiden clean." To save his unwilling wife from further persecution, the great simple-heart takes her back to Grimsby. Grim is dead; but his children receive them with loud joy and promise of service.

> Thou shalt ben loverd,[5] thou shalt ben syre,
> And we sholen [6] serven the [7] and hire; [8]
> And ure [9] sistres sholen do
> Al that evere biddes sho.[10]

[1] go.   [3] off.   [5] lord.   [7] thee.   [9] our.
[2] take. [4] stockings nor shoes.   [6] shall. [8] her.   [10] she.

> He ¹ sholen hire clothes washen and wringen,
> And to handes water bringen.   (1229–1234.)

But Goldeboro, so soon as she knows Havelok's rank, urges him to win his Danish Kingdom. Every scene of their expedition has the epic definiteness of detail. Marvelling at Havelok's stature and at Goldeboro's beauty, Earl Ubbe had them to a feast, which is described in detail, and set a guard about their house under his faithful Bernard Brown. Nevertheless sixty men attacked the house at night.

> Bernard stirt ² up, that was ful big,
> And caste a brinie ³ upon his rig,⁴
> And grop an ax, that was ful god,
> Lep to the dore, so ⁵ he were wod.⁶ (1774–1777.)

The outlaws broke in the door with a "boulder-stone."

> Havelok it saw, and thider drof,⁷
> And the barre sone ut-drow,⁸
> That was unride ⁹ and gret ynow,¹⁰
> And caste the dore open wide,
> And seide, "Her shal I now abide;
> Comes ¹¹ swithe unto me."
>   . . . .
> Havelok lifte up the dore-tree
> And at a dint he slow ¹² hem three.
> Was non of hem that hise hernes ¹³
> Ne lay ther-ute again the sternes.¹⁴
> The ferthe ¹⁵ that he sithen ¹⁶ mette
> With the barre so he him grette ¹⁷

¹ they. ⁵ as if. ⁹ unwieldy. ¹³ brains.
² started. ⁶ mad. ¹⁰ enough. ¹⁴ stars.
³ coat of mail, byrnie. ⁷ drove, ran. ¹¹ Come right on to me. ¹⁵ fourth.
⁴ back. ⁸ drew out. ¹² slew. ¹⁶ then.
¹⁷ greeted.

Bifor the heved [1] that the riht eye
Ut of the hole made he fleye,
And sithen clapte him on the crune [2]
So that he stan-ded [3] fel ther dune [4]

. . . .

Sum smot with tre and sum with ston;
Sum putten with gleyve [5] in bac and side
And yeven [6] wundes longe and wide
In twenti stedes,[7] and wel mo [8]
Fro the croune til the to.
Hwan he saw that, he was wod,
And it was ferlik [9] hu [10] he stod;
For the blod ran of his sides
So water that fro the welle glides.
But thanne begin he for to mowe
With the barre. (1793–1853.)

Evidently the poet loved this fight. The idea of the hero defending the doorway against odds warmed his imagination to picture every detail — the big bar, the sturdy challenge, the manner of each great stroke. It is an epic situation, and epically he has described it. For here flashes out of the romance the old epic conception of the hero, not a gentleman keeping the chivalrous code of battle, but a popular strong man, king though he be, smiting his enemies with a door-bar. As if to complete the epic character of the scene, Hugh Raven, hearing the din, rushes up crying:

[1] head.
[2] crown.
[3] stone-dead.
[4] down.
[5] sword.
[6] gave.
[7] places.
[8] more.
[9] wondrous.
[10] how.

> Roberd! William! hware are ye?
> Gripeth [1] eyther unker a god tre,
> And late we nouht thise dogges fle
> Til ure louerd wreke be.
> Cometh swithe, and folwes me! (1881–1885.)

This is what the English poet felt and has made us feel. As for love, not only is there none of the French dwelling on tender passages, but there is no love-making at all. At the end of the tale all the principal characters are disposed in marriage. For the rest, the poet has this to say of Havelok and Goldeboro, after their battles were over:

> So mikel love was hem bitwene
> That al the world spak of hem [2] two.
> He louede hire and she him so
> That neyther other mihte be
> Fro other, ne [3] no joie se,
> But yf [4] he [5] were to-gidere bothe.
> Nevere yete ne [3] weren he [5] wrothe.
> For here [6] love was ay newe;
> Nevere yete wordes ne [3] grewe
> Bitwene hem, hwar-of no lathe [7]
> Mihte rise, ne no wrathe.   (2967–2977.)

Love before marriage the poet can dispense with altogether; love after marriage he dismisses with general, perfunctory praise; but his real interest, and

---

[1] Grip each of you a good tree,
And suffer we not these dogs to flee
Till our lord avenged be.
Come forthwith and follow me.
[2] them.
[3] not, nor.
[4] unless.
[5] they.
[6] their.
[7] harme.

consequently his real force, is in action. *Havelok the Dane*, though its incidents are romantic, is in interest largely epic.

(c) Sir Tristrem[n] (about 1300)

A north-English romance presents Tristram as a ruder figure than the French courtly lover. Huntsman, harper, lover of the fair Iseult as in all the versions, this Tristram, as the English Percival, is a wild, strong youth, a fighting man. Compressed within some three thousand short lines, the story is rapid, sometimes too abrupt for clearness, never elaborate. Its conciseness is not the unifying seen in *Gawain and the Green Knight;* it is simply reduction of scale, the telling of all the incidents more briefly.

There is more art in the verse. Three-beat lines riming alternately are tied into stanzas by a final "bob and wheel" (3a 3b, 3a 3b, 3a 3b, 3a 3b, 1c, 3b, 3c).

A forest fled thai tille,	Ysoude of joie hath her fille,
Tristrem and Ysoude the schene.	And Tristram withouten wene,
Ne hadde thai no won to wille	As thare So blithe as bydene
But the wode so grene.	Nar thai never are.[1]
By holtes and by hille	*Sir Tristrem*, 2454–2464.
Fore Tristram and the quene.	

[1] The stanza may be imitated thus: —
    They fled to forest hiding
    Far from hall and tower.
    Naught had they for their abiding
    But the greenwood bower.

Besides control of his pretty stanza, the poet has bright suggestions of wood and meadow. Tristram and Iseult live in an earth house wrought in old days by giants and approached by a secret path. Summer's heat and winter's cold they bear together. Without wine or ale or dainty food, they live on wild flesh and herbs. Not a forecast of the Forest of Arden, this is rather a reminiscence of an older escape.

(d) SIR PERCEVAL OF GALLES (late fourteenth century)

All these English developments, epic handling, stanza, love of nature rather than love of woman, are found also in *Sir Perceval of Galles*.[n] The English Perceval, brought up by his mother in the wildwood, is fair, strong, and rude. There is little care for courtesies; there is hardly a detail of lovemaking, in spite of the fact that love is the main motive of the original; there is no trace of the Grail legend which made later versions of the Percival story mystical. This Percival rejoicing in fight, simply humorous, is closely akin in conception to Havelok. In form the romance is like *Sir Tristrem*, summary in much the same manner, but with rather more skill in planning and with more direct and

---

> By holt and hillside guiding
> Went Tristram. Every hour
> Yseult in him confiding
> Felt all her joy in flower.
> Of pleasure,
> Beyond all jealous power,
> Had they brimming measure.

vigorous phrase. Brimful of action, it never pauses
in its swift course, and suddenly closes at line 2288.
The stanza has sixteen verses on five rimes: aaab,
cccb, dddb, eeeb.

Thus he welke [1] in the lande
With his darte in his hande.
Under the wild wode wande [2]
  He wex [3] and wel thrave. [4]
He wolde schote with his
  spere
Bestes and other gere
As many als [5] he mighte bere.
  He was a gude knave. [6]

Smal birdes wolde he slo, [7]
Hertes, hindes also,
Broghte his moder of tho [8];
  Thurte hir [9] none crave.
So wel he lernede him to
  schote,
Ther was no beste that
  welke [1] on fote
To flee fro him it was no
  bote [10]
  Whenne that he wolde him
  have.

2. *Conventional Romances*

(a) LIBEAUS DESCONUS[n] (Le Bel Inconnu, 1325–50?)

"The fair unknown" is handled quite conventionally in a version combining with it the equally
old story of the awakening kiss. The unrecognized
son of Gawain,

       Gingelein was fair of siht,
       Gentil of body, of face briht,
       All bastard if he were.
       His moder him kepte with her miht,
       That he scholde se no kniht

[1] walked.   [2] bough.   [3] waxed, grew.   [4] throve.   [5] as.   [6] lad.   [7] slay.
[8] those.   [9] no need for her to crave any.   [10] good, avail.

> Y-armed in no manere;
> For he was ful savage
> And gladly wolde do outrage
> To his felawes in fere.
> And all for doute of wikked los
> His moder kepte him in clos
> As doughty child and dere.
> *Libeaus Desconus*, stanza 2.

This opening situation, which is identical with that of *Sir Perceval of Galles*, is merely summarized, without any such detail as makes that story vivid. The main narrative of Gingelein's following a damsel to deliver her mistress tells briefly the same story as Malory's seventh book and Tennyson's *Gareth and Lynette*. To this is added the entirely separate story of freeing a maid from enchantment. Nor has the detail distinctive character.

> In the grene greves
> They dihte a logge of leves
> With swordes briht and broune.   (595–597.)

It shows neither observation nor feeling to call groves green and swords bright. Indeed, the only specific detail is of fighting and of the dress and trappings of the vague personages.

(b) SIR BEVIS OF HAMPTON (about 1300)

Equally conventional is *Sir Bevis*.[n] Though a few of its many scenes are laid in England, it has no distinctly English character. Rather it is a typically conventional romance of the middle age, belonging to every country in general and no country in particular, and consisting of a collection of adventures about a famous name. The story is known in four French versions and six Italian, besides Scandinavian, Dutch, and Celtic.

Sir Bevis of Hampton, in his boyhood banished among the Saracens by his wicked mother, grew in renown, won victory for the Saracen King Ermin, and the love of the King's daughter Josian. Josian embracing Christianity for his sake, Bevis was treacherously imprisoned and Josian forced to wed King Ivor of Mombraunt. Escaping after seven years, and finding Josian wedded in name only, Bevis carried her off. After various adventures they went to Cologne, where Bevis slew a dragon, and whence he made an expedition to recover his English inheritance. Meantime Josian, once more forced to marry, strangled the offender and was condemned to be burnt. Bevis arrived from England in time to save her, and took her back to his domain. Thence they returned to the East, where they assured domain for their two sons. Their English lands being threatened, they returned to defend these. In settlement, a daughter of the King of England was married to one of their sons. They went once more to the East, and died in each other's arms.

This is the old, old story of exile and return, of the long-lost heir who comes at last to his own. As told in this romance of 4600 lines, it has twenty-five characters that play a distinct part, and as many more characters, or groups of characters, whose action is subordinate. There are nine separate places of action, with rapid shifting back and forth, from England to Ermonie, to Damascus, to Jerusalem, to Mombraunt, to Cologne, to England, to Cologne again, to England, to Ermonie, and so on. So bewildering is the succession of persons and places that it is hard to keep the names in mind even while one reads. Beginning with Bevis's father, the romance proceeds chronologically by adding adventure until Bevis's sons are grown men. At the beginning, indeed, one's interest is held by the boy's breaking in on his wicked mother's second bridal as a rude child Hamlet. Whether or not this situation was the original English story of Bevis, from the time when the boy is sold, as Joseph, to heartless merchants, events follow so thick that the modern reader is soon weary.

There is little compensating grace of chivalry. The hero's fame is supported mainly by brute strength. Of courtesy he shows very little, even to his lady Josian. Otherwise he is a stock hero of romance. As the greater heroes, he has a marvelous horse Arondel and a marvelous sword Morgelay. There is no lack of giants and dragons. There is oriental setting enough to range this story with romances derived from the East. Love, though it has little space, is distinct as a motive, both in the guilty passion of Bevis's mother and in the patient devotion of Josian. In both cases the woman is the wooer. Finally there is not art enough to relieve the unreality of romantic stock-in-trade. Sir Bevis and his host slay sixty thousand men (1018). Attacked in a castle, instead of keeping the advantage of position, he leads his men out, previously warning the enemy by trumpet (3365). The lady of Aumbeforce, wishing to marry Bevis, and learning that he has a wife, suggests that he be her husband nominally for seven years. If within that time Josian should be found, the lady would marry Bevis's lieutenant (3837). Reduced thus to mere marvel, romance becomes absurd.

(c) GUY OF WARWICK (before 1325?)

The English romance of *Guy of Warwick*[n] is essentially of the same sort. It differs from *Bevis* mainly in being better.

Guy, son of the steward of the Earl of Warwick, fell in love with the earl's daughter Felice. Rejected by her, first until he should be a knight, then until he should have proved himself, and again until he should be the most famous knight of the world, he fought many battles in France, Germany, Italy, and Greece. When he had thus won both the greatest fame and his lady, he was suddenly smitten with remorse for the waste of his life. Forsaking his wife, his domain, and even his country, he spent the rest of his life as a pilgrim. Though he still fought, it was only as a deliverer. In his old age he freed England from the Danes by defeating the giant Colbrand in single combat. Warned of his end, he summoned Felice to his hermitage, kissed her once, and died. She survived him but a fortnight.

For all its twelve thousand lines, this is less tedious and confusing than *Bevis*. Through most of the story the incidents are less crowded. Each situation being told more fully, there is less change of scene. Characterization there is not. All the men are merely knights, brave or cowardly, true or false, but otherwise alike. Yet Guy is preëminent among them not merely, as Bevis, by his strength and daring, but by his courtesy and fine feeling. The romance is truer to the spirit of chivalry in giving space to the tenderness and devotion of love and to the sensitive honor of knighthood. Conventional though it is, it shows both finer feeling and finer art.

3. *Romancing of Recent History*

The flourishing of poetry in the north awoke in patriotic John Barbour, Archdeacon of Aberdeen, the conception of applying romantic verse to a hero still living in men's memories. His long poem, the *Bruce*,[n] appeared (1375) within fifty years of the death of its hero (1329). Though he deals not with legend, but with history, with facts to be had almost at first hand, his love for the romances and his generous desire to make the figures of Bruce and Douglas inspiring color his story romantically. James of Douglas, even more than the Bruce himself, appears as a pattern of chivalry. Riding to support Sir Thomas Randolph at the battle of Bannockburn, he checks his troop on seeing the enemy waver, lest he should mar Sir Thomas's honor of routing a superior foe alone (xii. 114); and this is but one of the instances by which Barbour loves to show his hero a perfect knight. Thoroughly a figure of romance is the Douglas carrying the heart of the Bruce to the Holy Land for burial. As the paladins, he fights with the Saracens in Spain.

> The Bruces heart, that on his brest
> Was hinging, in the field he kest

> Upon a stane-cast and well more;
> And said: "Now passe thou foorth before,
> As thou wast wont in field to be;
> And I sall follow or els de." (xx. 423–428.)

As the great paladin Roland, he is overwhelmed by the Saracens (xx. 470); and he is lamented as Lancelot by Ector.

Early in the story, Bruce comforts his little fellowship through a tedious delay by reading the romance of Sir Firumbras (iii. 437); and the poet in his own person cites to point the moral of his tale, not only the heroes of classical antiquity, but also the Celtic Gall MacMorna (iii. 68), and Gandifer, one of the heroes of the romance of Alexander the Great. The fighting of these meager outlaw days is clearly shown as guerilla warfare. Bruce rarely had more than a few hundred men. But in the midst of these raids and surprises the poet makes the English Sir Aymer de Valence issue the stock romantic challenge to fight on a day appointed under Loudoun Hill. There is no doubt that Barbour intended to be romantic.

But the romances that he loves most and quotes are the historical romances, the "matter of France" (page 66). And his Scotch pride, his race feeling, and his local knowledge make him dwell on the fights of Bruce or Douglas with epic fulness of specific concrete detail. Though the many actors of the story are not sharply distinguished, yet their actions are realized fully. Douglas surprising and sacking his own castle (v. 396), Sim Ledoux scaling the walls of Roxburgh (x. 352), and the successive scenes of the great national victory at Bannockburn (xi–xiii) stamp themselves on the mind by sheer concrete abundance. One of the most intense of these passages, and one of the most thoroughly epic, is in Book vi. The king, having just escaped assassination twice, is tracked by his pursuers with a sleuth-hound through a morass:

> The king took with him two servants, leaving Sir Gilbert de la Hay to rest with his troop. He came to the water and listened intently if he heard aught of their coming; but yet he could hear nothing. Along the water on the other side he went a great space. He saw the braes standing high, the water running through unbroken, and found no ford by which men might pass but where he himself had passed. And so strait was the upcoming that two men might not crowd so as to take the land together. His two men he then bade go to their fellows to rest, for he would keep the watch there. "Sir," said they, "who shall be with you?"
>
> "God," he said, "forouten ma.
> Pass on; for I will it be swa."
>
> When he had bided there a while, he heard as it were a hound's whistling afar, which ever came nearer and nearer. . . . But he still thought he would stand there till he heard more tokenings; for he would not waken his companions for a hound's whistling. . . . The moon was shining right clearly. . . . And so long he stood hearkening till he saw at hand the whole rout coming in full great haste. Then he bethought him that, if he went to fetch his company, the pursuers would all have passed the ford before he could return, and that then he must

choose either to flee or to die. But his heart, which was
stout and high, counseled him to abide alone and keep
them at the ford and defend well the upcoming, since he
had on mail to guard him from their arrows. For if he
were of great manhood, he might daunt them all, since
they could come on but one by one. He did even as his
heart bade him. Stark outrageous courage he had when
he so stoutly took upon himself to fight alone with two
hundred and more. Therewith he went to the water; and
they upon the other party, who saw him stand there alone,
rode thronging into the water; for they had little fear
of him and rode to him in full great haste. He smote the
first so rigorously with his spear, which cut right sharply,
that he bore him down to the earth. The rest came then
in a rush. But the horse of the man that was borne down
cumbered the pass; and when the king saw that it was so
he stabbed the horse, who kicked and then fell in the pass.

> The rest with that came with a shout;
> And he that stalwart was and stout
> Met them right stoutly at the brae,
> And so fully he did them pay
> That some five in the ford he slew.
> The rest a little space withdrew,
> That dreaded his strokes wondrous sore,
> For he in nothing them forbore.
> Then one said "Certes, we are to blame.
> What shall we say when we come hame,
> When one man fights against us all?
> Who wist ever men so foully fall
> As we if we this way fight shy?"
> With that together they raised a cry
> And shouted "On him! he cannot last."
> With that they pressed on him so fast

> That had he not the better been,
> He had been dead, as ye may ween.
> But his defense so stemmed that folk
> That where he hit with even stroke
> There might nothing against it stand.
> Shortly there fell beneath his hand
> So many that the ford was then
> Clogged with slain horses and men,
> So that his foes, for that stopping,
> Might not come to the upcoming.
> Ah! dear God! he who had been by
> And seen how he so hardily
> Addressed himself against them all,
> I wot well that he should him call
> The best that lived in all his day.
>   (VI. 67–175, slightly modernized.)

With rudeness of verse and style, there is epic force of national feeling and of telling detail. The parallel of Tydeus, by which Barbour illustrates this splendid holding of the ford, may have been drawn from Statius; but the example of a hero holding a pass against a throng of enemies is typically epic.

Barbour's narrative skill goes no further than this force of sheer incident abundantly realized. As his verse is often diffuse and monotonous, so his story moves at an even gait in simple chronological order without much plan. Description of natural scenery occurs only in a few passages so conventional as to borrow for poetic adornment even the nightingale, which never sings in Scotland. What is realized is action. The *Bruce* is a Scotch *chanson de geste*.

CHAPTER VI

MIDDLE-ENGLISH ARTHURIAN ROMANCES

1. *The Stanzaic Morte d'Arthur*[n] (late fourteenth century)

THIS simple, lucid Arthur story, beginning after the Grail quest, tells how the love of Lancelot and Guinevere was used to bring about the downfall of the Round Table.

> The knightis of the table round,
>   The sangrayle whan they had sought,
> Aunturs [1] that they byfore them found
>   Fynisshid and to ende brought.
> Their enemyes they bette and bound;
>   For gold on lyf [2] they lefte them noght.
> Four yere they lyved sound,
>   Whan they had these werkis wroght.
>   (Stanza 2.)

The verse is crude. The stanza is a simple alternation of rimes, and rarely rises much higher than in this passage above doggerel. But the presentment of characters shows some distinctness. "Nice clerk," cries Mordred to the reproving Archbishop of Canterbury, "trowest thou to hinder me of

---

[1] adventures. [2] alive.

my will?" (3010). The fair Elaine, purest figure of
the Arthurian stories, is nowhere presently more
distinctly in her sweet simplicity than here.

> Therle had a doughter that was hym dere;
> > Mykell Launcelott she beheld.
> Hir rode [1] was rede as blossom on brere
> > Or floure that springith in the feld.
> Glad she was to sitte hym nere,
> > The noble knight undir sheld.
> Wepinge was hyr moste chere,[2]
> > So mykell on hym hyr herte gan held.[3]
>
> Up than rose that mayden stille
> > And to hyr chamber wente she tho.[4]
> Downe uppon hir bedde she fille,
> > That nighe hyr herte brast in two. (177–188.)

And when Lancelot will go away,

> Sir, if that your willes were,
> > Sith I of the ne may have mare,
> Som thing ye wolde beleve me here,
> > To loke on whan me longeth sare. (556–559.)

The composition leads consistently to the tragic
outcome of the whole. Gawain's bitter hatred of
Lancelot, for which even Malory shows no sufficient
motive, springs here from the killing of Gawain's
two brothers in Lancelot's rescue of the queen.
Thus we see clearly the fatal sequence leading to the
wreck of the Round Table. In details the manner
is traditionally popular. Dialogue often begins
abruptly, without explanatory transition.

[1] blush.   [2] mien.   [3] incline.   [4] then.

> Launcelott forth wendys he
> Unto the chambyr to the quene,
> And sette hym down upon his kne
> And salues there that lady shene.
> "Launcelott, what dostow here with me?" (65–69.)

As in *Sir Perceval*, one stanza is often linked to another by repetition of a verse as a sort of refrain. When the broken Guinevere, turned nun, bids Lancelot leave her forever and take a wife, he indignantly refuses, declaring that he too will enter a monastery and pray for her always. "Wilt thou so?" cries the queen.

> Lancelot sayd, "If I sayd nay,
> I were wel worthy to be brent."

The next stanza begins:

> "Brent to bene worthy I were,
> If I wold take non such a lyf." (3696–3699.)

Occasionally even a whole stanza is repeated with similar slight variation. Note the artistic refrain seen in *Pearl* (page 170), this is rather the simple connective used in the Bible story of Isaac and Rebekah. Both abrupt shift to dialogue and connective refrain are heard in many popular ballads (page 182); and this romance is sometimes like the ballads also in such homely traditional phrase as "rede as blossom on brere."

> Now thou levest for hyr sake
> All thy dede of armys bolde,
> I may wofully wepe and wake
> In clay till I be clongen [1] colde. (748–751.)

[1] shriveled.

2. *The Alliterative Morte Arthure* (about 1360)

The adoption of rime from the French did not put an end to alliteration. At first rime was merely added. Layamon[n] in his *Brut*, a romantic, half-mythical chronicle drawn early in the thirteenth century from the Norman French of Wace, rimes his staves now and then, often clumsily.

For north beoth tha Peohtes swithe ohte cnihtes,
The ofte ledeth in mine londe ferde swithe stronge,
And ofte doth me muchele scome and therfore ich habbe grome.[1] (13951–6.)

Feeble as is this riming — Layamon evidently meant to rime the last pair of staves, and perhaps the first — it has already admitted another verse scheme beside alliteration. But though the pattern was more and more determined by rime, alliteration persisted as an additional correspondence. The stanzaic *Morte d'Arthur* has a great deal.

  Bold men with Bowes Bent
   Boldely up in Botes yode;
  And Ryche hauberkes they Ryve and Rent,
   That throwowte Braste the Rede Blode.
  Grounden Gleyves throw hem wente;
   Tho Games thoght theym nothyng Gode.
  But by that Stronge Stoure was Stente
   The Stronge Stremes ran all on blode.
         (3074–3081.)

---

[1] Northward are the Picts, very brave knights,
Who often lead into my land host very strong,
And often do me much shame; and therefore have I vexation.

Here the alliteration is both excessive and, according to the old use, irregular. So in *Sir Perceval* it is evidently an additional correspondence used as the poet chooses.

> Scho Sente hir Socour ful gode,
> Mary that is Mylde of Mode.
> As he come thurgh the wode,
>   A Ferly he Fande;
> A Bird Brightest of Ble
> Stode Faste Bondene til a tre,
> I say it yow certainly,
> Both Fote and hande.
>
> (1825–1832.)

But alliteration also survived as a verse principle, sufficient without rime. Conspicuous in *Piers Plowman* (page 158), it is found in the Grail romance *Joseph of Arimathie*[n] (about 1350), and animates a strong and lively *Morte Arthure*.[n] Known as the alliterative *Morte Arthure*, this verse narrative is out of line with the contemporary development of the Arthur stories not only in verse, but in choice of events and in emphasis.

Arthur, sitting in royal state as conqueror and ruler of Britain, is approached by the envoys of Lucius, Emperor of Rome, who demands tribute. In reply Arthur leads a host to the Continent and utterly defeats the emperor in several battles. But Mordred, who has been left as regent, turns traitor, marries Arthur's queen Gaynour, and raises a host. In crushing this rebellion Arthur loses his best knights, including Gawain, and is buried at Glastonbury.

There is no Merlin, no Grail, no love-motive, no passing to Avalon. Lancelot is barely mentioned. Arthur himself, instead of merely presiding, fights his own battles as the epic kings. His chief knight is Gawain, who here keeps his old glory. Details of armor and fighting are specified with epic pleasure. Preparing to fight the giant of St. Michael's Mount, Arthur went to his wardrobe, armed him in a jacket with a rich border, over that donned a jerkin of Acres, and then a jesseraunt of fine mail and a slashed "jupon of Jerodyn." He drew on a helmet of burnished silver, "the best that was in Basil, with borders rich", the crest and the coronal enclosed fairly with clasps of clear gold set with stones (900–909). As the epic poets, he tells not only that a man was hit, but just how.

Than the comlyche kynge castes in fewtyre;
With a crewell launce cowpes full even
Abowne the spayre a spanne, among the schorte rybbys,
That the splent and the spleen on the spere lenges.
The blode sprente owtte and sprede as the horse sprynges,
And he sproules full spakely, bot spekes he no more.[1]
(2058–2063.)

Through the same specific detail we see the embarking of an English host, as we see the embarking of a Greek host in the *Iliad*.

[1] Then the comely king casts in rest,
With a cruel lance strikes full even
Above the waist a span, among the short ribs,
So that splinter and spleen stay on the spear.
The blood sprang out and spread as the horse springs,
And he sprawls full soon, but speaks he no more.

When all was schyppede that sholde, they schounte no
    lenger,
Bot ventelde them tyte as the tyde rynnes.
Cogges and crayers than crosse thaire mastes,
At the commandment of the kinge, uncoverde at ones.
Wyghtly on the wale thay wye up thaire ankers,
By wyt of the watyr-men of the wale ythes.
Frekes on the forestayne faken theire cobles.
In floynes and fercostes and Flemesche schyppes
Tyt sailles to the toppe, and turnes the lufe,
Stande upon stere-borde, sterynly thay songen.[1]
(736–745.)

As the detail is epic, so are the communal feeling
and the distinct persons.

Than gud Gawayne, gracious and noble,
All with glorious gle he gladdis his knyghtes.
"Gloppyns noght, gud men, for gleterand scheldes,
Yof yon gadlynges be gaye on yon gret horses.
Banerettes of Bretayne, buskes up your hertes!
Be noght baist of yon boyes, ne of thaire bryghte wedis!
We sall blenke theire boste for all theire blode profire."[2]
(2851–2857.)

---

[1] When all was shipped that should be, they shunned no longer,
But spread sail straightway as the tide runs.
Cogs and crayers cross their masts,
At the command of the king uncovered at once.
Nimbly on the gunwale they weigh up their anchors
By wit of the watermen of the waves of ocean.
Bold lads on the capstan coil their cables,
In floyns and farcoasts and Flemish ships
Haul sails to the top, and turn the tiller,
Stand to starboard; sternly they sang.

[2] Then good Gawain, gracious and noble,
All with glorious glee he gladdens his knights.
"Be naught dismayed, good men, for glittering shields,
Though yon fellows be gay on yon great horses.

This "glorious glee" marks Gawain throughout the poem. Sir Kay seems to ride straight out of the *chansons de geste*. Mortally wounded from behind, he gives his last stroke and his last word in the dramatic key of the Elizabethan history plays.

"Keep the, cowarde," and calles hym sone,
Cleves hym with his clere brande clenliche in sondire.
"Hadde thow wel delte thy dynt with thi handes,
I hadde forgeffen the my dede, by Crist now of hevyn."
He wendes to the wyse kynge and wynly hym gretes:
"I am wathely woundide, waresche mon I never.
Wirke now thi wirchipe as the worlde askes,
And brynge me to beryell, byd I no more.
Grete wel my ladye the quene, yif the werlde happyne,
And all the burliche birdes that to hir boure lenge;
And my worthily weife, that wrethide me never,
Bid hire for hir wyrchipe wirke for my saulle."[1]
(2181-2192.)

Even descriptions of nature have touches of definiteness.

Bannerets of Britain, busk up your hearts!
Be not abashed at yon boys, nor at their bright clothes.
We shall blench their boast for all their bloody proffer."

---

[1] "Defend thyself, coward," and calls him soon,
Cleaves him with his clear brand clean asunder.
"Hadst thou well dealt thy dint with thy hands,
I had forgiven thee my death, by Christ now of heaven."
He wends to the wise king and winsomely him greets:
"I am perilously wounded; heal may I never.
Work now thy worship as the world asks,
And bring me to burial; ask I no more.
Greet well my lady the queen if the world happen so,
And all the stately ladies that belong to her bower;
And my worthy wife, who angered me never,
Ask her for her worship to work for my soul."

All the feules thare flesche that flye with wenges;
For thare galede the gowke on greves ful lowde;
With alkyn gladchipe thay gladden them selven.
Of the nyghtgale notes the noise was swette.
They threpide wyth the throstils, thre hundreth at ones,
That what swowynge of watyr and syngyng of byrdes,
It myghte salve hym of sore that sounde was nevere.[1]
(926–932.)

The tone is sterner and simpler than the usual tone of romance. No loose love-making undermines the old stress on loyalty; and there is strong faith in divine providence.

> Destiny and doughtiness of deeds of arms,
> All is doomed and dealt at God's will. (1563–4.)

The introduction, in spite of conventional pattern, is worth paraphrasing for its moral earnestness.

Now great, glorious God, through grace of himself
And the precious prayer of his peerless mother,
Shield us from shame and sinful works,
And give us grace to guide and govern us here
In this wretched world through virtuous living,
That we may come to his court, the kingdom of heaven,
When our souls shall part and sunder from the body,
Ever to be and to bide in bliss with himself;
And thrill me to throw out some word at this time
That neither void be nor vain, but worship to himself

---

[1] All the birds there flit that fly with wings;
For there sang the cuckoo in the groves full loud;
With every gladness they gladden themselves.
Of nightingales' notes the noise was sweet.
They strove with the throstles, three hundred at once,
So that what with soughing of water and singing of birds,
It might heal him of hurt who whole was never.

Pleasant and profitable to the people that hear.
Ye that lust have to listen, or love to hear
Of elders of old time and of their strange deeds,
How they were leal in their law and loved God almighty,
Hearken to me graciously and hold you still;
And I will tell you a tale that true is and noble.

3. *Gawain and the Green Knight* (about 1400)

Gawain, the same Gawain of the older tradition, has to himself the English romance of clearest distinction. *Gawain and the Green Knight*[n] (2530 lines) is eminent in both composition and detail. The nice adjustment of the story plan, the freedom and power of verse, are comparable with Chaucer's. The description turns conventional amplitude into a rich and precise realization not only of the social scene, but of the scenery.

As Arthur held high feast on New Year's Day, and would not eat till he had beheld some adventure, a huge knight, clad all in green, rode into the hall, in one hand a holly bough, in the other an axe, seeking the best knight to prove him. If any of the Table Round, he said, were brave enough to smite him with the axe, that knight should keep it for his own, but must agree to take a stroke in return within a twelvemonth and a day. Gawain receiving this adventure and beheading him, the Green Knight picked up the head and rode off with it, bidding Gawain meet him at the Green Chapel according to the promise for the return stroke. As the next New Year drew nigh, Gawain, riding wild ways afar in his search, was received and nobly entertained at Christmastide in a castle whose lord promised to escort him betimes to the

Green Chapel hard by. Meantime showing as a guest the noblest and most scrupulous courtesy, Gawain was three times tempted by his host's lady in vain. Then standing by the Green Chapel to receive the return stroke, he was but grazed; for the Green Knight, revealing himself as the lord of the castle and the deviser of the temptations, declared himself satisfied that Gawain was indeed worthy.

Though in this form the story may have come from Ireland, the romantic material is familiar. The originality is in the way of telling. Folklore and faery, suggested in the background, supply neither motive nor solution. Love is absent; and both adventure and chivalry are deepened. In a romance so originally shaped the sources are of quite secondary interest. The story is not retold; it is transformed. First, instead of reviewing many of Gawain's adventures, it is confined to one; and even within this single adventure, that our interest may be centered upon the victory of chivalry over base selfish gratification, all minor episodes are passed over swiftly. Gawain's adventures during his ride to the castle, which most medieval romancers would have told at as great length as the central theme of the temptation, are compressed within two stanzas out of the hundred. The first of these is remarkable for its description:

Many cliffs he climbed in countries strange;
Far flitted from his friends as a foe he rides.
At each way over water that the warrior passed
He found a foe before him — if not 'twas a wonder —

And that so foul and so fell that fighting was certain.
So many marvels at the mount there may be found,
It were too tedious to tell of the tenth part.
Sometimes with serpents he wars, and with wolves also.
Sometimes with were-wolves that dwelt in the knots;
Both with bulls and with bears and with boars other times,
And monsters that made after him from the high moors.
Had he not been doughty and daring and served God,
Doubtless he had been slain, or stricken full often.
For war wounded him not so much; but winter was worse,
When the cold, clear water from the clouds was shed,
And froze ere it fell to the fallow earth.
Near slain with the sleet, he slept in his harness,
More nights than enough in the naked rocks,
Where clattering from the crest the cold burn trickled
And hung on high over his head in hard icicles.
Thus in peril and pain and plights full hard
Across the country he comes till Christmas even
    Doth fall.
   The knight well that tide
   On Mary Queen did call
   To rede him where to ride
   And help him to some hall.[n]
        (713–739.)

Description becomes ampler within the field on which our attention is fixed. Interest is held not by the excitement of activity, but by the very vividness of the situation. Day after day, in order to give opportunity for the temptation, Gawain's host goes to hunt. Each hunt is described without tedious repetition; and the second is cleverly interrupted by the main story. Description of nature is at once so sharp and so delicate as to give of itself poetic distinction. Gawain rides through a wood

Of hoar oaks full huge, a hundred together.
The hazel and the hawthorn were huddled in a thicket,
With rough, ragged moss arrayed all over,
With many birds unblithe upon bare branches,
That piteously there peeped for pain of the cold.
(743–747.)

So we see his way to the Green Chapel.

They bent by the banks where the branches were bare;
They climbed by the cliffs where clutches the cold.
. . . .
Mist-mows were on the moor, melted on the mountains.
Each hillock had a hat, a mist-mantle huge.
Brooks bubbled and broke by the banks all about,
Shattering sheer on the shores as they shoved downward.
(2077–83.)

At the opening of Part II is a lyric of the seasons:

After Christmas came the crabbed Lent,
Which tries the flesh with fish and food more simple.
But then the weather of the world rebukes the winter.
Cold is clutching adown; clouds are uplifting,
Shedding the rain sheer in showers full warm.
Filled is the fair field; flowers there are blooming.
On the ground and in the groves the green is a garment.
Birds are busking to build and heartily singing
For solace of the soft summer now stretching along
     The dike;
  And blossoms are bursting to blow
  In rows all rich alike.
  Then notes noble enow
  Across the woodland strike.

Afterward summer ensues with the soft breezes,
When Zephyrus sighs himself on the seeds and the herbage.
Well is it with the wort that waxes thereout,
When the dampening dew drops from the leaflets,
To bide a blissful blush of the bright sunshine.
But then hies the harvest and hardens it soon,
Warns it for the winter to wax and ripen.
He drives with his drought the dust that rises
From the face of the field to fly full high.
Wildly winds of the welkin war with the sun.
The leaves are loosened from the limbs and light on the
  ground,
And all gray make the grass that green was before.
Then all ripens and rots that rose from the field;
And thus hastens the year into yesterdays many,
And winter is with us again; for no word gains us
            Delay.
      Lo! Michaelmas moon
      Was come with winter's pay.
      Then thinks Sir Gawain full soon
      He must be now away.   (503–535.)

Passing references in the romances to the seasons are usually both conventional and bare. The fulness and distinctness here are keenly appreciative. But fond as the poet is of the out-of-doors, he is fonder of in-doors. There is an even larger realization of the human setting, the chivalrous habits of lords and ladies. Few other works of many times the length have pictures so bright and clear of the life of the medieval castle. Even the conventional arming of the hero becomes picturesque (566–620). But though it is leisurely enough for picturesqueness, the tale does not lag. The abundance of description includes such delicate suggestions in speech and dialogue as bring out character. For though this romance opens with a most romantic marvel, the bulk of the story is focused on character. The Green Knight as seen in his own castle has more individuality than the usual personage of a romance. His lady is still more distinct; and Gawain emerges with something of that individuality which makes Chaucer's Cressida seem startlingly modern, and for which English literature in general was not ready until it had been taught by drama. The proving of a knight by a lady was already an old story; but this unknown poet reconceived it. He made it at once more delicate and more typical, made a commonplace adventure of errant knights suggest moral progress.

A modern reader is at first rebuffed by the style. It seems too allusive, too consciously literary. The overdone alliteration is not the only archaism. But these foibles are soon found to be part of an eager suggestiveness. The highly charged diction repays the attention that it demands. In the verse, on the other hand, the most marked trait is freedom. The dominant pattern is what was later called blank verse. Though the traditional division into two staves is felt, the cæsura is at once less marked than in *Piers Plowman* and more skilfully shifted. The stanzas, though alike in their "bob-and-wheel" close and in keeping their other lines, the bulk of each stanza, alliterative without rime, are not alike in length. The average is about twenty-four lines; but the stanzas vary from twenty or less to forty or more. Each stanza is treated as a kind of narrative paragraph, concluded, as the scenes of Elizabethan drama, with rime. So the verse too is made part of the sequence of the story.

4. *Malory's Morte d'Arthur*

No survey of English medieval romance can omit the *Morte d'Arthur* of Sir Thomas Malory;[n] for this, though it was finished in 1470 and printed by Caxton in 1485, is thoroughly medieval. The Renaissance, by this time well advanced in Italy, had not yet widely affected England, and, even if it had, would not have deeply affected Sir Thomas Malory. Writing some seventy years after the death of Chaucer, he is distinctly less modern. Chaucer looks forward into the Renaissance; Malory looks back. Not only does he turn away from the Wars of the Roses to the far wars of Arthur, but in his wistful sympathy with the ideals of a passing chivalry he keeps the medieval spirit. Besides, his *Morte d'Arthur* has been far more popular than any other English version of the Arthur stories. For both these reasons it fairly sums up the influential traits of English medieval romance.

The spirit of romance and something of its history are reflected even in Caxton's preface; for the first English printer, being also publisher, editor, and man of letters, could estimate Malory's work with literary appreciation.

After that I had accomplysshed and fynysshed dyuers hystoryes as wel of contemplacyon as of other hystoryal and worldly actes of grete conquerours & pryncez, and also certeyn bookes of ensamples and doctryne, many noble and dyuers gentylmen of thys royame of Englond camen and demaunded me many and oftymes wherfore that I haue not do made & enprynte the noble hystorye of the saynt greal and of the most renomed crysten kyng, fyrst and chyef of the thre best crysten and worthy, kyng Arthur, whych ought moost to be remembred emonge us englysshe men tofore al other crysten kynges. For it is notoyrly knowen thorugh the vnyuersal world that there been ix worthy & the best that euer were; that is to wete, thre paynyms, thre Iewes, and thre crysten men. As for the paynyms, they were tofore the Incarnacyon of Cryst, whiche were named, the fyrst, Hector of Troye, of whom thystorye is comen bothe in balade and in prose; the second, Alysaunder the grete; & the thyrd, Iulyus Cezar, Emperour of Rome, of whome thystoryes ben wel kno and had. And as for the thre Iewes, whyche also were tofore thyncarnacyon of our lord, of whome the fyrst was Duc Iosue, whyche brought the chyldren of Israhel in to the londe of byheste; the second, Dauyd, kyng of Iherusalem; & the thyrd, Iudas Machabeus; — of these thre the byble reherceth al theyr noble hystoryes & actes. And sythe the sayd Incarnacyon haue ben thre noble crysten men stalled and admytted thorugh the vnyuersal world in to the nombre of the ix beste & worthy, of whome was fyrst the noble Arthur, whos noble actes I purpose to wryte in thys present book here folowyng; the second was Charlemayn, or Charles the grete, of whome thystorye is had in many places bothe in frensshe and englysshe; and the thyrd and last was Godefray of boloyn, of whos actes & lyf I made a book vnto thexecellent prynce and kyng of noble memorye, kyng Edward the fourth. The sayd noble Ientylmen instantly requyred me temprynte thystorye of the sayd noble kyng and conquerour, kyng Arthur, and of his knyghtes, wyth thystorye of the saynt greal and of the deth and endyng of the sayd Arthur, affermyng that I ought rather tenprynte his actes and noble feates than of godefroye of boloyne or ony the other eyght. . . . I haue after the symple connynge that god hath sente to me, vnder the fauour and correctyon of al noble lordes and gentylmen, enprysed to enprynte a book of the noble hystoryes of the sayd kynge Arthur and of certeyn of his knyghtes after a copye vnto me delyuerd, whyche copye Syr Thomas Malorye dyd take oute of certeyn bookes of frensshe and reduced it in to Englysshe. And I, accordyng to my copye haue doon sette it in enprynte, to the entente that noble men may see and lerne the noble actes of chyualrye, the ientyl and vertuous dedes that somme knyghtes vsed in tho dayes, by whyche they came to honour, and how they that were vycious were punysshed and ofte put to shame and rebuke, humbly bysechyng al noble lordes and ladyes, wyth al other estates, of what estate or degree they been of that shall see and rede in this sayd book and werke, that they take the good and honest actes in their remembraunce and to folowe the same. Wherin they shalle fynde many Ioyous and playsaunt hystoryes and noble & renomed actes of humanyte, gentylnesse, and chyualryes. For herein may be seen noble chyualrye, Curtoyse, Humanyte, frendlynesse, hardynesse, loue, frendshyp, Cowardyse, Murdre, hate, vertue, and synne. Doo after the good and leue the euyl; and it shal brynge you to good fame and renommee.

Sir Thomas Malory had seen knightly service under that mirror of chivalry, Richard Beauchamp, Earl of Warwick, who traced his lineage to the legendary Guy. From the bitter feuds of dislocated feudalism he had been taken to Newgate jail. The pathos thus cast on his doom of the goodly fellowship of the Round Table heightens the romantic motive of escape from the bewildering present. He has none of the Celtic eeriness; he is not at home in fairyland. Though he accepts courtly love as part of the courtly code, he cannot dilate upon wooing. His theme is the chivalry of the good old times.

That Malory cherished chivalry in a day when it was passing there is ample evidence in every chapter. His whole long task shines as a labor of love; and he is at his best in so praising the high deeds of knighthood as to stir generous emulation. To take one instance out of a hundred, the combat of Beaumains and Lancelot carries beneath the frank directness of the rendering a fine suggestion of the gallantry of youth.

Thenne he profered sir launcelot to Iuste and eyther made hem redy, and they came to gyder soo fyersly that eyther bare doune other to the erthe, and sore were they brysed. Thenne sir launcelot arose and halpe hym fro his hors. And thenne beaumayns threwe his sheld from hym and profered to fyghte with sir launcelot on foote; and soo they rasshed to gyders lyke borys, tracynge, rasynge, and foynynge to the mountenaunce of an houre; and syre launcelot felte hym soo bygge that he merueylled of his strengthe, for he fought more lyker a gyaunt than a knyght, and that his fyghtynge was durable and passynge perillous. For syr launcelot had so moche adoo with hym that he dred hym self to be shamed, and sayd, "Beaumayns, fyghte not so sore; youre quarel and myn is not soo grete but we may leue of." "Truly that is trouthe," sayd Beaumayns; "but it doth me good to fele your myght, and yet, my lord, I shewed not the vtteraunce." "In goddes name!" sayd syr launcelot; "for I promyse you by the feythe of my body I had as moche to doo as I myght to saue my self fro you vnshamed, and therfore haue ye no doubte of none erthely knyghte." "Hope ye so that I maye ony whyle stand a proued knyght?" sayd Beaumayns. "Ye," sayd Launcelot; "doo as ye haue done, and I shal be your waraunt." "Thenne I praye you," sayd Beaumayns, "yeue me the ordre of knyghthode."

MALORY, *Morte d'Arthur*, VII. iv–v.

Such passages warm the heart; and Malory has warmed more English hearts than any other English romancer of the older day. This affection has led some of his admirers to claim for him a large achievement of composition. Sir Edward Strachey speaks of his "epic unity." Whether or not epic has unity, whether or not the *Morte d'Arthur* is epic, has Malory achieved unity? His version of the Tristram story is no better welded to the Arthur cycle than by other compilers. In fact, it remains so distinct that it could be detached without the least disturbance. His version of the Grail story, though woven in, does not consistently further the main narrative. Instead, it is partly told several times; and the story in which it appears first, the fine tale of

Balin and Balan, has no specific relation to the neighboring books. Though others of the component stories are better joined, the *Morte d'Arthur* remains a typical collective romance, made as the earlier Arthur cycles had been made, by aggregation. Its only large constructive excellence is a certain culmination toward the close. It is composed, as others of its kind, by books, not as a whole. Even in single books Malory does not often approach the composition of *Gawain and the Green Knight*. For choosing from the huge Arthurian mass of his time, and sometimes for reconciling different versions in a clear account, he may well be praised, but not for composing his materials in a compelling sequence.[n]

But no other English collection of this scope approaches Malory in style.

Syr launcelot rode ouerthwart and endlonge in a wylde forest, and held no pathe but as wyld aduenture led hym. And at the last he came to a stony Crosse whiche departed two wayes in waste land; and by the Crosse was a stone that was of marbel, but it was so derke that syr launcelot myghte not wete what it was. Thenne syre Launcelot loked by hym and sawe an old chappel, & ther he wende to haue fond peple; and sir launcelot teyed his hors tyl a tree, and there he dyd of his sheld and henge hit vpon a tree. And thenne wente to the chappel dore and fonde hit waste and broken. And within he fond a fayr aulter ful rychely arayed with clothe of clene sylke; and there stode a fayre clene candelstyk whiche bare syxe grete candels; and the candelstyk was of syluer. And whanne syre Launcelot sawe thys lyght, he had grete wylle for to entre in to the chappel; but he coude fynde no place

where he myghte entre; thenne was he passynge heuy and
desmayed. Thenne he retorned and cam to his hors and
dyd of his sadel and brydel and lete hym pasture, &
vnlaced his helme and vngyrd his swerd and laide hym
doune to slepe vpon his shelde to fore the Crosse.
MALORY, *Morte d'Arthur*, XIII. xvii.

This passage fairly exemplifies Malory's prose.
It is less terse than the one quoted above, less terse
than many others that might be quoted; but in this
respect it is the more typical of Malory's usual
leisurely and lingering manner. The childish compound sentences are characteristic, not of Malory,
but of the half-formed sentence habit of his time.
But the imaginative realization of the scene in direct
simplicity of phrase is Malory's singular virtue. He
has the distinction and the charm of the great chroniclers, of Herodotus, of Froissart, of Villani, the
ability to tell a story, not rapidly indeed, but at once
sweetly and strongly while always telling it simply.
At his moments of deeper emotion he rises to eloquence. Tennyson's more elaborate rendering has
not dimmed Malory's Passing of Arthur.

"Tyde me deth, betyde me lyf," sayth the kyng; "now
I see hym yonder allone, he shal neuer escape myn handes;
for at a better auaylle shal I neuer haue hym." "God
spede you wel," sayd syr bedwere. Thenne the kyng
gate hys spere in bothe his handes & ranne toward syr
Mordred, cryeng "tratour, now is thy deth day come."
And whan syr Mordred herde syr Arthur, he ranne vntyl
hym with his swerde drawen in his hande. And there
kyng Arthur smote syr mordred vnder the shelde wyth a

foyne of his spere thorughoute the body more than a
fadom. And whan syr Mordred felte that he had hys
dethes wounde, he thryste him self wyth the myght that
he had vp to the bur of kynge Arthurs spere. And
right so he smote his fader Arthur wyth his swerde
holden in bothe his handes on the syde of the heed, that
the swerde persyd the helmet and the brayne panne;
and therwythall syr Mordred fyl starke deed to the erthe.
And the nobyl Arthur fyl in a swoune, and there he
swouned ofte tymes. And syr Lucan de butlere and
syr Bedwere ofttymes heue hym up. And soo waykely
they ledde hym betwyxte them bothe to a lytel chapel
not ferre from the see syde. . . . "Alas!" sayd the
kyng; "thys is to me a ful heuy syght, to see thys noble
duke so deye for my sake; for he wold haue holpen
me that had more nede of helpe than I. Alas! he wold
not complayne hym, hys herte was so sette to helpe me.
Now Ihesu haue mercy vpon hys soule." Then syr bedwere
wepte for the deth of his brother. "Leue thys mornyng
& wepyng," sayd the kyng; "for al this wyl not auaylle
me; for wyte thou wel and I myghte lyue my self, the
deth of syr Lucan wolde greue me euer more; but my
tyme hyeth fast. . . . Than syr bedwere cryed "A,
my lord Arthur, what shal become of me, now ye goo
from me and leue me here allone emonge myn enemyes?"
"Comfort thy self," sayd the kyng, "and doo as wel as
thou mayst; for in me is no truste for to truste in. For
I wyl in to the vale of auylyon to hele me of my greuous
wounde. And yf thou here neuer more of me, praye for
my soule."

MALORY, Morte d'Arthur, XXI. iv-v.

The diction of such passages was bequeathed to
the King James version of Old Testament narrative.

And David sat between the two gates; and the watchman went up to the roof over the gate unto the wall, and lifted up his eyes and looked, and behold a man running alone. And the watchman cried and told the king. And the king said, "If he be alone, there is tidings in his mouth." And he came apace and drew near. And the watchman saw another man running; and the watchman called unto the porter and said, "Behold another man running alone." And the king said, "He also bringeth tidings." And the watchman said, "Me thinketh the running of the foremost is like the running of Ahimaaz the son of Zadok." And the king said, "He is a good man, and cometh with good tidings." And Ahimaaz called and said unto the king, "All is well." And he fell down to the earth upon his face before the king and said, "Blessed be the Lord thy God, which hath delivered up the men that lifted up their hand against my lord the king." And the king said, "Is the young man Absalom safe?" And Ahimaaz answered, "When Joab sent the king's servant and me thy servant, I saw a great tumult; but I knew not what it was." And the king said unto him "Turn aside, and stand here." And he turned aside, and stood still. And, behold, Cushi came; and Cushi said, "Tidings, my lord the king; for the Lord hath avenged thee this day of all them that rose up against thee." And the king said unto Cushi, "Is the young man Absalom safe?" And Cushi answered, "The enemies of my lord the king, and all that rise against thee to do thee hurt, be as that young man is." And the king was much moved, and went up to the chamber over the gate, and wept; and as he went, thus he said, "O my son Absalom, my son, my son Absalom! would God I had died for thee, O Absalom, my son, my son!" *2 Samuel*, xviii, 24–33.

CHAPTER VII

MEDIEVAL LYRIC

LYRICS are not estimated by periods. The more we admire a lyric, the less likely we are to associate it with its time or its place. This habitual attitude is warranted by history. Any people that has reached a stable civilization may begin to produce lyrics, and may continue without much of that literary progress which is found in other poetic forms. The ancient lyrics of Sappho have been exemplars everywhere; and certain American lyrics of our time have been stimulated by China. Whereas verse narrative has a significant history, evidently developing from medieval century to century, lyric seems to have no history. Its art seems full-blown, perennial, and universal.

But though this is true of lyric essentials, there remain interesting variations of place and time. Love, death, hope, the wistfulness of childhood — such universal lyric themes may be expressed by images Chinese in their decorativeness or Greek in their love of light. Their setting may be Roman stoicism or monastic obedience or the imitative paganism of the Renaissance or the second-hand chivalry of the Cavaliers. Though in the last analysis these are incidental, they have their poetic value. Medieval lyric, more than either ancient or modern, is marked by its period.

The outstanding medieval achievement in lyric and the most pervasive influence are the Latin hymns.[n] From the death of Boethius, last of the ancient Roman poets, to the Renaissance relapse into imitation of antiquity a thousand years of Latin lyric are distinctively medieval. New with St. Ambrose, throwing the classical metric of Prudentius into new rhythms, the hymns developed with the Church. While popular conception and communal sentiment were continuously expressed in simple measures, the liturgy was expanded artistically in ritual, music, and poetry. Two of the greater sequences, the *Pange, lingua* of St. Thomas Aquinas for Corpus Christi and the *Dies irae* of Thomas of Celano for requiems, show that final fusion of conception and vision with emotional appeal which achieves truly lyric simplicity. Meantime Notker and Hermann of Reichenau had elaborated strophe and antistrophe, and Adam of St. Victor had explored stanza in various and exquisite recurrences. The art of the Latin hymns had range enough to be an ample exemplar for vernacular lyric.

Medieval Latin verse is accentual. By the time of Bede the preponderance of popular stress rhythm over the literary quantitative rhythms had become habitual. Though good verse, of course, used time values also, the rhythm, the pattern of the verse, was set and held by beats, as in English. The length and the number of syllables was secondary. St. Gregory's *Ecce jam noctis tenuatur umbra* looks like Horace's *Integer vitae scelerisque purus*, and so it may have been composed; but it came to be said and sung with a different rhythm. To render Horace's poem in its ancient time-rhythm, then sing it to the familiar college tune, then render it accentually, is to feel the change that by St. Gregory's time was coming over Latin verse composition. Whether he composed quantitatively or not, his poem came to be read accentually; and later hymns were so composed. Quantitative verse was written in school as part of the study of grammar, or afterward as a literary exercise; but hymns made to be sung in concert were composed accentually.

The commonest hymn line is of four beats, iambic in the Ambrosian hymns, as *Aeterne rerum conditor;* or trochaic in measures derived from the *Corde natus* of Prudentius, as *Apparebit repentina*. The former is used oftenest in a four-line stanza with alternate rime; the latter in a great variety of rimed stanzas, of which *Stabat mater dolorosa* became a favorite. Trochaic also is the commonest stanza of the Latin student songs: [n] *Mihi est propositum / in taberna mori*. A graver measure, derived perhaps from Boethius, developed in Carolingian times an accentual equivalent of the ancient spondee: *Sancti, venite; Christi corpus sumite*. These are the most frequent verses in a wide variety of stanza.

Though single accentual dactyls are often used in lyrics as a variation, a whole dactylic measure is rare except in long poems. Commonest in riming hexameters, it is conspicuous as the insistent rhythm of Bernard of Cluny's *De contemptu mundi*, which is often called from its first words *Hora novissima*.

> Hora novissima, tempora pessima sunt; vigilemus.
> Ecce minaciter imminet arbiter ille supremus;
> Imminet, imminet, ut mala terminet, aequa coronet;
> Recta remuneret, anxia liberet, aethera donet.

A pilgrim hymn assigned to tenth-century Verona is read most easily as a dactylic measure throughout.

> O Roma nobilis, orbis et domina,
> Cunctarum urbium excellentissima,
> Roseo martyrum sanguine rubea,
> Albis et virginum liliis candida,
> Salutem dicimus tibi per omnia,
> Te benedicimus, salve per saecula.
> . . . .
>
> *Analecta Hymnica*, 51 : 219.

Translation of the hymns into English, facilitated by the common accentual rhythm, made the Latin stanzas even more familiar. It exemplifies also the freedom of English verse in the number of unstressed syllables. The first line, for instance, of the following is felt to be metrically equivalent to its Latin original.

Vexilla regis prodeunt,	The rode tokne is nou to-
Fulget crucis mysterium,	sprad,
Quo carne carnis conditor	Whar he that wrought had
Suspensus est patibulo.	al mankinne
. . . . .	An-hanged was for oure-
The kynges baneres beth forth y-lad,	sinne.

Quo vulneratus insuper	Ther he was wounded and
Mucrone diro lanceae,	first y-swonge,[1]
Ut nos lauaret crimine,	Wyth sharpe spere to herte
Manauit unda et sanguine.	y-stonge,[2]
	To wasshen us of sinne clene,
	Water and blod ther ronne at ene.[3]
Impleta sunt quae concinit	Y-fulfild is Dauides sawe,
David fidelis carmine	That soth was prophete of
Dicendo nationibus	the olde lawe,
Regnauit a ligno Deus.	That sayde: men, ye mowen y-se
	How godes trone is rode tre.
Arbor decor et fulgida,	Ha tre! that art so faire
Ornata regis purpura,	y-cud [4]
Electa digno stipite	And wyth kynges pourpre
Tam sancta membra tangere.	y-shrud,[5]
. . . . . .	Of worthy stok y-core [6] thou
(Fortunatus, sixth century.)	were,
	That so holy limes up-bere.

(Text normalized from Carleton Brown's *Religious lyrics of the XIV century*, page 15.)

The following is even freer.

Aurora lucis rutilat,	On ernemorwe [7] the daylight
Caelum laudibus intonat,	spryngeth,
Mundus exultans iubilat,	The angels in heuene murye
Gemens infernus ululat,	syngeth,
	The world is blithe and ek glad,
	The fendys of helle beth sorful and mad,

[1] scourged. [3] once. [5] clad. [7] daybreak.
[2] pierced. [4] made known. [6] chosen.

Cum rex ille fortissimus,
Mortis confractis viribus,
Pede conculcans tartaros
Soluit catena miseros.

. . . . . .

(*Analecta hymnica*, 51 : 89.)

Whanne the kyng, godes
   sone,
The strength of the deth
   hadde ouercome,
Helle dore he brak with his
   fot,
And out of pyne us wrecches
   he tok.

. . . . .

(*Ibid.*, page 53.)

By the middle of the thirteenth century English lyric skill is clear in the popular round *Sumer is icumen in*. Its verse, though less remarkable than its music, shows a pretty control of variation within the pattern. By the fourteenth century English stanza is an established art.[n] The unknown author of a spring song (about 1310) in spondaic or dactylic variations, in adding alliteration to rime, and in light movement was an expert metrist.

Lenten is come with loue to toune
With blosmen and with briddes roune,
That al this blisse bryngeth :
Dayeseyes in thise dales,
Notes swete of nyhtegales;
  Ech foul song singeth.
The threstelcoc him threteth oo ;
Away is here wynter woo,
  When woderoue springeth.

Thise foules singeth ferly fele,
And wlyteth on here wynter wele,
  That al the wode ryngeth.
The rose rayleth hire rode ;
The leues on the lyhte wode
  Waxen al with wille.
The mone mandeth hire blee ;
The lilie is lossom to see,
  The fenyl and the fille.
Wowe thise wilde drakes ;

Miles muryeth here makes
    As strem that striketh stille.
Mody meneth, so doth mo;

Ichot Icham on of tho,
For loue that likes ille.[1]
. . . . . .

(Text normalized from Cook's *Literary Middle English Reader*, page 407.)

A livelier measure from the same period is the anonymous *Alison*.

Bytwene Mersh and Averil,
    When spray biginneth to springe,
The litel foul hath hire wil
    On hire lud [2] to synge.
I liue in loue-longinge

For semlokest [3] of alle thinge;
She may me blisse bringe;
Icham [4] in hire baundoun.[5]
An hendy hap I chaue y hent; [6]

[1] Spring is come with love to the farmstead, with blossoms and with rune of birds, which bring all this bliss. Daisies in these dales, notes sweet of nightingales, each bird sings its song. The throstlecock ay makes his plaint; [but] gone is their winter woe when the woodruff springs. These birds sing wondrous many and look at their winter comfort, that all the wood rings. The rose puts on her red; the leaves in the light wood grow all with a will. The moon sends forth her hue; the lily is lovely to see, the fennel and the chervil. Wild drakes are wooing, animals delighting their mates as stream that flows calmly. The moody moan, and so do others; I know I am one of them, for love that pleases me ill.

    Or, roughly to imitate the meter:

        Springtime is come with love to the dwelling.
        The blossoms and the birds are telling
            What all this rapture bringeth:
        Daisies over all the meadows,
        Nightingales within the shadows;
            Each bird song singeth.
        Complaineth but the throstlecock;
        The rest of winter make their mock
            When yellow woodruff springeth.
        But winter joys full many twitter,
        Southward beyond our tempests bitter,
            That all the woodland ringeth.

[2] language.   [3] fairest.   [4] I am.   [5] power.   [6] I have caught good luck.

Ichot[1] *from heuene it is me sent;*
From alle wymmen my loue is lent,[2]
And lyht on Alysoun.
  On heu hire here is fayr ynough,
  Hire browe broune, hire eye blake;
With lossum chere [3] she on me lough;[4]
With middle smal and wel y-make,
But [5] she me wol to hire take,
For to been hire owne make,[6]
Long to liuen I shal forsake,
And fey [7] fallen adoun.
An hendy hap, etc. . . .
(Text normalized from Cook, page 410.)

Friar William Herebert, who died in 1333, put a *memento mori* into simple popular stanza.

Sithe [8] man shal henne [9] wende
And nede [10] deyen at the ende
  And wonien he not whare,[11]
God is that he trusse his pak
And tymliche [12] put his stor in sak
  That not [13] when henne fare.

Ech man thenke for to spede,
That he ne lese the grete mede
That God us dihte yare.[14]

This lyf nis but sorewe alway;
Unnethe [15] is man gladful o [16] day,
  For sorewe and tene [17] and care.

[1] I wot (know).
[2] turned.
[3] lovely mien.
[4] laughed.
[5] unless.
[6] mate.
[7] doomed.
[8] since.
[9] hence.
[10] needs (necessarily).
[11] dwell he knows not where.
[12] timely (betimes).
[13] knows not (ne wot).
[14] prepared of old.
[15] hardly.
[16] one.
[17] distress.

MEDIEVAL LYRIC

Man with sorewe is first y-bore,	Ech man thenke, etc. . . .
And eft¹ with sorewe rent and tore,	(Text normalized from Carleton Brown's *Religious*
If he riht thenketh of his ware.²	*lyrics of the XIV century,* page 25.)

On the English side of the struggles narrated by Barbour (page 113) Laurence Minot, who lived in the first half of the fourteenth century, wrote popular verse in praise of King Edward and in scorn of the Scots. As an offset to Bannockburn he extols the victories of Halidon Hill and Neville's Cross; but most of his poems deal with the war in France. They are short, usually cast in rather rude stanzas, and depend for poetic effect on alliteration and biting phrase. For instance, the noble and pathetic story of the burgesses of Calais is told simply as follows:

> Lystens now, and ye may lere,³
>   Als men the suth may vnderstand,
> The knightes that in Calais were
>   Come to sir Edward sare wepeand,⁴
>   In kirtell one and swerd in hand,
> And cried, Sir Edward, thine we are;
>   Do now, lord, bi law of land
> Thi will with us for evermare.
>
> The noble burgase and the best
>   Come unto him to have thaire hire.
> The comun puple war ful prest ⁵
>   Rapes to bring about thaire swire.⁶

¹ again.   ³ learn.   ⁵ ready.
² goods.   ⁴ weeping.   ⁶ to bring ropes about their necks.

Thai said all, Sir Philip oure syre
And his son, sir Iohn of France,
　　Has left us ligand¹ in the mire
And brought us till this doleful dance.

Our horses that war faire and fat
　　Are etin up ilkone bidene.²
Have we nowther conig³ ne cat
　　That thai ne er etin and hundes kene.
　　All er etin up ful clene.
Is nowther levid biche ne whelp.
　　That is wel on oure sembland⁴ sene;
　　　　Hall's edition, Oxford, 1887, page 29.

The boasting verses sound as if they had been made at or near the very time.

Was thou noght, Franceis, with thi wapin
　　Bitwixen Cressy and Abuyle,
Whare thi felawes lien and gapin⁵
　　For all thaire treget⁶ and thaire gile?
Bischoppes war there in that while
　　That songen all withouten stole.
Philip the Valas was a file;⁷
　　He fled and durst noght tak his dole.
　　　　　　Hall's edition, page 25.

Courtly medieval lyric, the poetry reflecting the social code of courtly love, derived its stanzas from the patterns of the Provençal troubadours.[n] Often ingeniously elaborate, these most generally show the metrical values of refrain. The *balade*, one of

---

¹ lying.　　　　　　³ rabbit　　　　　　⁵ lie and gape.
² every one eaten up at once.　⁴ semblance, countenance.　⁶ magic, trick.
　　　　　⁷ vile, *i.e.* coward.

the simpler forms and one of the most widespread
in time and place, has three stanzas ending each
on the same line, and often adds an envoy. It is
heard at its prettiest in Chaucer.

> Hyd, Absolon, thy gilte tresses clere;
> Ester, ley thou thy meknesse al adoun;
> Hyd, Jonathas, al thy frendly manere;
> Penalopee and Marcia Catoun,
> Mak of your wyfhod no comparisoun;
> Hyde ye your beautes, Isoude and Eleyne;
> My lady cometh, that al this may disteyne.
>
> Thy faire body, lat hit nat appere,
> Lavyne; and thou, Lucresse of Rome toun,
> And Polixene, that boghten love so dere,
> And Cleopatre with al thy passioun,
> Hyde ye your trouthe of love and your renoun;
> And thou, Tisbe, that hast of love swich peyne;
> My lady cometh, that al this may disteyne.
>
> Herro, Dido, Laudomia, alle yfere,
> And Phyllis, hanging for thy Demophoun,
> And Canace, espyed by thy chere,
> Ysiphile, betraysed with Jasoun,
> Maketh of your trouthe neyther boost ne soun;
> Nor Ypermistre or Adriane, ye tweyne;
> My lady cometh, that al this may disteyne.
>   Prologue to the *Legend of Good Women*.

The enumeration of famous persons is a *balade*[n] convention. Chaucer's French contemporary Machaut, beginning one also with Absalom, goes on to Ulysses, Samson and Dalila, Pygmalion, and Solomon, and ends with Venus and Jupiter. The *Ubi sunt* type,

as it is called, is best known in the fifteenth-century
Balade des dames du temps jadis of Villon, which has
the envoy.

> Dictes moy où, n'en quel pays,
> Est Flora, la belle rommaine;
> Archipiada, ne Thaïs,
> Qui fut sa cousine germaine;
> Echo, parlant quand bruyt on maine
> Dessus riviere ou sus estan,
> Qui beaulté ot trop plus qu'humaine?
> Mais où sont les neiges d'antan!
>
> Où est la tres sage Helloïs,
> Pour qui fut chastré et puis moyne
> Pierre Esbaillart à Saint Denis?
> Pour son amour ot cest essoyne.
> Semblablement, où est la royne
> Qui commanda que Buridan
> Fust gecté en ung sac en Saine?
> Mais où sont les neiges d'antan!
>
> La royne Blanche comme lis,
> Qui chantoit à voix de seraine;
> Berte au grant pié, Bietris, Allis;
> Haremburgis qui tint le Maine,
> Et Jehanne, la bonne Lorraine,
> Qu'Englois brulerent à Rouan;
> Où sont elles, Vierge souvraine?
> Mais où sont les neiges d'antan!
>
> *Envoi*
>
> Prince, n'enquerez de sepmaine
> Où elles sont, ne de cest an,
> Que ce reffrain ne vous remaine:
> Mais où sont les neiges d'antan!

The prevalence of the *balade* throughout the fifteenth century is seen in a large collection of courtly lyrics, the *Jardin de Plaisance*, printed in 1501. The same collection shows the continuance of another courtly form, the rondel, in which the stanza is cumulative.

> Now welcom somer with thy sonne softe,
> That hast this wintres weders overshake,
> And driven awey the longe nightes blake!
>
> Seynt Valentyn, that art ful hy onlofte,
> Thus singen smale foules for thy sake:
> Now welcom somer with thy sonne softe,
> That hast this wintres weders overshake.
>
> Wel han they cause for to gladen ofte,
> Sith ech of hem recovered hath his make.
> Ful blisful may they singen whan they wake:
> Now welcom somer with thy sonne softe,
> That hast this wintres weders overshake,
> And driven awey the longe nightes blake!
>
> CHAUCER, *Parlement of Foules*, 680–692.

Balade and rondel, with rondeau and virelay, are set forms, used generally for compliment, condolence, or celebration — in a word, for occasional poetry. Among the hundreds of *balades*, French and English, in Chaucer's time few have the lyric depth of his *Balade de bon conseyl*.

Flee fro the prees, and dwelle with sothfastnesse;
Suffyce unto thee good, though hit be smal;
For hord hath hate, and climbing tikelnesse,[1]

[1] instability.

Prees hath envye, and wele blent overal.[1]
Savour no more than thee bihove shal;
Werk wel thyself, that other folk canst rede; [2]
And trouthe shal delivere, hit is no drede.[3]

Tempest thee noght al croked to redresse,
In trust of hir that turneth as a bal.[4]
Gret reste stant in litel besinesse;
And eek be war to sporne ageyn an al.[5]
Stryve noght as doth the crokke with the wal.
Daunte thyself, that dauntest otheres dede;
And trouthe shal delivere, his is no drede.

That thee is sent receyve in buxumnesse; [6]
The wrastling for this worlde axeth [7] a fal.
Her nis non hoom, her nis but wildernesse.
Forth, pilgrim, forth! Forth, beste, out of thy stal!
Know thy contree, look up, thank God of al;
Hold the hye wey, and lat thy gost [8] thee lede;
And trouthe shal delivere, hit is no drede.

Envoy

Therfore, thou vache,[9] leve thyn old wrecchednesse
Unto the world; leve now to be thral.[10]
Cry him mercy that of his hy goodnesse
Made thee of noght, and in especial
Draw unto him; and pray in general
For thee, and eek for other, hevenlich mede; [11]
And trouthe shal delivere, hit is no drede.

[1] wealth (prosperity) blinds everywhere.
[2] advise.
[3] never fear.
[4] *i.e.*, of fortune.
[5] "kick against the pricks."
[6] submission.
[7] asketh.
[8] spirit.
[9] ox.
[10] slave.
[11] reward.

But though the set forms are less apt for such fervor than for virtuosity, they are always a school of verse. Before the *balade* had faded, Petrarch had made the sonnet the occasional form of the future.

CHAPTER VIII
MEDIEVAL SYMBOLISM

THE simplest form of allegory is the fable (page 90). Still presenting types, but ampler, is the popular medieval debate[n] (*débat, conflictus*). With more or less thread of story, sometimes with descriptive elaboration, this pits against each other two typical figures. *The Owl and the Nightingale*,[n] one of the liveliest, personifies in the two birds the old strife between wisdom and art. Written early in the thirteenth century, the 1794 four-stress lines of dialogue are more than mere moralizing. With bright or sharp descriptive touches, they have hints of that interaction which later enlivened Chaucer's *Parlement of Foules*.

The French *Roman de la Rose*,[n] most popular of medieval allegories, presents the typical figures of Courtesy, Disdain, Fair-seeming, Shame, and other qualities as ladies and gentlemen. The rose-lady is love; and such story as there is tells of how love is finally won. For the allegory is of *amour courtois*, the code of social conduct in wooing. So it was conceived by Guillaume de Lorris, who between 1200 and 1230 wrote his pretty, conventional descriptions in some 4000 fluent lines. With little more of his slight story to tell, he left the poem unfinished. It was continued by Jean de Meun some fifty years later in 18,000 lines and in quite different vein. The allegory is both expanded and turned to satire. The two poems thus put side by side under the single title presented the social conduct of love from two typical points of view: (1) the desired lady is the distant object of long, unswerving, chivalrous devotion; and (2) she is on the other hand a most approachable frail woman. The medieval reader could take his choice. Guillaume de Lorris offered the correct literary code; Jean de Meun, much stronger thinking.

1. *Moral Allegory*, *Piers Plowman* (late fourteenth century)

In a somer seson   whan softe was the sonne
I shop me into a shroud   a shepe as I were.[1]
In habite of an hermite   unholy of werkes
Wente I wyde in this world   wondres to here.
But in a Maye morweninge   on Malverne hilles
Me bifel a ferly,[2]   a feyry me thoughte.
I was wery of wandringe   and wente me to reste
Under a brod banke   by a burne side;
And as I lay and lenede   and lokede on the watres,
I slumberde in a slepynge,   it sounede so myrie.
Thenne gan I meten   a mervelous swevene,[3]
That I was in wildernesse, wiste I never where;
And as I beheld into the est   on-heigh to the sonne,
I sawe a tour on a toft   trighely imaked,[4]

[1] I put me into a garment as if I were a shepherd.   [2] marvel.
[3] dream a marvelous dream.   [4] a tower on a knoll, squarely made.

A depe dale binethe, a dongeon therinne,
With depe dich and derk and dredful of sight.
A fair feld ful of folk fond I ther-bitwene,
Of alle maner of men, the mene and the riche,
Worching and wandring as the world asketh.
           Prologue, 1–19, normalized from the A text.

To dream in May is so common among medieval poets as to be a conventional introduction. Suspecting an allegory, we have to remind ourselves that it need not follow the lifeless pattern of the *Roman de la Rose*. Allegory no longer seems necessarily dull when we remember the *Pilgrim's Progress;* and in medieval England allegory was touched by genius in much the same way. A group of alliterative allegorical poems about Piers Plowman,[n] type of the honest laborer, is attributed to an unknown William Langland. Its prologue goes on to describe vividly the various people on this fair field the earth. Pilgrims, for instance —

Pilgrims and palmers pledged themselves together
For to seek Saint James and saints at Rome;
Went they forth on their way with many wise tales,
And had leave to lie all their lives after.
Hermits in a heap with hookéd staves
Went on to Walsingham and their wenches after.
Great lubbers and long that loth were to swink
Clothed themselves in capes, to be known for friars.
   .   .   .   .   .
There preached a pardoner as he a priest were,
And brought up a bull with bishops' seals,
And said that himself might absolve them all
Of falseness and fasting and of vows that were broken.

Unlearned men liked him well and believed his speech,
And came up cowering and kissed his bull.
He banged them with his brevet and bleared all their eyes.
. . . . . .
Ditchers and delvers that do their deeds ill
And drive forth the long day with "*Dieu vous sauve, dame Emma.*"
Cooks and their scullions cry their "Hot pies, hot!
Good geese and pigs! Go we dine, go!"
Taverners to them told the same tale,
With "Good wine of Gascony and wine of Alsace,
Of Rhine and of Rochelle, the roast to digest."
All this I saw sleeping and seven times more.
(Prologue, from line 46.)

Piers Plowman is marked off at once from conventional allegory by such characterization. These are real people — types, to be sure, and described very briefly, but flashed upon us as individuals. For even as the pardoner is not merely typical of his class, but stands out as an individual, so do the abstract qualities and institutions. Of these latter the first is Holy Church:

What this mountain meaneth, and this darksome dale,
And this fair field full of folk, fairly I shall show you.
A lady lovely of look in linen apparelled
Came adown from the cliff and called me fairly
And said: "Son, sleepest thou? Seest thou this people,
How busy they be about the maze?
The most part of the people that are passing now on earth
Have their worship in this world; care they for no better.
Of other heaven than here hold they no account."

I was afraid of her face, fair though she were,
And said "*Merci, ma dame,* what is this to mean?"
"This tower and this toft," quoth she, "Truth is therein;
And would that ye wrought as his word teacheth."
(I. 1–13.)

Truth, says the lady, is the guide to conduct. The dungeon in the deep dale is the castle of Care. "And who," asks the dreamer, "are you?"

"Holy Church I am," quoth she; "thou oughtest me to know.
I fostered thee first and thy faith taught thee.
Thou broughtest me bondsmen my bidding to work
And to love me loyally while thy life endured."
Then kneeled I on my knees and cried her of grace.
(I. 73–77.)

In answer Holy Church says, "When all treasure is tried, truth is the best," shows how this works out in humility, and goes on:

"For though ye be true of tongue and true in your winning,
And eke as chaste as a child that in church weepeth,
Unless ye live truly and also love the poor,
And such goods as God sends truly divide,
Ye have no more merit in Mass or in hours.

. . . . . .

For James the gentle judgeth in his books
That faith without fruit is feebler than naught,
And dead as a door-nail, unless the deed follow."

. . . . . .

Yet kneeled I on my knees and cried her of grace
And said "*Merci, madame,* for Mary's love, of heaven,
That bare the blissful Bairn that bought us on the rood,
Teach me the true way for to tell the false."

"Look on thy left hand," quoth she "and see where he
    standeth,
Both False and Favel and all his whole crew."
I looked on the left hand as the lady told me;
Then was I ware of a woman wondrously apparelled,
Fair with all her furs, the richest upon earth,
Crowned with a crown — the king hath no better.
All her five fingers were fettered with gems
Picked of the preciousest that prince ever wore.
In red scarlet she rode, be-ribboned with gold.

       .   .   .   .   .   .

"What is this woman," quoth I, "thus wondrously at-
    tired?"
"That is Meed the maiden," quoth she, "that hath me
    marred full often!"
                           (end of I, opening of II.)

    Lady Meed is presented not only thus by her looks, but also by her speech and actions. She is made to characterize herself, as a person in a play. With the aid of Simony and Favel, she is to be married to False; but, their project being scented, they are forced to carry the case before the king. Thereupon all the lying crew flee except Lady Meed herself, who is much courted by the justices, and shriven by a venal confessor on her promise to put a window in his church. She intercedes with the mayor to wink at the oppression of the poor by landlords and tradesmen. The king proposing to marry her to Conscience, she professes willingness; but Conscience refuses in an arraignment of her and all her works, and adds a stout rebuttal to her meek and crafty defence.

"Cease now," said the king; "I suffer you no more.
Ye shall assent, forsooth, and serve me both.
Kiss her," quoth the king, "Conscience, I bid thee."
"Nay, by Christ," quoth Conscience; "congé me rather.
Unless Reason rede me thereto, rather will I die!"
(IV. 1-5.)

Reason, being fetched to court, sees justice done in a suit against Wrong, in spite of the intercession of Lady Meed, and undertakes to rule the realm.

"By Him that reached on the rood," quoth Reason to the king,
"But I rule thus thy realm, rend out my ribs,
If it be so that Buxomness be at mine assent."
"I assent," quoth the king, "by Saint Mary my Lady,
Once my counsel is come of clerks and of earls.
But readily, Reason, thou ridest not hence;
For as long as I live let thee I will not."
"I am ready," quoth Reason, "to rest with thee ever.
So that Conscience be our counselor, care I for no better."
"I grant gladly," quoth the king. "God forbid that he fail.
And as long as I live let us bide together."
(end of IV.)

Thus ends the first vision. In the second part Conscience comes with a cross to preach repentance. Pernel Proudheart is smitten with contrition. Envy and Covetousness and the other deadly sins as they come to confession are characterized quite as clearly by their own words as the people of early Elizabethan drama. Most dramatic of all is the episode of Gluttony:

Now beginneth the Glutton for to go to shrift.
His course is to church-ward his shrift for to tell.
Then Betty the brewster bade him good morrow,
And straightway she asked of him whither he would.
"To holy church," quoth he, "for to hear Mass;
And soon I shall be shriven, and sin no more."
"I have good ale, gossip," quoth she. "Glutton, wilt thou assay?"
"Hast thou aught i' thy purse," quoth he, "any hot spices?"
"Yea, Glutton, gossip," quoth she, "God wot, full good.
I have pepper and peony and a pound of garlic,
A farthing-worth of fennel-seed for these fasting days."
Then goeth Glutton in, and great oaths after.
Cissy the souter's wife sat on the bench.
Wat the warrener and his wife too,
Tomkin the tinker and two of his helpers,
Hick the hackney-man, and Hodge the needler,
Clarice of Cock Lane and the clerk of the church,
Sir Pierce of Pridie and Pernel of Flanders,
Davy the ditcher and a dozen other,
A rebeck-player, a rat-catcher, a raker from Cheapside,
A rope-maker, a riding-man, and Rose the disher,
Godfrey of Garlickhithe and Griffin the Welshman,
Second-hand men a heap, — early in the morning
Give Glutton with good will good ale to handsel.
. . . .
There was laughing and leering and "Let go the cup."
Bargains and beverages began to arise;
And they sat so till evensong, and sang now and then,
Till Glutton had gulped a gallon and a gill.
. . . .

MEDIEVAL SYMBOLISM

He had no strength to stand till he his staff had.
Then began he for to go like a gleeman's dog,
Sometimes aside and sometimes aback,
As he that sets a snare to seize birds with.
When he drew to the door, then dimmed his eyes;
And athwart the threshold he was thrown to the ground.
Clement the cobbler caught Glutton by the middle,
And for to lift him aloft laid him on his knees;
And Glutton was a great churl and grim in the lifting.

. . . . . .

With all the woe of this world his wife and his daughter
Bare him home to his bed and brought him therein.
And after all this surfeit such a sloth he had
That he slept Saturday and Sunday till sun was going to
    rest.
Then he wakened from his wink, and wiped his eyes.
The first word that he spake was "Where is the cup?"
His wife warned him then of wickedness and of sin.
Then was he rueful, the rascal, and rubbed his ears;
Began to groan grimly and great dole to make
For the wicked life that he so long had lived.
"For hunger or for thirst, I make here mine oath,
On Friday not even fish shall fill my maw,
Ere Abstinence, mine aunt, have given me leave.
And yet have I hated her all my lifetime."
           (V. 146–221; B text, 304–391.)

We must go to Falstaff's cronies at the Boar's Head in this same London neighborhood to find a company of folk from the city streets comparable to this in concise force of rendering.

Force, not beauty; for evidently the poet of *Piers Plowman* has no such thought of beauty as the poet of *Gawain* or of *Pearl*. Realization he has; he makes us see what he saw. The conventional vision form made popular by the *Roman de la Rose* he animates with dramatic power. But he wished men, imagining these people, to be moved with the evil and the aspiration of the time. He would make them cry out, like Christian in Bunyan's allegory, "What shall I do?" He is a moralist, a reformer, a preacher. His story, with all its pictures, is to stir men's souls.

A thousand of men then thronged all together,
Weeping and wailing for their wicked deeds,
Crying upward to Christ and to His clean Mother
To have grace to seek for Saint Truth.   God grant they so
    may!   (V. 260–263; B text, 517–519.)

It is like a wood-cut by Dürer.

The throng asks guidance of a palmer fresh from the Holy Land; but he has never heard of Saint Truth. Then suddenly appears the Plowman, the honest and faithful laborer who can show men how to live.

"Peter," quoth a plowman, and put forth his head.
"I know him as naturally as a student his books.
Clean conscience and wit kenned me to his dwelling,
And did ensure me straightway to serve him forever.
Both to sow and to set while I swink might,
I have been his fellow this fifteen winter."
           (VI. 28–33; B text, V. 544–549.)

So the Plowman becomes their guide to Saint Truth. But first he teaches them to work, each in his station.

> "That were a long letting," quoth a lady in a veil.
> "What shall we women be working the while?"
> "Some shall sew the sacking for saving of wheat;
> And ye women that have wool work at it fast;
> Spin it all speedily; spare not your fingers,
> But if it be holyday or else be holy even.
> Look over your linen and labor thereon fast.
> The needy and the naked, take note how they lie,
> And cast on them clothes; for so would Truth.
> (VII. 7–15; B text, VI. 7.)

The knight, who wishes to lend a hand, is told that his office is to defend the laborers. The idle and the malingerers, on the other hand, have to be goaded to their stint by Hunger. So the Plowman teaches them to work out their salvation.

> Therefore I counsel all Christians to cry Christ mercy,
> And Mary his Mother, to be mean between,
> That God give us grace, ere we go hence,
> Such works to work while that we are here
> That after our death-day Do-well rehearse
> That at the day of doom we did as he bade us.
> (end.)

The vitality of this message and the vividness of its preaching were enough to fix the Plowman as a proverbial figure in English literature. He was turned by later reformers to their own purposes. We read again and again of the Plowman until he is superseded by Bunyan's Pilgrim.

As a story *Piers Plowman* is not easy to follow. The allegorical persons are more distinct than the allegory itself. The episode of belling the cat, for instance, and the entrance of the plowman himself, are so sudden as to be disconcerting; and the sequence of the whole is not always clear. The opening prospect of the Church ill served by churchmen, of the state with king, knights and commons, of the professions and trades, does not specifically lead to the apparition of Holy Church and to her message of truth. Nor are we quite certain whether truth is to be taken in its usual medieval sense of loyalty. The action of Lady Meed, again, is more distinct than its function. What is the significance of her marriage? Why should we then turn to the seven deadly sins?

More light comes from considering the sequence as rather of ideas than of events. Thus may be discerned first the duties of the ordinary man in the world, then those that are common ground to him and to the clergy, and then the special function of priests. So (1) the purification of society, (2) the purification of the individual, and (3) the way of salvation in the active life, have their counterpart later in (1) theology and Church government, (2) the special devotion of monastic life, and (3) the mission of the Church to save society.[n] But though such leads can be found by the reader, they are not emphasized by the writer. "He is the victim, not the master of his thought," says Jusserand. Though the epigram is hardly just, *Piers Plowman* has fired more readers than it has enlightened. We see what the author saw; we feel his passion for righting the world; but we are often uncertain what is to be done next.

The verse is a return toward the old staves. More conscious and more varied in *Gawain and the Green Knight*, these seem here merely a popular tradition. The old two-stave habit suffices to make sentences by adding one idea or image to another with little subordination. The diction is popular in the sense of appealing to that wider audience which enjoyed ballads, and more generally in being oral. Thus it reflects, as the verse does, the sharp contrast with the Gawain poem. That too implies a moral allegory, but an allegory of individual knighthood heightened by religion. This in both style and scope is wider.

The tone and the point of view are English. The zeal is a sober earnestness; the commonsense, as strong as the sense of law and order. A faithful son of Church and State is pleading for reform, not for revolution. By the time of the *Pilgrim's Progress* hundreds of the common people had broken with both Church and State. For Bunyan, as for them, salvation lay with the individual. But *Piers Plowman* keeps the principle of obedience. In other respects the earlier and the later allegory are alike, most of all in that concrete vividness and homely force which are the salt of English literature. Both are full of homely proverbs; both have that popular style which is the oral habit of the preacher. Both are English in the same ways; but *Piers Plowman* is also medieval.

2. Mystical Allegory, *Pearl* (about 1370)

That spot of spyses mot nedes sprede
Ther such ryches to rot is runne.
Blomes blayke and blewe and rede
Ther shyne ful shyr again the sunne.
Flor and fruite may not be fede
Ther it doun drof in moldes dunne.
For ech gresse mot grow of graynes dede;
No whete were elles to wones wonne;
Of good ech good is ay bigonne.
So semly a sede moghte fayle not
That spryngand spyces up ne sponne
Of that precios perle wythouten spotte.
                                        (Stanza 3 normalized.)

The beauty of verse, which is one of the charms of *Gawain and the Green Knight*, is more conspicuous in *Pearl*.[n] Both poems are marked by an artistic sense of form, a shaping of the whole and a delicate use of detail. *Pearl* has one hundred stanzas in twenty groups of five, each group bound together by a refrain, that is, by the recurrence of a word or phrase in the last line of each stanza. "Precious pearl without spot," for instance, recurs at the end of each stanza of the first group; and each stanza must have a rime to *spot*. In other words, the poet rimes on one sound six times in each stanza, and on another sound ten times in each group. This complicated metrical scheme is handled with the smoothness of high art. Other fourteenth-century poets than Chaucer had wide and sure command of metric.

MEDIEVAL SYMBOLISM

The pattern of the *Pearl* stanza, with its alliterations, rimes, refrain, and metrical movement, can be followed better in imitative rendering. The third stanza, quoted above, runs thus.

> That spot with spices must grow and spread
> Where such richness to rot is run.
> Blooms of yellow and blue and red
> Are pure in their pride to meet the sun.
> Flower and fruit are unwitheréd
> Where it down drove in mold all dun.
> For each grass must grow from grains that are dead;
> No wheat were else for our winter won;
> Of good each good is ay begun.
> So seemly a seedling suffers not
> That springing spices the grave should shun
> Of that precious pearl without a spot.

The tenth stanza describes the river of Paradise.

> The comeliness of its current keeping,
> Were beauteous banks of beryl bright.
> Swiftly and sweetly the water was sweeping,
> With the rune of the ripples running aright;
> And its depths a hoard without hands was heaping,
> As glimpsed through glass aglow to the sight,
> As starlight when stolid souls are sleeping
> Streams from the welkin some winter night.
> For never a pebble in pool there pight
> But was emerald, sapphire, or sard to guess,
> That all the length was liquid light,
> So clear was all that comeliness.

Teaching him her happiness, the Pearl at last bows the poet to the divine will and the heavenly hope (stanza 92).

Right as the moon in might doth rise
Ere yet is driven down the day,
So suddenly in a wondrous wise
I beheld the heavenly array.
This noble city of rich emprise,
Unbidden, as aye the blest obey,
Was full of virgins in the very guise
Of her whose happiness I say;
And crowned were all in the selfsame way,
Apparelled in pearls and in weeds of white.
Bound on their bosoms all display
The blissful pearl with great delight.

Yearning toward this vision, he struggles to cross the river — and awakes. But Paradise has taught him peace. The poem closes:

To please the prince and be at peace with him is full easy for the good Christian. I have found him, day and night, a God, a Lord, a true friend. Such as I have now told was the fortune that befell me at this mound, bowed in grief for my Pearl; and straightway I gave her up unto God in Christ's dear blessing and mine own — he whom in the form of bread and wine the priest showeth unto us each day. And now may Christ our Prince grant that we become servants of his own household, and precious pearls to delight him ever. Amen.

Osgood's prose translation.

The poem has been interpreted as an elegy on the death of an infant child, and again as an allegory. It may be both; it certainly is the latter. Clearly its goal is vision. The conventional poetic dream is quite surpassed in these sharp images of physical beauty; but the sensuous imagery, never dilated as

MEDIEVAL SYMBOLISM 173

in the *Faërie Queene,* is consistently used for spiritual suggestion. The dream is not mere escape from grief, nor mere consolation; it suggests a spiritual progress. Thus the Mass (862), leading to the Apocalypse (1057–1068), reminds of Corpus Christi and of the Holy Grail. Thus the poetic sequence, even within its little compass, reminds of the *Divina Commedia.*[n] The allegory of *Piers Plowman* is moral, stressing conduct in this world. The symbolism of *Pearl* is mystical; it is an apprehension of heaven.

3. *Symbolism as a Medieval Habit*

Simple fable of types, debate of types as in the *Owl and the Nightingale,* description of types in the ideal setting of the *Roman de la Rose,* allegory of conduct as in *Piers Plowman,* allegory of aspiration and vision as in *Pearl* — underlying all these is a medieval habit of symbolism. Though symbolism is not peculiar to the middle age, it has in no other period been so pervasive a habit.[n] A commonplace of medieval preaching was to expound a text literally in the immediate meaning shown by the context, then morally for its typical significance in conduct, then mystically for its vision of divine providence. Warrant was found not only in parables, but also in apostolic teaching.

It is written that Abraham had two sons, the one by a bondmaid, the other by a freewoman. But he who was of the bondwoman was born after the flesh; but he of the freewoman was by promise. Which things are an allegory:

for these are the two covenants; the one from the Mount Sinai, which gendereth to bondage, which is Agar. For this Agar is Mount Sinai in Arabia and answereth to Jerusalem which now is and is in bondage with her children. But Jerusalem which is above is free, which is the mother of us all.
Galatians, iv, 22–26, King James version.

The Psalms were constantly used thus in the liturgy, the monastic offices, and the hymns. So used, a psalm expressed not only David or some other ancient in grief or aspiration, but also every man feeling the common human experience, and finally *the* Man who "hath borne our griefs", "*the* Word made flesh." Medieval readers were so familar with this that they readily saw in *Piers Plowman* at once a particular man and every man, and in the end a type of the Christ. The great abbey church of the Magdalen at Vézelay is sculptured not with the story of her life in gospel and legend, but with scenes typical of temptation, sin, repentance, and redemption.

Thus the Old Testament is made part of the New. Messianic psalms and prophecies are repeated in preparation for Christmas; Isaiah's "Who is this that cometh from Edom, with dyed garments from Bozrah?", in preparation for Easter. The Word of St. John is Isaiah's Wisdom and his Key of David. The Virgin Mother is hailed not only as Moon or Star of the Sea, but as the bush, burning and unburnt,[n] that guided Moses, as the fleece that guided Gideon, as the stem bearing the flower from the root of Jesse; and cathedrals have "Jesse windows."

> Than myght the mylde may [1] synge,
> Ysaye, the word of thee.
> Thou seydest a yerd [2] sholde sprynge
> Out of the rote of gentil Jesse,
> And sholde floure with florisshing
> With primeroses greet plente.
> Into the croppe [3] sholde come a kyng
> That is Lord of power and pyte.
> My swete sone, I see
> I am the yerde; thou art the flour.[4]

The view of the whole Bible as revealing one continuous scheme of divine providence for the redemption of mankind interprets also secular history. The statues thronging cathedral porches are not only of apostles and other saints, but of kings and queens. For all the arts, sculpture and glass as well as poetry, have this unifying poetic conception. Vergil's conception of the progress of mankind toward ordered peace is extended by Dante to reveal the gift and achievement of eternal life. The *Divina Commedia* is the supreme medieval vision.

Medieval symbolism, then, is a general poetic habit of vision. Its ordinary allegory, indeed, typifying the seven deadly sins or the seven liberal arts in verse or sculpture or illumination, is much the same as ancient or modern personification of War, or Industry, or Power; but it has distinctive character

---

[1] maiden.   [2] stem, rod (modern *yard*).   [3] topmost branch.
[4] The stanza is the second (normalized) of the lyric reprinted in Cook's *Literary Middle English Reader*, 465.

in a preoccupation with vision, in a poetic habit of looking through the transitory things of sense toward the unseen eternal. This is the common ground of poems as different as *Piers Plowman* and *Pearl* because it is the common ground of all medieval art. Modern symbolism, unable to appeal to such a general habit, runs far greater risk of extravagance and obscurity. It has the medieval appeal only where poet and audience think in the same tradition. Otherwise it may need footnotes or a guide-book. The medieval artist and his audience had the same symbols by heart. Again, in a modern symbolistic poem the individual persons and events may be primary; the symbolism, secondary. But in a medieval poem we may expect the symbolism to be the main intention. The medieval reader would thus approach *Gawain and the Green Knight*. He would hardly inquire whether Dante's Beatrice were reminiscent of a particular Florentine maiden, or whether the poet of *Pearl* had lost an infant child. For symbolism was habitual in medieval conception and interpretation.

CHAPTER IX

MIDDLE-ENGLISH POPULAR COMPOSITION

1. *Ballads*

APART from medieval literary fashions, written down seldom and late, are the popular verse-tales called ballads.[n] They are oral not only in the sense of being composed to be read aloud or recited, but as if to be chanted or sung, and in the further sense of being orally transmitted. From the late middle age into modern times they have been handed down orally among common people. Thus popular and oral, they are distinct also in composition, a clearly marked type of verse narrative.

KEMP OWYNE

1 Her mother died when she was young,
    Which gave her cause to make great moan;
  Her father married the warst woman
    That ever lived in Christendom.

2 She served her with foot and hand,
    In everything that she could dee,[1]
  Till once, in an unlucky time,
    She threw her in ower Craigy's sea.

[1] do.

3 Says, "Lie you there, dove Isabel,
    And all my sorrows lie with thee;
Till Kemp Owyne come ower the sea,
    And borrow [1] you with kisses three,
Let all the warld do what they will,
    Oh borrowed shall you never be!"

4 Her breath grew strang, her hair grew lang,
    And twisted thrice about the tree,
And all the people, far and near,
    Thought that a savage beast was she.

5 These news did come to Kemp Owyne,
    Where he lived, far beyond the sea;
He hasted him to Craigy's sea,
    And on the savage beast looked he.

6 Her breath was strang, her hair was lang,
    And twisted was about the tree,
And with a swing she came about:
    "Come to Craigy's sea, and kiss with me.

7 "Here is a royal belt," she cried,
    "That I have found in the green sea;
And while your body it is on,
    Drawn shall your blood never be;
But if you touch me, tail or fin,
    I vow my belt your death shall be."

8 He stepped in, gave her a kiss,
    The royal belt he brought him wi;
Her breath was strang, her hair was lang,
    And twisted twice about the tree,
And with a swing she came about:
    "Come to Craigy's sea, and kiss with me."

[1] ransom.

9 "Here is a royal ring," she said,
   "That I have found in the green sea;
  And while your finger it is on,
   Drawn shall your blood never be;
  But if you touch me, tail or fin,
   I swear my ring your death shall be."

10 He stepped in, gave her a kiss,
    The royal ring he brought him wi;
   Her breath was strang, her hair was lang,
    And twisted ance about the tree,
   And with a swing she came about:
    "Come to Craigy's sea and kiss with me."

11 "Here is a royal brand," she said,
    "That I have found in the green sea;
   And while your body it is on,
    Drawn shall your blood never be."

12 He stepped in, gave her a kiss,
    The royal brand he brought him wi;
   Her breath was sweet, her hair grew short,
    And twisted nane about the tree,
   And smilingly she came about,
    As fair a woman as fair could be.

Here is a fairy story.[n] The old myth behind it suggests the folklore behind the earlier romances. Many other ballads give the same eerie suggestion. Some are not merely like the romances in subject; they are the same tales. The ballad of *Fair Annie* is the same story as Marie's *Lai del Fresne* (page 77). There is a ballad, as well as a romance, of Horn (page 94). *Child Waters* is essentially like the story of patient Griselda; and *Sir Hugh* is the *Prioress's Tale* (page 207). Though they were not diffused in the same ways, nearly all the most popular English ballads have been found in other countries. At bottom they are no more English than they are German or Scandinavian.

But here the resemblance to romance ends. These likenesses, though interesting, are less significant than the differences. *Kemp Owyne* is unlike any form of narrative so far considered. It shows a distinct way of story-telling. Similar as its subject matter is to that of the tale of Henno (page 51) for instance, its method and effect are as different as possible. Ballads can hardly be explained, then, as abbreviated and debased versions of the romances. Even those that may have been borrowed from romances are not abbreviated. We must explain their brevity otherwise. Nor are they debased. Different as their narrative is, it is not inferior. It has its own success; it fulfils its own purpose.

The ballad form, first of all, answers the peculiarly oral character. We read ballads today only because oral verse-narrative is no longer usual. Many of them, as this of *Kemp Owyne*, were first written down in modern times by collectors. A few manuscripts go back to the fifteenth century; many are of the seventeenth century, the eighteenth, even the nineteenth. But the ballads thus finally written had been circulating orally, some of them since Shakespeare's time, some of them apparently since Chaucer's. Their history has little to do with

MIDDLE-ENGLISH POPULAR COMPOSITION 181

manuscript. They are anonymous; and they are essentially oral. Daughters, learning them from their mothers' singing, sang them in turn to their children, or in village groups. Barbour, referring in the fourteenth century to the three times when fifty men defeated a host, says:

> I will not rehearse all the manner;
> For whoso wishes, he may hear
> Young women when they will play
> Sing it among them any day.
> *Bruce*, xvi, 519, modernized.

Thus surviving traditionally in unlettered communities even down to our own time, they help us to guess what oral tradition was in the days before the education of the masses.

Romances too were changed in transmission, but deliberately by poets who could hold to their copy when they chose. For a ballad there might be no copy. A singer, rendering it as he remembered it, changed it as often accidentally as deliberately. Thus most ballads, and practically all the best known ones, appear in several versions; and if every oral version could have been preserved, the number would be increased indefinitely. Yet through the various versions there is in most cases something constant, a story clearly recognizable as the same and a definite manner of telling.

Popular thus in circulation, they were popular in other ways. Their folklore seems less transformed than in the romances from its original eerie strength.

Kemp Owyne, even in its modern version, is still told much as old wives may be imagined to have told those wild tales which Marie and Walter Map turned into sweet verse and elegant prose. Here is neither sweetness nor elegance. As the ballads tell often of violence and sometimes of crime, so they tell the tale bluntly. There is no description except rude conventional terms; there is no sentiment. But though *Kemp Owyne* is brief almost to bareness, without elaboration of any sort, it pauses to give three separate stages by which this British Perseus released his Andromeda; and these three stages are told in almost the same terms. Indeed, the triad with its slightly varied refrain comprises half the tale; and the refrain begins even earlier. This refrain, then, is not a poetic embellishment; it is a kind of nucleus; it determines the composition. The tale is conducted by the refrain. Emphasizing the narrative pattern, the refrain may echo an older participation by the audience. No ballad as we have it is communal to that extent. Every ballad that has survived may have been retouched, or even reshaped, both by oral repetition and by conscious art. But the ballads remain peculiarly popular in the directness of their appeal to the audience. That direct appeal, however it arose, marks them off in method and in movement. The whole body of ballads, some three hundred in English, is fairly homogeneous. In spite of many minor variations due to the accidents of time and place and transmission, it is yet unmistakably recognizable as a distinct form.

MIDDLE-ENGLISH POPULAR COMPOSITION

In defining the form we may begin by setting aside those few longer tales, often called ballads, of which the type is *Robin Hood*. This "geste" is rather a collection of ballads woven together about a traditional hero into a rude sort of epic. The stirring tales of *Chevy Chase* and *Otterburn* again, though they too have ballad traits, are carried beyond the usual ballad scope. The typical ballad tells, not the whole story, but its crisis.

SIR PATRICK SPENS

1 The king sits in Dumferling toune,
   Drinking the blude-reid wine:
"O whar will I get a guid sailor,
   To sail this schip of mine?"

2 Up and spak an eldern knicht,
   Sat at the kings richt kne:
"Sir Patrick Spence is the best sailor
   That sails upon the se."

3 The king has written a braid letter,
   And signd it wi his hand,
And sent it to Sir Patrick Spence,
   Was walking on the sand.

4 The first line that Sir Patrick red,
   A loud lauch lauched he;
The next line that Sir Patrick red,
   The teir blinded his ee.

5 "O wha is this has don this deid,
   This ill deid don to me,
To send me out this time o' the yeir,
   To sail upon the se!

6 "Mak haste, mak haste, my mirry men all,
   Our guid schip sails the morne:"
  "O say na sae, my master deir,
   For I feir a deadlie storme.

7 "Late late yestreen I saw the new moone,
   Wi the auld moone in hir arme,
   And I feir, I feir, my deir master,
   That we will cum to harme."

8 O our Scots nobles wer richt laith
   To weet their cork-heild schoone;
   Bot lang owre a' the play wer playd,
   Thair hats they swam aboone.

9 O lang, lang may their ladies sit
   Wi thair fans into their hand,
   Or eir they se Sir Patrick Spence
   Cum sailing to the land.

10 O lang, lang may the ladies stand,
   Wi thair gold kems in their hair,
   Waiting for thair ain deir lords,
   For they'll se thame na mair.

11 Haf owre, haf owre to Aberdour,
   It's fiftie fadom deip,
   And thair lies guid Sir Patrick Spence,
   Wi the Scots lords at his feit.

As *Kemp Owyne*, this is almost pure narrative. Description is reduced to similar conventional phrases. Omission is carried to the extreme of narrative conciseness. The tale does not explain how the king happened to be sitting in Dumferling,

how he happened to have a new ship, why he
wished to send it; it does not explain who Sir
Patrick was, how he happened to have men at
hand, what the grudge was against him, who
brought him the letter, where he found his men,
who the man was that spoke of the weather. Though
some of the other versions tell what happened between stanzas 7 and 8, none of them tells it at length.
The method in all is substantially the same. Where
modern imitators have succeeded in this, we must
sometimes remain uncertain whether a ballad is old
or new.

This compression is not, of course, mere omission;
it is a focusing of imagination on the salient scenes.
The story is a little tragedy. The story-teller has
focused on those scenes which most suggest the
tragic significance. Narrative swiftness, though it is
not always so well achieved, is more or less characteristic of all ballads. It distinguishes them as a
class. They usually omit, as *Sir Patrick Spens;*
they usually crowd the necessary information and
some of the action into dialogue; they usually limit
the time and place; they almost always achieve
climax. This typical ballad compression evidently
arises from a narrative purpose to tell not so much
a series of events as a situation. A ballad begins, as
Gray[n] said, in the fifth act of the play. The English
romance of *King Horn* (page 94) is unusually short,
some fifteen hundred lines; but the ballad of *Hind
Horn* has less than a hundred because it tells the
main situation instead of the story,

HIND HORN

1 In Scotland there was a babie born,
   Lill lal, etc.
  And his name it was called young Hind Horn.
   With a fal lal, etc.

2 He sent a letter to our king
  That he was in love with his daughter Jean.

3 He's gien to her a silver wand,
  With seven living lavrocks sitting thereon.

4 She's gien to him a diamond ring,
  With seven bright diamonds set therein.

5 "When this ring grows pale and wan,
  You may know by it my love is gane."

6 One day as he looked his ring upon,
  He saw the diamonds pale and wan.

7 He left the sea and came to land,
  And the first that he met was an old beggar man.

8 "What news, what news?" said young Hind Horn;
  "No news, no news," said the old beggar man.

9 "No news," said the beggar, "no news at a',
  But there is a wedding in the king's ha."
        . . . . . .

Thereupon, as in the romance, Horn goes to the hall in disguise and wins his bride. This is indeed the fifth act. The first part omits so much that it is hardly clear. Crudely handled, as here, the ballad compression may be merely abrupt; highly developed, as in *Sir Patrick Spens*, it intensifies a situation.

These strong tales of legendary lore, of the bitterness of hate and the doom of passion, ran their course apart from the course of literature long enough to fix their own form for their own purpose. They might inspire a poet like Coleridge to compose something of his own at once similar in detail and very different as a whole; they might be mutilated or extended, garbled or "improved", by transcribers; but they were too vitally distinct to be merged in other forms of composition. In 1765 Bishop Percy published *Reliques of Ancient Poetry*,[n] a collection of ballads taken from a manuscript then about a century old. The seventeenth-century collector who made this Percy Folio revealed to modern literature some of the essentials of popular verse narrative.

With this history the ballads, though some of them may have been composed in the middle age, are hardly medieval. They give us glimpses, indeed, into early popular composition; but as we have them they come from the fifteenth and later centuries. One of the most characteristic, as one of the most poignant, *Mary Hamilton* has a modern scene. They need not be regarded either on the one hand as debased romances, or on the other hand as survivals of epic, to claim attention in the history of medieval literature. Enough that they show sometimes, beside the manipulations of the medieval romances, the very stuff out of which these were made, and that oftener they exhibit the force of folk-lore as composed not for wistful gentry, but for the folk.

2. *Miracle Plays*

More characteristically medieval and equally popular, the miracle plays[n] are rather a developing form than a developed. Whereas the ballad is fairly constant for centuries, medieval drama is less distinct in composition. Feeling its way, hardly finding its way till the sixteenth century, it had achieved, even in the fifteenth, the essentials of dramatic appeal. More immediately than any other form of composition a play is measured by its hold upon the people who see it. From its very origin drama has always been in this sense popular. Among the Greeks the common human love of acting was applied to certain popular observances of religion. Greek drama thus began in the rites celebrated annually by the whole village to honor Dionysus, the god of fertility and enthusiasm. In the shouting, singing chorus there may have been improvised verse by individuals, refrain by the crowd. Out of this impersonation at the vintage of the story of Dionysus grew more regular responses. The leader of the chorus became an actor in the modern sense of taking a fixed part. In time other fixed parts were assigned, till the mimic action had a definite dialogue; but the chorus persisted as representatives of the community.

Medieval drama began afresh, without derivation from classical models, and in a society centuries beyond the Greek village chorus. But though its rise was different in these respects, it was like in others. Medieval society was similar in communal religious observance and in wide ignorance of reading. The medieval community center was the church; and medieval drama sprang, not by any popular action indeed, but from the communal observance of the great annual Church festivals. "Whom seek ye?" came the thrilling chant at Easter, when the whole village or city district would be gathered in the parish church; and then, in further response, "He is not here; he is risen." To make this more impressive, the clergy had it chanted responsively by singers representing the angel and the women. So at Christmas there were responses of the angels and the shepherds. Such responses were dramatic further in revealing and developing character. In the sequences for Easter the Magdalen's meeting with the angels, with the Lord, with the apostles, is rendered in dialogue.

> Speak, Mary, thou sawest
> Aught in thy watch to guide us?
>
> I saw the tomb of the living,
> The glory of Christ arising and giving,
> The angels who guarded
> The grave-clothes discarded.
> He rose, my hope; he came to me.
> He goeth before you to Galilee.

The Magdalen thus became personally distinct;

and in the eleventh century the sequences written for the observance of her own feast on July 22 advanced the characterization.

Responsive recital and characterization within the liturgy were dramatic thus and no further. They did not constitute drama. That took shape when the scenes from sacred history were brought out of the church into the street. At York, Chester, or Coventry the whole community, through its trade-guilds, maintained an annual series of dramatic representations, setting the main scenes of the Bible. Each scene, provided by a guild, was mounted on a cart and drawn to the market-place before the church, where the spectators were assembled in the open air. *Miracles* these series were called, as representing dramatic scenes of Revelation and of the lives of saints; or *mysteries*, as representing the supernatural truths of the creed; but in England both sorts were commonly called *miracles*. Medieval drama, beginning thus as a popular performance, was always answerable to the people.

Filling the market-place in the fine weather of Corpus Christi, the medieval community saw the masons, perhaps, give Cain and Abel, the tilers give Noah's Ark, the tanners give Abraham and Isaac, and so on through a procession of Bible history. The scenes thus represented were not tableaux; they were definite dialogue learned and acted. Further the composition did not usually go; but to that extent the miracles were drama. There was no unity binding the whole series; there was not

MIDDLE-ENGLISH POPULAR COMPOSITION

always unity even of a single play; but there was always dialogue and action. Further dramatic effect was reached by the development of characterization. Interpreted by natural gesture and action, a part demanded further expression in words; and this the unknown medieval playwrights supplied. The Brome *Abraham and Isaac*, for instance, may fairly be called a play because it has such dramatic realization as comes from expanding the representation of character. The Bible story says merely:

And Abraham took the wood of the burnt offering, and laid it upon Isaac his son; and he took the fire in his hand, and a knife; and they went both of them together. And Isaac spake unto Abraham his father, and said, My father: and he said, Here am I, my son. And he said, Behold the fire and the wood; but where is the lamb for a burnt offering? And Abraham said, My son, God will provide himself a lamb for a burnt offering. So they went both of them together. And they came to the place which God had told him of; and Abraham built an altar there, and laid the wood in order, and bound Isaac his son, and laid him on the altar upon the wood. And Abraham stretched forth his hand, and took the knife to slay his son.   *Genesis*, xxii, 6–10.

The writer of the Brome play expands throughout in the following manner:

ABRAHAM

Rise up, my child, and fast come hither,
My gentle bairn that art so wise,
For we two, child, must go together,
And unto my Lord make sacrifice.

ISAAC

I am full ready, father. Lo!
  Given to your hands, I stand right here,
And whatsoever ye bid me do, even so
  It shall be done with glad cheer,
  Full well and fine.

ABRAHAM

Ah, Isaac, mine own son so dear,
  God's blessing I give thee, and mine.
Hold this fagot upon thy back,
  And I myself here fire shall bring.

ISAAC

Father, all this here will I pack.
  I am full fain to do your bidding.

ABRAHAM

Ah, Lord of Heaven, my hands I wring;
  This child's words wring like death my heart!

So the dialogue goes on to the crisis, which gives even more play to feeling.

ISAAC

I pray you, father, let me know the truth,
  Whether I shall have any harm or no.

ABRAHAM

Not yet may I tell thee, sweet son, in sooth,
  My heart is now so full of woe.

ISAAC

Dear father, I pray you, hide it not from me,
  But some of your thought tell ye me, your son.

ABRAHAM

Ah, Isaac, Isaac, I must kill thee!

ISAAC

Kill me, father? Alas, what have I done!
If in aught I have trespassed against you, God wot,
    With a rod ye may make me full mild —
And with your sharp sword kill me not,
    For in truth, father, I am but a child.

ABRAHAM

I am full sorry, son, thy blood to spill,
    But truly, my child, it is not as I please.

ISAAC

Now would to God my mother were here on this hill!
    She would kneel for me on both her knees
        To save my life.
And since that my mother is not here,
    Change your look, I pray you, father dear,
    And kill me not with your knife.

(From the modernized text in *The Second Shepherds' Play, Everyman, and other early plays* . . . by Clarence Griffin Child, Boston and New York, 1910.)

To this extent the miracle plays developed dramatic characterization. Noah's wife became a comic character from the hint of her being loth to enter the ark; Herod became a furious ranter; and there are many finer touches worthy to stand beside the Brome writer's Abraham. Finest of all, perhaps, is the address in the York *Nativity* of Mary to the new-born Prince of Peace, which must stand in its original poetry:

>Nowe in my sawle grete ioie haue I.
>I am all cladde in comforte clere.
>Now will be borne of my body
>Both God and man togedir in feere.[1]
>>Bliste mott he be!
>Jesu! my son that is so dere!
>>now borne is he!
>Hayle my lord God! hayle prince of pees!
>Hayle my fadir! and hayle my sone!
>Hayle souereyne sege [2] all synnes to sesse![3]
>Hayle God and man in erth to wonne![4]
>>Hayle thurgh whos myht
>All this worlde was first begonne,
>>merknes [5] and light!
>Sone, as I am sympill sugett [6] of thyne,
>Vowchesaffe, swete sone, I pray the,
>That I myght the take in the armys of myne,
>And in this poure wede [7] to arraie the.
>>Graunte me thi blisse,
>As I am thy modir chosen to be
>>in sothfastnesse.

In larger movement the medieval drama did not generally advance. Even after the middle age the conditions of presentation did not further dramatic sequence. But there are striking exceptions, most striking, perhaps what is known as the *Secunda Pastorum*, or Second Shepherds' Play, of the so-

---

[1] in company. [3] cease, stop. [5] darkness. [7] clothing.
[2] seat, throne. [4] dwell. [6] subject.

called Towneley Cycle. In putting on the stage the shepherds who heard the angels and adored the Holy Child the writers of miracle plays were working with familiar characters. For in the frank medieval way the Syrian herdsmen were made English shepherds; and in characterizing them the playwrights naturally pleased the audience with English rustic manners and dialogue, and thus with rustic repartee. Of the two shepherd scenes one became an English comedy. The Towneley writer gave it a coherent plot of its own. Without a hint from Scripture he developed such complication and solution by the reaction of character on character as make it a unified and coherent one-act play. Other exceptions, though less marked, show that the writing of miracle plays sometimes awakened a sense of dramatic sequence; but in general medieval drama prevailed sufficiently for its time by the dramatic fundamentals, representation before a crowd, and broad characterization.

3. *Prose*

Middle English prose was popular mainly in the sense that it was popularizing. It was a means of instructing the people. Prose had long meant Latin prose, for works of instruction were written in Latin; but in the fourteenth century this field too was entered by the vernacular. The most frequent and obvious cases were translations. A familiar narrative instance from the Wiclifite translation of the Vulgate will show the simplest differences of the English habit from the Latin.

4. Quis ex vobis homo qui habet centum oves, et si perdiderit unam ex illis, nonne dimittit nonaginta novem in deserto, et vadit ad illam quae perierat, donec inveniat eam?

5. Et cum invenerit eam, imponit in humeros suos gaudens.

6. Et veniens domum, convocat amicos et vicinos, dicens illis: congratulamini mihi, quia inveni ovem meam quae perierat.

7. Dico vobis quod ita gaudium erit in caelo super uno peccatore paenitentiam agente quam super nonaginta novem justis qui non indigent paenitentia.

8. Aut quae mulier habens drachmas decem, si perdiderit drachmam unam, nonne accendit lucernam et everrit domum et quaerit diligenter donec inveniat?

9. Et cum invenerit, convocat amicas et vicinas, dicens: congratulamini mihi, quia inveni drachmam quam perdideram.

What man of you that hath an hundrith sheep, and if he hath lost oon of hem, whether he leveth not nynti and nyne in desert, and goeth to it that perishide, til he fynde it?

And whan he hath founden it, he joyeth and leyeth it on his shuldres.

And he cometh hoom and clepeth togider his freendes and neighboris and seith to hem: be ye glad with me, for I have founde my sheep that hadde perishid.

And I seye to you so joye shal be in hevene on o synful man doynge penaunce more than on nynti and nyne juste that han no nede to penaunce.

Or what woman havyng ten besauntes, and if she hath lost oo besaunt, whether she teendeth not a lanterne and turneth upsodoun the hous, and seketh diligently, til that she fynde it?

And whan she hath founden, she clepeth togider freendes and neighbores and seith: Be ye glad with me, for I have founde the besaunt that I hadde lost.

10. Ita dico vobis gaudium erit coram angelis Dei super uno peccatore paenitentiam agente.

11. Ait autem, homo quidam habuit duos filios;

12. Et dixit adolescentior ex illis patri: pater, da mihi portionem substantiae quae mihi contingit. Et divisit illis substantiam.

13. Et non post multos dies, congregatis omnibus, adolescentior filius peregre profectus est in regionem longinquam; et ibi dissipavit substantiam suam vivendo luxuriose.

14. Et postquam omnia consummasset, facta est fames valida in regione illa; et ipse coepit egere.

15. Et abiit et adhaesit uni civium regionis illius; et misit illum in villam suam, ut pasceret porcos.

16. Et cupiebat implere ventrem suum de siliquis quas porci manducabant; et nemo illi dabat.

So I seye to you joye shal be bifor aungels of God on o synful man doynge penaunce.

And he seide a man hadde twei sones;

And the yonger of hem seide to the fader: fader, yeve me the porcioun of catel that falleth to me. And he departede to hem the catel.

And not after many dayes, whan alle thinges weren gedered togider, the yonger sone went forth in pilgrymage into a fer contre; and there he wastede his goodes in lyvynge lecherously.

And after that he hadde ended alle thinges, a strong hungre was maad in that contre; and he bigan to have neede.

And he went and drough him to oon of the citeseyns of that contre; and he sent him into his toun, to fede swyn.

And he coveitede to fille his wombe of coddes that the hogges eeten, and no man yaf him.

17. In se autem revertens, dixit: quanti mercenarii in domo patris mei abundant panibus; ego autem hic fame pereo!

18. Surgam et ibo ad patrem meum, et dicam ei: pater, peccavi in caelum et coram te.

19. Jam non sum dignus vocari filius tuus; fac me sicut unum de mercenariis tuis.

20. Et surgens venit ad patrem suum. Cum autem adhuc longe esset, vidit illum pater ipsius, et misericordia motus est, et accurrens cecidit super collum ejus, et osculatus est eum.

21. Dixitque ei filius: pater, peccavi in caelum et coram te. Jam non sum dignus vocari filius tuus.

22. Dixit autem pater ad servos suos: cito proferte stolam primam et induite illum, et date annulum in manum ejus et calceamenta in pedes ejus.

And he turnede ayen to him self and seide: hou many hired men in my fader hous han plente of looves, and I perishe here thorough hunger!

I shal rise up and go to my fader, and I shal seye to him: fader, I have synned into hevene and bifor thee.

And now I am not worthy to be cleped thy sone; mak me as oon of thin hired men.

And he roos up and cam to his fader. And whan he was yit afer, his fader seigh him, and was stirred bi mercy, and he ran and fel on his necke and kissed him.

And the sone seide to him: fader, I have synned into hevene and bifor thee; and now I am not worthi to be cleped thy sone.

And the fader seide to his servauntes: swithe brynge ye forth the firste stole and clothe ye him, and yeve ye a ring in his hond and shoon on his feet.

23. Et adducite vitulum saginatum, et occidite, et manducemus et epulemur.
24. Quia hic filius meus mortuus erat, et revixit; perierat, et inventus est.
(*Evang. S. Luc. xv.*)

And brynge ye a fat calf, and slee ye, and ete we, and make we feeste.
For this my sone was deed and hath lyved ayen; he perished and is founden.
(English text normalized from the 1879 Oxford edition of Forshall and Madden.)

The translation is sometimes less distinct than the original in tense. *Cupiebat* (16) means rather "used to long" than simply "longed" (*coveitede*). But this is hardly more than difference of idiom. The difference of construction is more significant. The Latin says, for instance: "he lays it on his shoulders rejoicing, and, coming home, calls his neighbors, saying,' etc. The English rendering is: "rejoices and lays it on his shoulders, and comes home and calls and says." The Latin throws the merely connective actions into participles; it subordinates. The English puts them all on a par; it coördinates. Such making of sentences by mere series of statements is one of the marks of early prose. In comparison with the poetry of the period, fourteenth-century English prose is undeveloped in composition. It has little range of logical habit. Lively homeliness of diction is carried by the simplest narrative sentences.

So foreign wonders are described in a late fourteenth-century pilgrimage guide to the Holy Land, the *Voiage and Travaile*. Current under the doubtful name of Sir John Mandeville,[n] it is a compilation in French, then in English and other languages, from several medieval travel books.

And there [in Constantinople] is the most fayr chirche and the most noble of alle the world; and it is of Seynt Sophie. And before that chirche is the image of Justynyan the emperour, covered with gold; and he sit upon an hors ycrowned. And he was wont to holden a round appelle of gold in his hand; but it is fallen out therof. And men seyn there that it is a token that the emperour hath ylost a gret partie of his landes and of his lordshipes; for he was wont to ben emperour of Romayne and of Grece, of alle Asye the lesse and of the land of Surrye, of the land of Judee, in the whiche is Jerusalem, and of the lond of Egypt, of Percye, of Arabye. But he hath lost alle but Grece; and that land he halt alle only. And men wolden many tymes put the appelle into the images hand ayen; but it wil not holde it. This appelle betokeneth the lordship that he hadde over alle the world, that is round. And that other hand he lifteth up ayenst the Est, in tokene to manace the mysdoeres. This image stant upon a pylere of marble at Costantynoble (Chapter i).

Without distinction of phrase, as in such passages, the aggregation becomes tiresome. Though the *Voiage and Travaile* shows some firmer composition, it readily lapses into series without definite sentence boundaries.

What serves most to redeem this early looseness is rhythm. A sentence imperfectly defined by logic may yet be sufficiently guided by its cadences.

The second degree of grace is more special, that God gives frely til ilke man that is gode and skilful creature;

MIDDLE-ENGLISH POPULAR COMPOSITION 201

and this grace standes ever atte yates of our hertes, and knokkes on our free wille, and biddes lat him in (normalized from Horstman's edition of the Works, I. 133).

Richard Rolle,[n] to whom this treatise on Grace is ascribed, seems sometimes to remember certain cadences of medieval Latin.[n]

Prayere is evermore plesande to God, with lowe bryghtly brennande in a meke herte, withouten smokynge smelland ful swetly, in all meke mindes haldand the love of our lord God hot in our hertes (*ibid.* 299).

But he runs as readily into a traditional rhythm of English verse. Parallel printing will show that some passages have essentially the same composition as the *Piers Plowman* (page 158).

  Riche men with theire servants   that the poure harmed;
  domesmen that wold noght deme   but it were for mede;
  countours that the wronge   by theire sotilte maintened;
  demesters that leal men dampned and delivered starke theves;
  werkmen that falsly swinkes   and takes ful hire;
  tilmen that falsly tendes; prelates that han cure of menes soules, that neither chastise ne teche them.
  Of all lede of men   that wrongly has wroght
  there I sawe that echon bitterly it boght.
For there I sawe defaute of al godenes and plente of pine and sorowe,
  as hote fire ay brennand,   brimstone stinkand;
  gredy devels as dragons   wide gapand;
  hunger and thrist   for ever lastand;
  nedders and tades on the sinful gnawand (*ibid.* 153).

Even in rhythm, then, as well as in logic, prose composition in the fourteenth century has less definite habits than verse. Though it has occasional beauty, it is generally undeveloped. Chaucer, so sure and various in verse, often labors with the prose of his beloved Boethius. A greater strain, of course, is put upon undeveloped prose by such reflection and exposition than by narrative. Narrative prose was the sooner stabilized. In the fifteenth century Malory had it under control (page 139). With little need for logic, he was sure enough in rhythm to save his sentences from either monotony or trailing. At the same time the expository and argumentative prose of Pecock[n] was still cumbrous; and even the smoother sentences of Fortescue show that English prose had not yet firm habits of composition.

CHAPTER X

CHAUCER (1340? 1345?-1400)

MEDIEVAL narrative is best reviewed through its greatest poet. His use of current conventions, his experiments in method and scope, the achievements of his mature art within medieval habits and beyond, are an epitome of medieval literary history.

1. *Biography* [n]

Chaucer was a London man of business. Sprung from a business family that had patronage in high society, and himself knowing both magnates and nobles, he moved in two worlds; but his own social world was the world of affairs. His family had been for generations engaged in that important commerce of medieval England which exported wool and imported wine; and he himself spent his prime in the government regulation of this as Controller of Customs. Even earlier his diplomatic missions had to do with commerce. Business was his career; writing was his avocation.

What was probably his first schooling, the learning of Latin through plainsong, may be echoed in that charming passage of the Prioress's Tale which glimpses the boys about their "antiphoner." The

Canterbury Tales recall also two of his later schoolbooks: Geoffrey of Vinsauf's *Nova Poetria* in the satirical reference of the Nun's Priest (B. 4537), and a passage from an elegy of Maximian translated, and transformed by its new application, in the tale of the Pardoner (C. 727). Both were probably items in his study of *grammatica*, which regularly included the analysis and the writing of Latin verse. Whether school took him on in the Trivium with some training in rhetoric and perhaps in logic, or whether he picked up these, as other things, by himself, he acquired a learning exceptional in his time. Reading the usual Latin authors (page 12), he was especially fond of Boethius. Besides translating the *Consolatio*, he used it often enough to show that it was always in the back of his mind. Of the *Roman de la Rose* he translated most of the first part, but made more use of the second. French, still the dominant literary vernacular of western Europe, he probably both heard and spoke daily through most of his life. Though he may not have commanded Italian till he went to Italy, there is equal probability that he was chosen to go because he knew it already.

A different sort of education began in 1357 with his service at court. The pay for this in money was less important than its opportunities to learn courtly ways, to hear courtly poetry, and, in the days when publication depended on patronage, to win recognition. His military service, capture, and ransom (1359–60) were followed, perhaps by some study of law in the Temple, certainly by his return to court. In 1368 he was esquire; and his wife Philippa had already been made damoiselle. After another slight military experience he spent much of the years 1370–78 on diplomatic commissions for the improvement of commerce. Among these were two of cardinal importance to himself, the missions of 1373 and 1378 to Italy. To hear Italian daily, to see Italy and its new painting, to buy Italian books, to feel the stirrings of the Renaissance, were large literary opportunities. The Italian author who stimulated him most was not Dante, whose great conception and composition seem to have meant less to Chaucer than his style. It was not Petrarch; for he slighted the sonnets and preferred a Latin prose version of a tale to the laureate's ambitious Latin verse. It was Boccaccio, perhaps the *Decameron*, but mainly the *Teseide* and the *Filostrato*. The widening of literary range, evident first in Chaucer's verse, led him far; for he is among those greater literary artists whose quick responses to new experiences at once stir initiative.

On his return he went into the Customs. After some twelve years of this business life, about 1386, he brought out his *Troilus and Criseyde* and was greeted by the French poet Deschamps in a *balade* as a "grant translateur." He may have spent a few years as a country, or at least a suburban gentleman; but he was in Parliament, and from 1389 to 1391 Clerk of the King's Works. His remaining years he must have given increasingly to writing and revision. He knew Froissart, perhaps Wiclif. Besides friends whom he mentions, Scogan, Bukton, the poet Gower, and the "philosophical" Strode, he had friends important in wealth or position. His own position was secure, comfortable, and dignified.

Uneventful on the surface, his life was yet large; and he made it progressive. He studied both the Englishmen of the future, among whom he had been born, and the higher classes that they were beginning to enter. He advanced his art to the creation of individuals at once so medieval and so distinct that we may live with them personally in their time. This sureness in making us live with significant people has made him singularly attractive. Various as his persons are, brutes and frauds as well as knights and saints, he neither offers them for praise or blame nor merely analyzes; he carries us into their lives. To call him either a skeptic or a reformer is to misunderstand not only certain passages, but his whole trend. He understood otherworldly people without being ascetic; he understood crooked people without believing that the world was out of joint. If his retractions suggest that he found himself too indulgent, even readers who wisely skip some of his tales are glad that he was genial. The geniality and poise that have so long been a refuge from narrative fret and propaganda suggest that he brought his life, as well as his art, to serenity.

2. Development of Verse Narrative

Chaucer's tales may be classified by their medieval types. Those in the *Legend of Good Women* are of the medieval form derived from Ovid. The Nun's Priest chooses a beast-fable (page 90). The Monk and the Pardoner offer *exempla* (page 78). The saint's legend (page 80) underlies the tales of the Man of Law, the Prioress, the Second Nun, and the Clerk. The Miller, Reeve, Shipman, Friar, and Merchant tell *fabliaux* (page 91); the Knight, Squire, Franklin, and Wife of Bath, romances. But the classification shows little of Chaucer. The medieval types, though discernible, do not generally control his narrative method. Only in the *Legend of Good Women* and in the *fabliaux* are they usually followed. In the best tales they are mere background of suggestion. The tale of the Nun's Priest, for instance, though obviously drawn from the popular Cock and Fox, ranges far beyond the beast-fable, and beyond some longer Reynard stories that it seems to use. It becomes a comedy of the Cock and Hen, and is animated by the same motive as that of Rostand's *Chantecler*. The Prioress's Tale, again, though derived from a saint's legend, is transformed into a narrative lyric of a child's devotion to the Virgin, and turned from horror to pathos and worship. The saint is there, but not the form of the saint's legend. The Pardoner's Tale, introduced as an *exemplum*, leads an extraordinarily swift and compelling sequence of scenes to a tragic solution. Of the romances, the Tale of the Wife of

Bath is nearest to type. The Knight's, relying less on adventures than on the pageantry sketched in the prologue to the *Legend of Good Women*, closes upon philosophy. How to interpret romance was for Chaucer a long study. He often smiles at it in asides. He parodies it in Sir Thopas. He exposes its fundamental falsity in *Troilus and Criseyde*. He gives it in the Tale of the Franklin a new sequence of character. In a word, the medieval types were in Chaucer's characteristic work not so much patterns as points of departure. In his most striking mature work they are ignored. The opening of the Pardoner's Tale and the prologue of the Wife of Bath are dramatic monologues; the interludes of the *Canterbury Tales* bring the audience into interaction; and the *Troilus and Criseyde* is a novel.

Originality so various was a slow achievement through apprenticeship, experiment, and critical study. Chaucer gained his first expertness in verse. Catching from Boccaccio the superiority of a longer line than the French octosyllabic for narrative, he explored in the couplet adjustments unused three centuries later by Dryden. His stanza is more fluent and flexible than even Byron's, and pointed more narratively. To the gift of an extraordinarily sensitive ear, to the constant hearing of two rhythms, French and English, he added both experiment and anxious revision. The modern student of his verse must remember, first, that its rhythm, control, or pattern is the same as ours of today; secondly, that it was composed to be read aloud. The suggestions added to story by verse depend on being heard. A mere list of his verse-forms shows that he ranged widely; and within any given meter of his mature work will be found such manifold variations of stress and pause, tempo and substitution, as avoid monotony without weakening the pattern, answer the movement of the action, or suggest its mood.

Troilus and Criseyde, the text on which we can most rely, gives clear evidence of revision. Its close has a passage at once pathetic and ominous.

>   And for ther is so gret diversite
>   In Englissh, and in writyng of oure tonge,
>   So prey I god that non myswrite the,
>   Ne the mysmetre for defaute of tonge.
>
>   (V. 1793–1796.)

No other English poet has suffered so much as Chaucer from the shifting of language. Changes in speech and in habits of reading were accelerated by his time. The early printed editions so miswrote and mismetred him as to misguide even Spenser. One of the more important gifts of modern scholarship to literature is the gradual restoration of Chaucer to his eminence among the greatest English artists in verse.

In story-telling his progress, though equally sure, had to overcome more prejudice. Not a few verse tales that he heard and read in his youth were admired in spite of being diffuse or rambling. Ovid's lucid plots were too brief to show how narrative should be sustained; and his composition encouraged the use of description separably for dilation. Guillaume de Lorris conceived the *Roman de la Rose*[n] not as a story, but as a group of fashionable descriptions. Chaucer, discerning that descriptive dilation is an intrusion of rhetoric into poetry, studied how poetry might follow its own ways by drawing description into the narrative course. More and more he saw this course as the goal of a livelier, more fluent, more compelling art. In the Squire's Tale he pauses at the heroine's walk in the wood, where convention called for expanded description, to insert instead this satirical criticism, the most explicit declaration of his creed.

> The knotte, why that every tale is told,
> If it be taried til that lust be cold
> Of hem that han it after herkned yore,
> The savour passeth ever lenger the more
> For fulsomnesse of his prolixitee.
> And by the same reson thinketh me
> I sholde to the knotte condescende,
> And maken of hir walking sone an ende.
> (F. 401–408.)

But he arrived at the creed of narrative sequence through experiment. His early *Bok of the Duchesse* opens with a description of sleeplessness caused by love and alleviated by reading Ovid's *Ceyx and Alcyone*. This tale he paraphrases at length before beginning the dream which it brought on, and which introduces his own story. Still postponing by a description of a hunt, he finally puts his story into the mouth of a strayed hunter and concludes it, upon a brief dialogue, with his own awakening. The introduction and the frame are conventional; the conduct is conventionally descriptive; and the poem as a whole has no narrative sequence. Chaucer's art has been spent on phrase and verse, not on story.

He still used the conventions of his time in the *Parlement of Foules*, but with significant modification. The opening dream and book have comparatively less space. The induced story, after much description of the *Roman de la Rose* type, passes into a debate of the birds[n] that typify social classes. Instead of merely following the usual method seen in the *Owl and Nightingale* (page 157), he livens the types with characteristic speech, and their dialogue with interaction. His quite superfluous young dog in the *Bok of the Duchesse* (388) had already come alive as a real puppy leaping out from the unreal background. In the *Parlement of Foules* he followed this clue much farther. The second tercel speaks as an assertive man. The code of courtly love is not merely upheld by the higher classes and challenged by the lower; it comes into actual clash of debate. The vulgar goose and duck speak as real bourgeois, and are answered by derisive aristocratic laughter. The beast-fable, which Chaucer used again, and quite differently, in the tale of the Nun's Priest, is imposed here upon the conventions of the *Roman de la Rose*, and enhanced by touches of drama. The value of these, we must remind ourselves, was much clearer in oral rendering, and could readily be heightened by gesture and manner. Far as it is still from narrative consecutiveness, the *Parlement of Foules* opens one of Chaucer's characteristic means, the use of dialogue to advance a story by interaction.

To advance a story, to add the spell of onward movement, demanded further practise. The step that he had already taken in turning from interruptive conventional description to individualizing suggestion of personal habit by speech and gesture led of itself to vivid realism. The preaching of all demagogues is embodied in the Pardoner. "I peyne me to han an hauteyn speche, And ringe it out as round as gooth a belle." To his recipe of sonorous oratorical bluff the Pardoner adds gesture.

> Than peyne I me to strecche forth the nekke,
> And est and west upon the peple I bekke,
> As doth a dowve sitting on a berne.
> Myn handes and my tonge goon so yerne
> That it is joye to see my bisinesse.
>
> (C. 330–331, 395–399.)

This is monologue; but the "bisinesse", our "stage business", will help make dialogue carry interaction. Chaucer used it to make his persons not only reveal themselves, but bring out each other in a situation. Thus he has something like a scene in a play; and his final step in achieving an onward course of action is to compose by scenes.

Such composition he uses for swiftness and inevitability in the Pardoner's Tale. After he has made this accomplished rascal exhibit himself in the introductory monologue, he carries the story with unsurpassed conciseness from its ominous opening to its fatal close by a progression of scenes. I. Three ruffians drinking in a tavern are interrupted by the corpse-bell, learn that the last victim of the Black Death is one of their companions, and take a frenzied oath not to wait their turn, but to seek and conquer this monster that slays youth. II. At their very outset they meet a strange Old Man, whom they insult, but cannot pass. "Why do you live on and on, you old scarecrow?" "Because no one will exchange his youth for my age; nor will Mother Earth let me in." "No, you are in league with Death. Tell where he is, or die yourself." "If you must, you will find him under yon oak. 'Nat for your boast he wil him nothing hyde.'" III. Under the oak they find a chest of gold, forget their quest in their greed, and, to stop dispute, draw lots for the one who shall fetch food and drink while the other two remain on guard. So soon as the one goes, the two agree to kill him on his return. IV. The one, buying poison of an apothecary, puts it into the bottles that he hands to the two. V. Thus they kill him, and he them. Stripped for action, this tale of 250 lines is never bare. It is vividly suggestive of the physical scene and the terror behind it, of the legendary mystery of the Old Man, of mood after mood through speech. All this is led to the issue with cumulative force by a progress strictly narrative. Each scene is distinct for itself; the tempo varies from the wild oath and the wild dash to the pause before the Old Man, and again to the summary culmination; but the story has unbroken and compelling movement.

This purely narrative economy, in which the story is all story, in which at every moment we are moving on toward the end, is the more Chaucer's triumph because there had been little, outside of the ingenuity of the *fabliaux*, to guide him. Boccaccio, making a similar discovery for the prose *novella* about the same time in his *Decameron*, had used it little. Nor did Chaucer adopt it as his personal form. Rather he seems to have been interested in applying sequence more widely and in other ways. The much longer tale of the Franklin is just as clearly composed by scenes not merely in a series, but in a compelling order. As in the still longer *Troilus and Criseyde*, its critical scene functions as the turning-point of a play.

> "Is ther oght elles, Dorigen, but this?"
> "Nay, nay," quod she, "God help me so as wis,
> This is to muche, and it were Goddes wille."
> "Ye, wyf," quod he, "lat slepen that is stille.
> It may be wel, paraventure, yet to-day.
> Ye shul your trouthe holden, by my fay!
> For God so wisly have mercy on me,
> I hadde wel lever ystiked for to be,
> For verray love which that I to yow have,
> But if ye sholde your trouthe kepe and save.
> Trouthe is the hyeste thing that man may kepe."
> But with that word he brast anon to wepe.
> (F. 1469–1480.)

In the Knight's Tale, though he both shortened Boccaccio's rendering and afterward revised his own, he preferred to present the transitory brilliance of high life as a pageant in its own light and then to throw back on it the light of a higher philosophy. Instead of relying on one narrative achievement, however distinguished, he continued to seek variety.

His goal was to make the sequence of action a sequence of characterization. A mere *fabliau* may dispense with characterization; the Tale of the Nun's Priest or of the Knight may offer it generally in types; but Chaucer's triumphs are in creating persons who are at once individuals and eloquent of our common humanity. The Wife of Bath's self-revelation is far greater than her tale; the Pardoner's, at least equal to his far stronger one. The Franklin's Tale fuses character with plot by making it operate progressively as motive. For full development of this mastery we turn to the *Troilus and Criseyde;* for variety in its application, to the scheme of the *Canterbury Tales*.

3. *Troilus and Criseyde*[n]

To retell Troy in terms of medieval life was a settled literary habit. Whether or not this is less true than the laborious classicism of the Renaissance, it is at least consistent. The romances make Hector and Diomed dukes or knights in feudal society, as Italians continued to paint the Blessed Virgin in Italian costume against an Italian background. So for both Boccaccio and Chaucer the setting of the Trojan lovers is neither Homer's nor Vergil's; it is medieval high society cultivating the fiction of courtly love. Chaucer makes this setting not only ampler than Boccaccio's, but more active. For since he is bent on putting courtly love to the test of real life, he keeps that life before us in details of daily habit which at the same time reveal the characters. Setting, character, plot, are all woven together. Thus Pandarus goes to visit Criseyde:

> And fond two othere ladys sete, and she,
> Withinne a paved parlour; and they thre
> Herden a mayden reden hem the geste
> Of the sege of Thebes whil hem leste.
>
> Quod Pandarus, "madame, God yow see,
> With al youre book and al the compaignie."
> "Ey uncle, now welcome iwys," quod she;
> And up she roos, and by the hond in hye
> She took hym faste, and seyde, "this nyght thrie,
> To goode mot it turne, of you I mette;"
> And with that word she doun on bench hym sette.
>
> (II. 81–91.)

The lively and easy dialogue is edged with significance at critical moments. Pandarus brings the first love-letter of Troilus. At Cressid's hesitation to receive it, he protests his amazement. Then suddenly:

> "But for al that evere I may deserve,
> Refuse it nat," quod he, and hente hir faste,
> And in hire bosom down the lettre he thraste,

And seyde hire: "cast it now awey anon,
That folk may seen and gauren on us tweye!"
Quod she: "I kan abyde til they be gon,"
And gan to smyle, and seyde hym: "em, I preye,
Swich answere as yow list youre self purveye;
For trewely I nyl no lettre write."
"No? than wol I," quod he, "so ye endite."
                              (II. 1153–1162.)

Speech and gesture, tone and manner, are sharpened in this scene not merely to brighten the social comedy, but by interaction to advance the story. For that onward movement of *Troilus and Criseyde*, at once leisurely and constant, is the development of character. It makes impulse stir habit, and mood reveal motive, in order to lead through decision after decision to the inevitable issue of character.

Thus has been transformed a Troy story already old. Chaucer, as well as Boccaccio, knew the episode as it was scattered in seven different passages through Benoît de Sainte-More's *Roman de Troie*, and as it was told again in Latin prose by Guido delle Colonne.[n] Boccaccio in his *Filostrato*[n] had made out of them a new story of love at first sight, wooing, winning, loss, and heartbreak at the desertion. Fatal passion leads his Troilus through rapture to ruin. That love should be irrevocable was the code. Change of love was outlawed. Yet real life showed passion not only shifting, but essentially transitory. As if recognizing in Boccaccio's presentation of passion something truer than the romantic code of courtly love, and at the same time discerning deeper springs of character, Chaucer made the *Filostrato* over.

Of the 5512 lines in the *Filostrato* Chaucer used 2730, or about half; but his *Troilus and Criseyde* has 8239 lines. That is, using half of Boccaccio's story, he made his own half as long again as Boccaccio's whole. His additions are mainly his second and third books with the latter part of the first, the parts that tell the gradual and elaborate conquest of Cressid. In Boccaccio's conception no such approach is necessary. His Cressid falls as easily into the arms of Troilus as later into the arms of Diomed. Chaucer's agent in the winning is Pandarus. For this purpose he transforms Boccaccio's gay and facile cousin of Cressid into her middle-aged uncle, shrewd, cynical, but covering his immorality with engaging frankness and wit. The interaction of these three main characters, with subsidiary use of their princely society, is led with dramatic suspense and complication to the climax of possession; it has sharp reverse on Cressid's return to her father in exchange for a Trojan prisoner; it makes her yielding to Diomed bring about Troilus's despair and death; it concludes upon his looking back from a higher sphere with derision at a life devoted to "the blinde lust, the which that may not laste."

Obviously Chaucer has shifted the focus from Troilus to Cressid; but he has done much more. He has made her one of the most distinct creations of English fiction by making her story a character development. The story moves with her. Gracious

and subtle, lovely and practical, she enacts in the
real world the literary fiction of passion. Out of
a passionate adventuress he made a noble lady
playing the dangerous fashionable game with discretion, but in vain. Far more interesting than
Shakspere's Cressid, she is drawn with that sympathy, at once penetrative and delicate, which gives
life to Shakspere's greater heroines. Very moving
is the graciousness that survives her degradation;
and the ruin of Troilus, as well as her own, is drawn
gradually and inevitably from the interaction of
their characters.

4. *The Scheme of the Canterbury Tales*

"Sir parish prest," quod he, "for goddes bones,
Tel us a tale, as was thy forward yore.
I see wel that ye lerned men in lore
Can moche good, by goddes dignitee!"
The Persone him answerde, "benedicite!
What eyleth the man, so sinfully to swere?"
Our hoste answerde, "O Iankin, be ye there?
I smell a loller in the wind," quod he.
"How! good men," quod our hoste, "herkneth me.
Abydeth, for goddes digne passioun;
For we shal han a predicacioun.
This loller here wil prechen us somwhat."
"Nay, by my fader soule! that shal he nat,"
Seyde the Shipman; "heer he shal nat preche;
He shal no gospel glosen heer ne teche.
We leve alle in the grete god," quod he.
He wolde sowen som difficultee,

> Or springen cokkel in our clene corn.
> And therfor, hoste, I warne thee biforn,
> My Ioly body shal a tale telle;
> And I shal clinken yow so mery a belle
> That I shal waken al this companye.
> But it shal nat ben of philosophye,
> Ne *physices*, ne termes queinte of lawe.
> Ther is but litel Latin in my mawe.
> (B. 1166–1190.)

This interlude between the Man of Law's Tale and the Shipman's is more interesting than the links between tales in other medieval collections. It is suggestive both by itself and for the series. The rude teasing of the host, the shocked protest of the innocent priest, and the humor of the fuddled sailor's rising to the defense of orthodoxy are composed in a scene. The pilgrim auditors take the stage and comment on one another. With incidental hints of medieval life Chaucer's interludes add to his tales a human setting. They are part of the whole scheme. Their art and its function in the scheme become clearer by comparison with other medieval "framework tales."

(a) Gower's Confessio Amantis

Gower's collection was nearly contemporaneous; and the two authors were long spoken of together without much critical discrimination.[n] The tales of the *Confessio Amantis* deserved their popularity by their terseness and lucidity. Content with the Ovidian model, Gower achieved neither salience nor variety. His inferiority to Chaucer is obvious also in his collective scheme. After a long prologue the lover (*amans*) is bidden in a May-morning vision by the queen of love to make confession to Genius, her priest. To exemplify sins against love and instruct in its lore, the priest tells his penitent some hundred tales. Sins of seeing are exemplified by the legends of Actaeon and of the Gorgons; sins of hearing, by those of Aspis and of the Sirens. The penitent having confessed briefly his sins under these heads, the priest proceeds to expound the seven deadly sins and exemplify them in their various aspects, pausing between tales to hear the lover's confession and to moralize. This framework of confession with its categories of sins, far from having literary value, is so unwieldy that it breaks down, and so formal that it soon becomes a tiresome intrusion. A convention borrowed from the *Roman de la Rose*, it does not serve to enhance the tales by effective grouping. The 33,000 lines are none too many for the telling of the tales; but too many of them are spent on mere machinery.

(b) THE DECAMERON

No less obviously to be compared is that famous Italian collection of one hundred prose tales, the *Decameron* (1353). Most of its stories are composed either as short romances (*novelle*) or as amplified anecdotes (*parabole*, i.e. *exempla*). Of the latter some compress the main situation within one day or night. Only five or six of the hundred have the stricter consistency and sequence of the *fabliaux* (*favole*).

The framework of the *Decameron* is far superior to that of the *Confessio Amantis* in literary value. "I propose," says Boccaccio in his preface, "to tell a hundred tales . . . told in ten days by a noble company of seven ladies and three youths in the time of the late pestilence . . . in the which tales appear pleasant or rude chances of love and other incidents of fortune happening as well in modern times as in ancient." After describing the plague in Florence, the "noble company," and the fair country house to which they withdrew for safety, Boccaccio makes each of his ten persons tell a tale each day on the same general theme. Thus he arranges ten groups of ten tales each, with charming interludes of conversation, song, and description. But it is only the charm of style that saves the connective scheme from monotony. The narrators are merely mouthpieces; the grouping of the tales is not used, as by Chaucer, to bring about contrast and personal interchange; the setting, though vastly more attractive than the heavy allegorical fiction of the *Confessio Amantis*, is merely repeated with variations.

(c) THE SEVEN SAGES

No less monotonous in its similarity to that of the *Arabian Nights* is the framework of the *Seven Sages*.[n] An oriental collection of great antiquity, this is found in many western versions, of which the most widely influential was the French *Sept Sages*. The English versions range from the fourteenth century to the sixteenth. The framework common to these numerous and various versions is the following:

"A young prince is tempted by his stepmother, the queen. She, being rebuffed by him, accuses him of attempting to violate her, and he is condemned to death. His life is saved by seven wise men, who secure a stay of execution of the royal decree by entertaining the king through seven days with tales showing the wickedness of woman, the queen meantime recounting stories to offset those of the sages. On the eighth day the prince, who has remained silent up to that time, speaks in his own defence, and the queen is put to death."

Killis Campbell's edition, page xi.

Evidently the ancient framework is both simple and inflexible. For though it is superior to that of the *Confessio Amantis*, and even to that of the *Decameron*, in being itself a story, it affords slight literary opportunity. The king, stayed by the tale of the first sage, finds the queen in tears, and is won back by her counter-tale to reaffirm his sentence on the prince. With mere variation of the dialogue this scene is repeated six times. Instead of being always different, as in the *Canterbury Tales*, the interlude is always substantially the same. Not only are the tales generally alike in form, being all by the necessity of the plan *exempla*, but the plan itself is only a vehicle.

(d) Chaucer's Pilgrimage Setting

Chaucer's scheme is at once more flexible and larger in scope. The fiction of a traveling company offers more various opportunity than that of a confession, a trial, or even a house-party. Pilgrimage suggested to every medieval reader both the telling of tales and various company. Further, Chaucer's interludes, instead of being pauses, whether pleasant as Boccaccio's or tedious as Gower's, act upon the tales. They add an individualized teller in action and interaction. The General Prologue describes each teller by summary indications of make-up, costume, and personal style, not in order to review English social classes, but to prepare for the various interaction of the interludes. Far from exemplifying Chaucer's descriptive habit, it is specifically adjusted to a list of *dramatis personae*.

The parody of Sir Thopas gains in point by the rude interruption of the host. Revenge for this may be meant as excuse for the dulness of the following prose morality. At any rate, the host's rueful comparison of the wife of Melibeus to his own, and the domestic comedy of Chantecler and Pertelote, suggest cues for the prologue of the Wife of Bath; and her tale opens the way for other *maistrye* of women in marriage. Though the grouping remains conjectural because the scheme remained incomplete, there is no doubt that Chaucer projected a larger technic of dramatic setting, mediating as a Greek chorus between the fictitious audience on the scene and his actual hearers.

Medieval verse narrative was recited or read aloud. Chaucer had early learned to avoid such setting as delayed or interrupted its oral course. Trying to make description run instead in that course, he had found inanimate background both less tractable orally and less significant narratively than the surrounding men and women. Dialogue, the most oral means of liveliness, he pointed by gesture, and from mood and emotion advanced it to interaction. In the Canterbury plan he staged his tales by characterizing the tellers as actors and suggesting their interplay with an audience.

So Chaucer concluded the English middle age. We know it because his penetrating analysis and his tolerant philosophy served a consummate art. He was not content with types, nor with offering his own analysis as story. Story-telling he made, more than it had ever been before, more than it was to be for long afterward, a weaving of verse and image, speech and gesture, emotion and moral habit, into a living, moving sequence. Seeing through the faded fashions of romance and the social fiction of courtly love, he created both Cressid and Dorigen. Realistic and satirical, he transcended satire in the Pardoner and the Wife of Bath. His ranging from sinners to saints is more than variety, more even than the creation of individuals; it enables us to live, through stories of poetic truth, in the English medieval world.

APPENDIX

Introduction to Middle English Grammar

This introduction is based on the language of Chaucer not only because, as the greatest English poet of the middle age, he is usually read most and always read first, but also for two practical reasons: first, his diction follows that use which had become standard; secondly, his works, besides being the most available, are usually published in normalized texts, that is, without regard to those manuscript variations which are important for other kinds of study than those proposed here.

ABBREVIATIONS

1, 2, 3, 1st person, etc.
e- initial e; -e final e; -e- medial e.
g. genitive (modern possessive).
inf. infinitive.
M. E. Middle English.

mod. E. modern English.
p. plural.
pres. present.
pret. preterit (past tense).
ptc. passive participle.
s. singular.
subj. subjunctive.

I. PHONETIC

Read aloud. M. E. spelling being often different from that of mod. E., and always more variable, the clue to a word is rather for the ear than for the eye.

Generally pronounce every syllable except (1) -e elided in verse before a vowel, and (2) -es in the cases noted on page 231 (2).

Generally sound the consonants as in mod. E. But -gh, -h (commonest in -ght, -ht) is much like German -ch; k- and -l- are not silent as in mod. E. knife, half.

Begin by sounding single vowels as in modern French, German, Italian, or Spanish. The following equivalents are approximate.

M. E.	*mod. E.*	*M. E.*	*mod. E.*
a =	a in father	ĭ, y̆ =	i in sit; *e.g.*, -i- words now ending with a consonant and doubling that consonant before a suffix (as sitting)
au, aw =	ow in how (except before a nasal, where it = a above; *e.g.*, *aungel*)		
ai, ay ⎫ ei, ey ⎭ =	ay in day	ou, ow =	oo in fool (except *broughte*, etc., open as below, and *knowe*, etc., as in mod. E.)
ī, ȳ =	i in machine; *e.g.*, -i- words now written with silent -e (as bite).		

M. E. had two e sounds not usually rimed together: (1) e close, or tense = mod. E. a in ate; *e.g.*, many -e-words now written -ee- : *been, free, meek, seke, seme, slepe;* (2) e open, or lax = mod. E. e in there; *e.g.*, (*a*) especially words now written -ea- : *bere, bete, biquethe, bireve, breke, breeth, clene, cleve, dede, drede, drem, ese, ete, feste, grece, grete, heed, heeth, hele, hethen, heve, heven, hevy, lepe, mene, mete, pees, pecok, plese, reche, rede, reson* (*seson, treson*), *shere, spere, sprede, stele, strem, swere, teche, trede, wepne, were, wreke, yere.* (Though now showing four different sounds, these words are all written in mod. E. -ea-, and were all sounded in M. E. with open e.); (*b*) before r (*er, ther, were*); (*c*) in strong preterits of the 2nd class (*ches, crep*).

M. E. had two o sounds not usually rimed together: (1) o close, or tense (often written -oo-) = mod. E. o in note; *e.g.*, many words now written -oo- : *bōne, bōte, dōm, dōn, gōd, hood, rōte, shō, sōne, stōd* ('stood'), *tōk* (never sounded as mod. E. -oo-); (2) o open, or lax = o in mod. E. store; *e.g.*, (*a*) in the combination now written -ought (M. E. -*oh, -ouh, -ough*, as *brohte*); (*b*) before r (*bord, dore, lord, sory*); (*c*) in strong prets. of the 1st class (*drof*) and ptc. of the 2nd class (*chosen*).

M. E. u = mod. E. u in full. The sound is frequently written o; *e.g., bokeler, somer, mordre, thonder, come* (ptc.), *ronne* (ptc.).

M. E. unstressed e, as in -e, -er, -es, = mod. E. e in mantel, *i.e.*, is 'neutral.' So are unstressed a (as in *aboute*) and the rare unstressed o.

M. E. i and j, u and v, are freely interchanged in writing. Variation between -el and -le, -en and -ne, -er and -re, etc. (as in mod. E. theater and theatre) is often merely graphic; the pronunciation remains the same.

Practise on one of the parables in the Wiclifite version (page 196), and memorize one of Chaucer's short poems. For more exact pronunciation see S. Moore, *Historical outlines of English phonology and morphology*, Ann Arbor, Michigan, 1925.

II. INFLECTION

INFLECTION OF NOUNS

Mod. Eng. has only one declension, and for this only one inflectional sign, -(e)s, to mark the plural and (written 's) the genitive singular. Survivals of other declensions (*oxen, feet, deer*) are very few.

M. E. had already reached this stage of simplification. The only differences are:
(1) There are more survivals:
   (a) of old plurals; *e.g., thing, good, eyen*, and certain habitual expressions of measure, such as *five yere, hundred pound*, in which the noun was originally g. p. These still survive in mod. E. in such compounds as *fortnight, twelve-month*.
   (b) of old genitives; *e.g., herte rote, fader soule, lady grace*.
(2) -es is usually sounded as a separate syllable.
   But though this holds in most cases, such spellings as *angels, candels, squirrels, lyouns, lovers* show that after a liquid or a nasal the -es often coalesced, as in mod. E., with the preceding syllable; and this happens naturally after vowels; *i.e.*, in such cases the p. or the g. sign is not a separate syllable.

The dative case can often be distinguished in use (as in *on lyve*, 'alive'), but hardly in inflection. The -e, which in M. E. is its sign, may arise from other causes.

An old dative p. survives in the adverb *whilom* ('once upon a time').

INFLECTION OF ADJECTIVES AND ADVERBS

Adjective inflection survives in M. E. as -e:
(1) of the older p.: *swote dewes, gode werkes*.
(2) of the older "weak" or "definite" declension (as in

modern German *der arme Mann*): *the beste man, this wide world.*

But in many cases the *-e* may arise from other causes.

The commonest adverbial termination is dative *-e: foule, faste, lowe, stronge.*

Another common adverbial termination is g. *-es: ones, twies, thries.* So the noun *nedes* ('necessarily.' Compare the dative *nede* in the same sense).

Mod. E. *-ly* is not historically adverbial. M. E. adjectives and adverbs show it often in its older form *-lich.*

Aller (*alder, alther*) is an old g. p. occurring usually with other adjectives, especially superlatives: *allerbest, altherfairest, alderlast, alderfirst* ('best of all,' etc.). So *bother* (*bothe*) with pronouns in such phrases as *your bother love, our bothe labour,* is g. p.

Comparatives with vowel change, as in mod. E. *old — elder,* appear in *long — lenger, strong — strenger.*

Bettre is usually adjective, and *bet* adverbial. *More* (with superlative *mōst* or *mēst*) has p. and adverb *mo. Lesse* appears also as *lasse.* The comparative adverb of *fer* ('far') is *ferre;* of *nere, ner(r)e.*

INFLECTION OF PRONOUNS

Personal pronouns are generally as in mod. E.; but the neuter is commonly *hit,* with g. *his* (not *its*); 3 p. g. is *hir(e)* or *her(e)* (not *their*), the same form as 3 s. g. feminine; 3 p. objective (dative or accusative) is *hem* (not *them*); in 2 p. *ye* is nominative, *you* objective.

Thou sometimes contracts with a preceding verb: *seystow, wostow.*

That has p. *tho,* which is also the adverb; *this,* p. *thise; other,* p. *other.* *At the* is often contracted to *atte.* The correlatives *that oon* and *that other* are the source of the mod. E. colloquial *tother.*

An older indefinite pronoun survives in *men seith*, which is equivalent to *on dit* or *man sagt*.

The dative is clearest in the pronouns frequently used with impersonal verbs: *me list, him liste, me thoughte, were hir loth, him liketh*.

INFLECTION OF VERBS

-e(n) is the sign of the p., the inf., and the strong ptc.

-est, 2 s., sometimes contracts with the vowel of the stem; *e.g., seist*.

-eth is the regular ending of 3 s. pres.; but stems in *-d* and *-t* often contract: *forget* (for *forgeteth*), *fret* (for *freteth*), *stant* (for *standeth*). So *rit, sit, halt*, etc. Note that these forms are pres., not pret.

-eth is also the ending of the imperative p.: *trusteth, asketh;* i.e., trust (ye), ask (ye).

An old prefix of the ptc. (*ge-*, as in modern German) appears sometimes as *y-*, but has no longer either meaning or function.

The inflection of the verb in mod. E. is generally stable; in M. E. there was more variation.
(1) Any M. E. strong ptc. may end in either *-en* or *-e;* e.g., *songen* or *songe*. In mod. E. a given ptc. is fairly settled; e.g., *broken* (never *broke*, except colloquially), *sung* (never *sungen*).
(2) M. E. shows survivals of the earlier use by which the pret. p. of strong verbs has the vowel, not of the pret. s., but of the ptc.; e.g., *he rod, they riden; he swam, they swommen;* but in general the pret. p. in M. E. has already conformed to the pret. s.

These variations are among the causes of the double preterits seen in the following lists (either *wrang* or *wrong*, either *saugh* or *sey*). Some of these doublets are familiar in Shakespeare, and even to-day in colloquial speech.

(3) The tendency to conform to the predominant method carried many old verbs from the strong to the weak conjugation. This process being still active in M. E., some verbs show strong forms and weak forms side by side; e.g., *wēp* and *wepte*.

On the other hand, analogy created some strong forms. *Strive*, though a French derivative, conforms to such other verbs in *-ī-* as *drīve* (Class 1).

The M. E. forms of the following familiar mod. E. strong verbs should be especially noted: burst (*breste, brast, brosten*), choose (*chēse, chēs, chōsen*), fly (*flye, fleigh* or *fley, flowen*), get (*gete, gat, geten*), give (*yeve, yaf, yeven*).

The following sevenfold classification of strong verbs is of little use in learning to read. It is included here, first for students who know German, secondly for later linguistic study of any Germanic language.

MIDDLE-ENGLISH STRONG VERBS

1. rīde   rōd   riden   drīve   drōf   driven
(So (a)bīde, glīde)   (So rīve, shrīve, strīve, thrīve)
shīne   shōn   shinen   strīde   strade
rīse   rōs   risen   strīke   strake   striken
(So agrīse, 'shudder')   strōk   stroken

smīte   smōt   smiten   wrīe   wreigh   wrien
(So bīte, wrīte)   The *-ō-* is often written *-oo-*
                                      (*rood*)

2. *bēde   bēd   bōden   bowe   beigh   bowen
    chēse   chēs   chōsen   brewe   brew   browen
    clēve   clēf   clōven   flȳe   fleigh, fley   flowen
    crēpe   crēp   crōpen   shēte   shēt   shoten
    flēte   flēt   flōten   shove   shēf, shōf   shoven
    sēthe   sēth   sōden   The *-ē-* is often written *-ee-*.

* Often confused with *bidde* (Class 5).

APPENDIX

3. breste   brast   brosten   drinke   drank   dronken
   wreste   wrast   wrosten   (So shrinke, sinke, stinke,
   delve   dalf   dolven   swinke)
   helpe   halp   holpen   fighte   faught   foughten
   melte   malt   molten   swimme   swam   swommen
   kerve   carf   corven   wringe   wrang,   wrongen
   sterve   starf   storven   wrong
   renne   ran   ronnen   binde   bond   bounden
   swelle   swal   swollen   (So finde, grinde, winde)
   yēlde   yōld   yolden   climbe   clomb   clomben
   ginne   gan   gonnen   ringe   rong   rongen
   (So spinne, winne)   (So singe, springe, stinge,
                                     swinge, thringe)

4. bēre   bar   bōren   come   cam, cōm   comen
   (So shere, tere)   nime   nam, nōm   nomen
   brēke   brak   brōken   stēle   stal   stōlen
   spēke   spak   spōken

5. bidde   bad   beden   sitte   sat, seet   seten
   ēte   eet   eten   steke   stak
   gēte   gat   geten   trede   trad   treden
   līe, ligge lay   leyn   wrēke   wrak   wreken,
   see   saugh,   seyn   wroken
            sey   yēve   yaf   yeven

6. tāke   tōk   tāken   gnawe   gnow   gnawen
   (So forsake, shake, shape,   laughe   lough   laughen
    wake)   slee   slough,   slawen,
   bāke   bōk   bāken   slow   slayn
   cwāke   cwōk   wasshe   wesh, wish   wasshen
   steppe stōp   stapen   fāre   fāren
   stonde stōd   stonden   hēve   haf, hēf
   swēre   swōr   swōren   The -ō- is often written -oo
   drawe   drough, drawen   (stood).
           drow

7. blōwe   blew   blowen   wēpe   wēp   wēpen, wōpen
   (So crowe, growe, knowe,   honge   hēng
    throwe)   hōlde   hēld   hōlden
   bēte   bēt   bēten   falle   fel, fil   fallen
   lēpe   lēp   lōpen   walke   welk
   lēte   lēt   lēten   waxe   wēx   waxen
   slēpe   slēp   slēpen   The -ē- is often written -ee-.

APPENDIX
Finding List

Agrīse	1	fighte	3	See	5	strīve	1
Bāke	6	finde	3	sēthe	2	swelle	3
bēde	2	flēte	2	shāke	6	swēre	6
bēre	4	flȳe	2	shāpe	6	swimme	3
bēte	7	forsāke	6	shēre	4	swinge	3
bidde	5	Gēte	5	shēte	2	swinke	3
bīde	1	ginne	3	shīne	1	Tāke	6
binde	3	glīde	1	shove	2	tēre	4
bīte	1	gnawe	6	shrinke	3	thringe	3
blōwe	7	grinde	3	shrīve	1	thrīve	1
bowe	2	grōwe	7	singe	3	thrōwe	7
brēke	4	Helpe	3	sinke	3	trede	5
breste	3	hēve	6	sitte	5	Wăke	6
brewe	2	hōlde	7	slee	6	walke	7
Chēse	2	honge	7	slēpe	7	wasshe	6
clēve	2	Kerve	3	smīte	1	waxe	7
climbe	3	knōwe	7	spēke	4	wēpe	7
come	4	Laughe	6	spinne	3	winde	3
crēpe	2	lēpe	7	springe	3	winne	3
crowe	7	lēte	7	steke	5	wrēke	5
cwăke	6	līe	5	stēle	4	wreste	3
Delve	3	Melte	3	steppe	6	wrīe	1
drawe	6	Nime	4	sterve	3	wringe	3
drinke	3	Renne	3	stinge	3	wrīte	1
drīve	1	rīde	1	stinke	3	Yēlde	3
Ete	5	ringe	3	stōnde	6	yēve	5
Falle	7	rīse	1	strīde	1		
fāre	6	rīve	1	strīke	1		

Weak Verbs

Weak verbs, *i.e.*, those making pret. and ptc. by adding -(*e*)*d*(*e*) or -*t*(*e*), contract more freely than in mod. E.: *kist*, *knet* ('knitted'), *blent* ('blinded'), *peynt* ('painted'), *kempt* ('combed').

Weak verbs in -*ch*- and soft -*g*- contract pret. and ptc. to -*eynt*(*e*) : *blenche* — *bleynt*, *drenche* — *dreynt*, *quenche* — *queynt*, *sprenge* — *spreynt*. *Senge* ('singe') makes ptc. *seynd*.

APPENDIX

Rēde makes pret. *radde*. So *drēde* — *dradde*, *lēde* — *ladde*, *sprēde* — *spradde*.
Tēche, as in mod. E., makes *taught(e)*. So *rēche* — *raughte* ('reached') and *strecche* — *straughte* ('stretched'). An old pret. *yēde* is sometimes used instead of *went(e)*.

ANOMALOUS VERBS

Be(en) has p. *be(en)*. *Can* has inf. and p. *con(ne)*, pret. *coude* or *couthe*. *May* has inf. and p. *mowe(n)*, pret. *might(e)*. *Must*, historically a pret., appears in M. E. as *moste*. The pres., meaning sometimes 'may', sometimes 'must', is *mōt*, p. *mōte(n)*. *Shal* occasionally has p. *shulle(n)*. *Wil* has 1 and 3 s. *wil* or *wol*, 2 *wilt* or *wolt*, p. *wil* or *wol*, pret. *wolde*. *Dar* has p. *dar* or *dorre*, pret. *dorste*. *Wite* ('know') makes 2 s. *wost*, 3 s. *wot*, p. *wite(n)*, pret. *wist(e)*. An old 3 s. *thar* ('needs') occurs rarely, with pret. *thurte*. It appears also as *tharf* — *thurfte*.

Several forms of *be*, *have*, *wil*, and *wite* contract with the negative *ne:* *nam* ('am not'), *nis* ('is not'), *nadde* ('had not'), *noot* ('knows not'), *nere* ('were not'), etc.

III. SYNTAX

SYNTAX: NOUNS

Maner is used as an adjective meaning 'kind of', 'sort of', *no maner vice;* *wonder*, as an adverb meaning 'wondrously' or merely 'very': *wonder glad, wonder lyk, wonder faste*.
Nedes ('necessarily') and *whiles* (usually a conjunction, 'while') are common instances of the M. E. adverbial g. The forms survive in mod. E. as *needs* and *whilst*. The adverbial g. *his (hir) thankes* means 'by his (her, their) will.'

Syntax: Adjectives and Adverbs

The use of adjectives as nouns, familiar in all periods, gives in each period certain set expressions; *e.g.*, M. E. says *the grete* ('the main points, the substance') as mod. E. says *the long and the short*. Similar are *the gentils* ('the people of birth'), *these olde wise* ('these old wise men').

A negative is quite commonly reinforced by another negative, as in French. A famous line of Chaucer's General Prologue has three: *He never yet no vileinye ne sayde*. There is no historical warrant for saying that two negatives make an affirmative.

The mod. E. relative adverbs *when* and *where* are transferred interrogatives. So M. E. *whan, wher;* but the transitional stage appears in *whan that*, and the relative adverb is also expressed by the demonstrative *ther*, with or without *as: ther as he was* ('where he was').

Syntax: Pronouns

Reflexive action is expressed usually by the personal pronoun alone, without mod. E. *self: peyned hem* ('exerted themselves'), *for Avarice to clothe hir wel* ('clothe herself'), *to kembe and tresse me* ('to comb and braid myself'). But compounds with *self* are used sometimes: *todasshte hirself, wel had she clad hirself*.

The interrogative *whether* means 'which of two', and may be used to introduce a direct question as well as an indirect.

Mod. E. relative pronouns *who, which, what*, are transferred interrogatives. In M. E. this transference has already been made: *through which the ground to preisen is, briddes whiche therinne were*. But this use being not yet stabilized, the relative is expressed in several other ways:

(1) by an interrogative + *that: whom that, which that*. This is the transitional form.

APPENDIX 239

(2) by *that* with a personal pronoun: *Ne she hath kin noon of hir blood that she nis ful hir enemy* ('nor hath she any kin of her blood whose enemy she is not'); *ther nas nat oo poynt that it nas in his right assyse* ('there was not one point which was not in its right position').

(3) occasionally by *as*: *in thilke place as they habyten* ('in the same place in which they dwell'). Compare *ther as* above.

(4) The compound relative expressed in mod. E. by *what* (= *that which*) is in M. E. regularly expressed by *that* alone: *entremete of that thou hast to done* ('meddle with what thou hast to do'). The use is common in the King James Bible: *take that thine is*, Matt. xx. 14. So the demonstrative adverb *ther* is used in the sense of *where*.

Syntax: Conjunctions

In English, as in other languages, the subordinating conjunctions have been developed from adverbs and prepositions; *e.g.*, *before* is adverb in *never before*, preposition in *before dawn*, conjunction in *before he came*.

The transition from adverb or preposition to conjunction is often through use with a noun clause introduced by *that*; e.g., *Nothing prevented him but* (noun) *blindness* is equivalent to *Nothing prevented him but* (noun clause) *that he was blind*. Thus in M. E., in the English of Shakespeare, and even in some mod. E. survivals, we find such transitional forms as *er that, but that, for that*, side by side with *er, for*, etc., used alone as conjunctions: *how Criseyde Troilus forsook, or at the leeste how that she was unkynde* (Troilus IV. 15); *I hate him for he is a Christian, but more for that . . . he lends out money gratis* (Merchant of Venice I. iii. 36).

So *for* (as a subordinating conjunction meaning 'because') appears in M. E. either as *for that* or as *for*. So we find *er* and *er that, til* and *til that, sin* or *sith* and *sin that, if* and *if that, though* and *though that, while* and *whiles that*, etc.

'Although' is expressed by *al* with a subj. immediately following: *al were it bad* ('although it were bad'); *al hadde he be* ('although he had been').

'As if' is expressed by *as* with the subj. *as she were al with dogges torn* ('as if she were all torn by dogs'); *it semed as they kiste alway*.

'Unless' is expressed by *but* or *but if; of fruyt hadde every tree his charge, but it were any hidous tree; never wel ferde but if she outher saugh or herde som greet mischaunce* ('never fared well unless she either saw', etc.).

SYNTAX: VERBS

M. E. uses the inf. without *to* oftener than mod. E.; *i.e.*, not only with auxiliaries, as in *ginneth waxen* and in mod. E. *may go, can see*, etc., but much more freely: *semed be, loved wel have*.

M. E. inf. with *for to* shows no distinction of meaning from the use with *to*.

The auxiliary with intransitive verbs of motion and of happening is usually *be*, as in modern French and German: *is befalle, been ypassed, was comen*.

The causative auxiliary with the inf., as mod. E. *make* in *he makes me do it*, is usually *do* or *let* (Compare French *faire* and German *lassen*, used with the inf. in the same sense.): *he dide hem bothe entaile and peynte* ('he caused (some one) both to carve and to paint them'; *i.e.*, he had them both carved and painted); *had don come* ('had caused to come'); *lat calle thy freendes* ('have they friends called'); *leet make a statue* ('had a statue made'). Note that whereas mod. E. idiom expresses this by the passive ptc. of the thing done, M. E. idiom has the active inf. of the doer.

M. E. sometimes uses *gan*, somewhat as mod. E. *did*, with the inf. as a sort of pret.: *unto sir Mirthe gan I goon* ('went I'); *Dame Richesse on hir hond gan lede a yong man* ('led').

APPENDIX 241

M. E. often uses *have* with the ptc. (the so-called perfect inf.), usually in expressions of unfulfilled or unreal condition, where mod. E. uses the simple inf.: *er that deeth us shal have nomen* ('before death shall take us', or as we commonly say, 'before death takes us'); *wel wende I ful sikerly have been in paradys* ('I thought myself to be in paradise'); *he wende to have reproved be if*, etc. ('he expected to be reproved if').

The subjunctive in mod. E. survives in certain set forms, which have remained so constantly in use as to resist a general tendency toward expressing distinctions of mood by auxiliaries (*may, should*, etc.). These set forms give the clues to the more extensive use of the subjunctive in M. E.

(1) *God bless you* and *Good bye* ('God be with you') preserve in mod. E. the use of 3 s. subj. as an expression of wish. So M. E.: *God it kepe, God me blesse, as helpe me God, God ynough alwey hir sende*.

(a) M. E. uses the subj. more widely, not only in expressions of wish and command, but in the object clauses following: *God graunte in gree that she it take* ('God grant that she may receive it with favor'); *commaundeth me that it be so; I pray God ever falle hir faire* ('I pray God that it may ever happen fairly for her', *i.e.*, that she may ever have good luck). So in the pret.: *it was not hir entente that fro that purs a peny wente* ('should go'); *no lenger wolde he that he kepte* ('should keep'); *she nolde hir owne fader ferde wel* ('she would not that her own father should fare well'). The *nolde* in this sentence is pret. subj., as the *had* in *had rather*. Compare the following section (2) and French *voudrait* in similar expressions.

(2) *If it were, as if it were*, and *I had rather* are survivals in mod. E. of an extensive M. E. use of the pret. subj. in so-called unreal conditions, or conditions contrary to fact, and in their conclusions: *she were worthy for to been an emperesse* ('she would be worthy to be an empress');

gret qualm ne were it noon, ne sinne, although hir lyf were gon ('it would be no great pain or sin, although her life should be gone'); *as she were al with dogges torn* ('as if'); *he semede as he were an aungel* ('as if'); *as it two yonge douves were.*

Mod. E. *I had rather = I should rather have; i.e.,* had is historically a pret. subj., as German *hätte,* in an unreal condition. In M. E. the expression is usually impersonal: *me (him, hir, hem) were lief* (or *lever*); *i.e.,* 'it would be agreeable (or more agreeable) to me (him, her, them).'

(3) *Be he rich, or be he poor* is a mod. E. survival of an extensive M. E. use of the subj., (*a*) in conditions, (*b*) in relative clauses implying condition.

(*a*) subj. with *if,* etc.: *if any aske me, if she see, if a man in honour rise, if it lyke yow.* 'Unless' in such clauses is expressed by *but* or *but if.*

(*b*) subj. in relative clauses implying condition (indefinite, or 'ideal' relative clauses): *in which half that he be* ('on whichever side he may be'); *whoso loke in that mirour* ('may look'). So when the implied condition is unreal: *He semede as he were an aungel that doun were comen fro hevene* ('he seemed as if he were an angel that might have come down from heaven'); *whoso dorste to hir trespace, he were ful hardy* ('whosoever should dare to trespass against her, he would be very bold'). Note that in many of these cases the subj., though distinguishable in use, is not distinguishable from the indicative by inflectional form. That is one reason for its fading in mod. E.

(4) *Till he come,* familiar from the King James Bible, but in mod. Eng. superseded by *till he comes* (indicative), is a similar M. E. use of the subj. to imply uncertainty of time in temporal clauses looking to the future: *er that age thee devoure* ('before age devour thee').

(5) The subj. in concessive clauses, now almost extinct, is regular in M. E. See 'although' under Conjunctions above.

(6) The subj. in purpose clauses with *that* and *lest,* now

APPENDIX 243

entirely superseded by auxiliaries, survives in M. E.: *lest it the tendre grasses shende* ('lest it should harm the tender grasses').

(7) The 1 p. subj. used as an imperative in such phrases as *go we in*, though familiar through the time of Shakespeare, is now quite superseded by *let us go in*.

For historical study of inflections and syntax see Moore, as above; Krapp, G. P., *Modern English, its Growth and Present Use*, New York, 1909; Jespersen, O., *Growth and Structure of the English Language*, Leipzig, 1905.

IV. SEMANTIC

COMMON MIDDLE ENGLISH MEANINGS NOW OBSOLETE OR UNUSUAL

buxom	yielding	*keep*	care
caste	plan	*kinde*	nature
catel	capital	*knave*	boy
chere	mien	*leche*	physician
clerk	scholar	*lewed*	ignorant
conceit	conception	*lore*	teaching
condicioun	rank	*lust* (*lest*)	desire
conning	skill	*make*	compose (poetry)
corage	spirit		
cure	care	*nice*	foolish
daunger	haughtiness	*outrage*	excess
defende	forbid	*parte* (*departe*)	divide
disese	discomfort	*peyne*	exert
doom	judgment	*pine*	torture
drenche	drown	*purchace*	procure
dresse	dispose	*queynt*	dainty
falle	happen	*religious*	monastic
fare	behavior	*route*	company
free	liberal	*sad*	settled
frete	devour	*science*	knowledge
gentil	well born	*sely*	innocent
glee	music	*sentence*	opinion
half	side	*shape*	plan
honest	honorable	*shrewe*	scoundrel
hool	sound	*sitte*	befit

APPENDIX

skile	reason	*tough*	difficult
sort	lot	*uncouth*	strange
spille	destroy	*vileinye*	baseness
sterve	die	*wait*	watch
storie	history	*wit*	intelligence
tide	time		

The M. E. dictionary of Stratmann has been revised by Bradley, Oxford, 1891. For serious study of the successive meanings of any word, the New English Dictionary on Historical Principles (called the Oxford Dictionary, or N. E. D.) is indispensable.

NOTES

The following notes, referring to the numbers of the preceding pages, add necessary or suggestive details for further study. They indicate the editions and discussions most available for beginners, and show how to carry out the exposition. General books of reference such as cyclopedias, and comprehensive manuals such as the Cambridge Medieval History, are taken for granted. Full bibliography will be found in John Edwin Wells's *Manual of the Writings in Middle English, 1050–1400*, New Haven, Yale University Press, 1916, with four supplements, of which the last appeared in 1929. The bibliographical notes below are therefore selective.

CHAPTER I. THE MIDDLE AGE

This chapter briefly surveys the typical directions of study in medieval literature. Opening the whole field, it is meant to show where all students should begin and how each may go on according to his particular interest and equipment. Medieval history, for instance, which is constantly involved with medieval literature, need not be mastered first and separately. The practical course is to look over a recognized, preferably a recent, brief manual, to consult it at need, and to use its bibliography and larger bibliographies such as the 1931 revision of Paetow's *Guide to the study of medieval history*, where further study is desired. So architecture, or sculpture, or music may be brought in first through general books of reference, then through special works, as each student finds that it serves his turn. Since the subject of this volume is the literature, the following notes on collateral studies are limited to such few indications as may not readily be found in reference books. The forms of medieval Latin literature and the composition of a few significant vernacular poems are set forth in C. S. Baldwin's *Medieval rhetoric and poetic*, New York, 1928.

3. Julius Caesar Scaliger, whose *Poetica* was influential in these centuries, calmly brings his history of Latin poetry through his own poems, but omits the whole middle age.
6. For the monasteries as centers of education and art see the section on Bede in chapter ii below.
7.1 K. P. Harrington's *Medieval Latin*, Boston & New York, 1925, is an interesting volume of typical selections with useful notes.
7.2 For the place of Anglo-Saxon in the history of the English language consult G. P. Krapp's *Modern English*, New York, 1909, or O. Jespersen's *Growth and Structure of the English Language*, Leipzig, 1905.
10. *The Philobiblon of Richard de Bury*, edited and translated by Ernest C. Thomas, London, 1888 (reissued, with preface and notes by Sir Israel Gollancz, in the Medieval Library of the Oxford University Press). For the availability of books in the late middle age see Eleanor P. Hammond, *English Verse between Chaucer and Surrey*, Duke University Press, 1927, page 13.
11.1 Thomas ed., page 206 ; **11.2** pages xlvi–xlvii.
11.3 *Cursor mundi* ed. R. Morris, London, 1874, etc. (Early English Text Soc.)
11.4 *Polychronicon*, with the English translation of John Trevisa, ed. Babington & Lumby, 1865, etc. (Rolls

series.) Caxton printed, 1482, the English translation with a continuation to 1460. A similar work is *The two cities, a chronicle of universal history to . . . 1146 . . . by Otto, Bishop of Freising*, translated by C. C. Mierow, New York, Columbia University Press, 1928.

12.1 For the medieval exposition of literary form by Vincent of Beauvais and other compilers see C. S. Baldwin, *Medieval rhetoric and poetic*, 172–182; for knowledge of science, W. C. Curry, *Chaucer and the medieval sciences*, Oxford, 1926.

12.2 For medieval use of classical authors refer to J. E. Sandys, *History of classical scholarship*. The most recent discussion is J. S. Beddie's in *Speculum*, 5 : 3–20 (January, 1930). For Boethius see C. S. Baldwin, *Medieval rhetoric and poetic*, 100.

14. The relations of the *chansons de geste* to the stations of the great pilgrimage routes are explored in the four learned volumes of Joseph Bédier's *Les légendes épiques;* the reflections of social life in the romances, in Langlois's *La vie en France au moyen âge*, and more briefly in Sarah F. Barrows's *The medieval society romances*, New York, Columbia University Press, 1924.

15. The art, *dictamen*, is explained in C. S. Baldwin's *Medieval rhetoric and poetic*, chapter viii.

CHAPTER II. THE EPIC CENTURIES: ANGLO-SAXON LITERATURE

W. P. Ker's *Epic and romance*, London, 1897, is an excellent guide to epic habits, both Germanic and French. Margaret Schlauch's *Medieval narrative*, New York, 1928, has concisely instructive introductions to its translations from the sagas, the *chansons de geste*, and the Nibelung cycle. To make acquaintance with Anglo-Saxon literature, use the two volumes of A. S. Cook and C. B. Tinker: *Select translations from Old English poetry*, Boston & New York, 1902; and *from Old English Prose*, 1908.

16. For medieval preaching see C. S. Baldwin, *Medieval rhetoric and poetic*, New York, 1928, chapter ix.

17.1 For the sagas see Ker and Schlauch (above) and W. A. Craigie, *The Icelandic sagas*, Cambridge, 1913. *Grettir* is translated in the Everyman Library. The saga of the *Volsungs*, translated by Magnusson and Morris with parts of the Elder Edda, London, 1888, and by Dr. Schlauch, New York, 1930, exhibits Germanic mythology, for which see also *Horned Seyfried* and the Nibelung cycle in the Schlauch collection. For the Prose Edda as a "textbook for apprentice poets" see A. G. Brodeur's introduction to his translation, New York, 1916. L. M. Hollander has translated the *Poetic Edda*, University of Texas, 1928. The Oxford Medieval Library has *Translations from the Icelandic*.

17.2 *The Song of Roland* is translated by Isabel Butler in the Riverside Literature Series; by Jessie Crosland in the Oxford Medieval Library; by Leonard Bacon (verse), New Haven (Yale University Press), 1914; by James Geddes, New York, 1925; *Raoul de Cambrai*, by Jessie Crosland in the Oxford Medieval Library; the *Pilgrimage of Charlemagne* and *Charles and Elegast*, in the Schlauch collection.

18. As guide to *Beowulf* use W. W. Lawrence's *Beowulf and epic tradition*, Cambridge (Harvard University Press), 1928, with its bibliography. Editions of the Anglo-Saxon text: A. J. Wyatt & R. W. Chambers, revised, Cambridge (England), 1920; F. Klaeber, Boston & New York, 1922. Translations: C. G. Child, Boston, 1904 (prose); F. B. Gummere, *The oldest English epic*, New York, 1909 (verse, with *Finnsburg, Waldhere, Deor, Widsith,* and *Hildebrand*);

NOTES 249

C. B. Tinker, New York, 1910 (prose); J. R. C. Hall, London, 1911 (prose); J. D. Spaeth in *Old English poetry*, Princeton, 1922 (verse).

19. In the verse translations on pages 18–23 and 45–47 first consideration has been given to the rhythm. Though this cannot be reproduced in modern English, it can, I hope, be echoed by translating the old staves, so far as may be, measure for measure, with the alliteration that binds them into verses, and by keeping intact, even at the risk of strangeness, the original sentence structure.

24. The prose translations in this section are quoted from C. B. Tinker's *Beowulf*, revised edition, New York, Newson & Co., 1910.

25. See the *Attack on Finnsburg* in Gummere's *Oldest English epic* (above).

29. James Ingram's translation of the *Chronicle* is reprinted in the Everyman Library.

32. The Everyman translation of Bede's *Historia ecclesiastica* has a suggestive introduction by Vida D. Scudder and a bibliography. The volume includes Bede's lives of St. Cuthbert and of the abbots Benedict, Ceolfrid, Easterwine, Sigfrid, and Huetberht. The Loeb Classical Library *Opera historica* (2 vols.) has the Latin text with a parallel translation (based on Stapleton's) by J. E. King. For Bede on metric see C. S. Baldwin's *Medieval rhetoric and poetic*, New York, 1928, 110–112.

36. Man's life is like a sparrow, mighty king,
That, while at banquet with your chiefs you sit
Housed near a blazing fire, is seen to flit
Safe from the wintry tempest. Fluttering,
Here did it enter, there on hasty wing
Flies out and passes on from cold to cold;
But whence it came we know not, nor behold
Whither it goes. Even such that transient thing,
The human soul; not utterly unknown

250   NOTES

> While in the body lodged, her warm abode;
> But from what world she came, what woe or weal
> On her departure waits, no tongue hath shown.
> This mystery if the stranger can reveal,
> His be a welcome cordially bestowed.
>
> Wordsworth, Ecclesiastical Sonnets, xvi.

42. C. W. Kennedy, *The Caedmon poems* translated into English prose, London, 1916; J. D. Spaeth, *Biblical Epic*, in *Old English poetry*, Princeton, 1922 (verse).

46. Translations: R. K. Root, *Andreas* (verse), New York, 1899 (Yale Studies in English); C. W. Kennedy, *The poems of Cynewulf* (prose), London & New York, 1910 (useful introduction). Cynewulf wrote the *Christ*, the *Fates of the Apostles*, *Elene*, and *Juliana*, possibly also *Andreas*, *Phoenix*, and *Dream of the Rood*. A. S. Cook's edition of the *Christ*, Boston & New York, 1900, has an introductory discussion of the composition interesting even to students unacquainted with Anglo-Saxon. Cook edited also the *Dream of the Rood*, Oxford, 1905, *Elene* and *Phoenix* (with *Physiologus*), New Haven, 1919; G. P. Krapp, *Andreas* and *Fates of the Apostles*, Boston & New York, 1916.

48.1 *Brunanburh* has been translated by Tennyson, by Spaeth in *Old English poetry*, and by others, often with *Maldon*.

48.2 *Maldon*, translated by Spaeth (above); by Cook and Tinker in *Select translations from Old English poetry*.

CHAPTER III. MEDIEVAL ROMANCE:
LITERARY MOTIVES

Use Ker and Schlauch (head-note to Chapter II). Add W. W. Lawrence, *Medieval story*, New York, 1911 (revised 1926). For bibliography from this point on consult J. E. Wells, *A manual of the writings in Middle English*,

1050–1400 (with its supplements), New Haven (Yale University Press). But the best introduction to medieval romance is romance itself in Malory's *Morte d'Arthur* or in the *Mabinogion* as translated from the Welsh by Lady Charlotte Guest.

51. Walter Map's collection, *De nugis curialium*, is largely a notebook of stories. The old edition of the Latin original, Thomas Wright's for the Camden Society, 1850, has been superseded by that of M. R. James, Oxford, 1914. James published a translation, London, 1923; F. Tupper and M. B. Ogle, another, London, 1924. Map is discussed below at pages 63–4, 78–80, 82–3.

54. For courtly love see the index to this volume and W. G. Dodd, *Courtly love in Chaucer and Gower*, Boston, 1913. The Provençal romance of *Flamenca* has been translated by H. F. M. Prescott, New York, 1930.

59. The symbolism of the ceremonies of knighting is explained in *Sir Hugh of Tabarie*, translated in E. Mason's collection (Everyman Library) *Aucassin and Nicolette and other medieval romances*.

62.1 Sometimes the Celts took back with interest what they had lent. Legends derived from oral Celtic tradition and put into French literary form were sometimes turned back into Welsh.

62.2 The latest version seems to be Mr. Kipling's in the *Jungle Book*. Two medieval French versions are *Bisclavret* and *Guillaume de Palerne*, the latter translated about the middle of the fourteenth century into English alliterative verse (*William of Palerne*, ed. W. W. Skeat, Early English Text Society, 1867).

65. The current prose compilation is entitled *I paladini di Francia*.

66. Geoffrey's *Historia* is translated by Dr. Evans (Everyman Library). For the long discussion as to its place in the development of Arthurian romance see W. Lewis Jones, *King Arthur in history and legend*, Cambridge, 1911; Acton Griscom's introduction to his edition of the Latin text, London, 1929; and the *Manual* of Wells.

70.1 Dr. Schlauch (above) includes translations from the Alexander legend. F. P. Magoun has edited with the Latin sources *The gests of Alexander of Macedon*, two middle English alliterative fragments, Harvard University Press, 1929. See also *King Alexander* (selections) in French and Hale (head-note to Chapter IV below).

70.2 See *Sir Lancelot of the Lake*, translated by Lucy A. Paton, New York, 1929.

72. Dr. Schlauch (above) translates from Robert de Boron and from the Greater Holy Grail. The Everyman Library has Dr. Evans's translation of *Perlesvaus* entitled *The high history of the Holy Grail*. Bibliography for the complicated and partly speculative history of the Grail legend will be found in the *Manual* of Wells.

CHAPTER IV. MEDIEVAL ROMANCE: LITERARY FORMS

To Dr. Schlauch's translations and introductions in her *Medieval narrative* (above) add W. H. French and C. B. Hale's *Middle English metrical romances*, New York, 1930 (texts, notes, glossary). In the Everyman Library the collection of translations by Eugene Mason, *Aucassin and Nicolette and other medieval romances and legends*, conveniently exhibits the shorter forms.

76. For the scheme of the *Divina Commedia* see C. S. Baldwin, *Medieval rhetoric and poetic*, New York, 1928, pages 269–280. Of the many transla-

NOTES 253

tions the only one rendering the whole in the characteristic composition by tercets is J. B. Fletcher's (New York, 1931), which is at once faithful and beautiful.

77.1 F. B. Luquiens, *Three lays of Marie de France retold in English verse*, New York, 1911 (useful introduction). Prose translations: Edith Rickert, London, 1901; Jessie L. Weston, London, 1900; Eugene Mason, in the Everyman Library.

77.2 *Sir Orfeo* is reprinted in Cook's *Literary Middle English Reader*, and in French and Hale (above).

78. For *exemplum* see the index to C. S. Baldwin's *Medieval rhetoric and poetic*.

80.1 *Gesta Romanorum*, translated by Swan, London, 1871; by M. Komroff, New York, 1928.

80.2 Three lives are included in the Schlauch collection (above). See also R. E. Parker, *The Middle English stanzaic versions of the life of Saint Anne*, London, 1928. The fifteenth-century English version of the collection called the *Golden Legend* (ed. Herrtage, London, 1879) is reprinted in Temple Classics.

81. Translated in the Mason collection, *Aucassin and Nicolette*, etc. (Everyman Library) and by Alice Kemp-Welch, with other "miracles", London, 1908 (Oxford Medieval Library).

82.1 Translated by Alice Kemp-Welch, London, 1903, with the French text and an introduction by Dr. L. Brandin.

82.2 Translated in the Mason collection (above) and by F. W. Bourdillon, but best by Andrew Lang.

83.1 Chrétien's *Erec*, *Cligés*, *Yvain*, and *Lancelot* translated (prose) by W. W. Comfort (Everyman Library); *Cligés*, by L. J. Gardiner (prose, Oxford Medieval Library); *Erec et Enide* (French) by Mme Lot (Myrrha Lot Borodine), Paris, 1924. See her *La femme et l'amour au xiie siècle d'après les poèmes de Chrétien de Troyes*, Paris, 1909. The latest comprehensive work on Chrétien, with bibliographical notes, and with many significant quotations in the original accompanied by translations into modern French, is Gustave Cohen's *Un grand romancier d'amour et d'aventure au xiie siècle, Chrétien de Troyes et son œuvre*, Paris, 1931.

83.2 This familiar translation, often reprinted, is in the Everyman Library. T. P. Ellis and John Lloyd have made a complete translation from the two texts of Dr. Gwenogvryn Evans, Oxford Library of Translations, 2 vols.

85. *Ywain and Gawain*, ed. G. Schleich, Leipzig, 1887; selections in French and Hale (above).

90.1 Marie de France translated an *Isopet*.

90.2 Caxton's 1481 History of Reynard the Fox is modernized as *Epic of the beast*, with *Physiologus*, in the series Broadway Translations.

91. Five *fabliaux* are translated in the Schlauch collection (above). The standard discussion is Joseph Bédier's *Les fabliaux, études de littérature populaire et d'histoire littéraire du moyen âge*.

CHAPTER V. MIDDLE ENGLISH ROMANCES, DISTINCTIVE AND CONVENTIONAL

For this chapter and the following the student should increasingly use texts rather than translations. The Appendix preceding this section of notes provides a compact Middle English grammar based on the language of Chaucer; quotations in the text from earlier works are either translated or glossed in footnotes; and the editions provide glossaries. The earlier period is exemplified in J. Hall's *Selections from early Middle English, 1130–1250* Oxford, 1920; the later, in K. Sisam's *Fourteenth-century verse and prose*, Oxford, 1922. W. A. Neilson and K. G. T. Webster's *Chief British poets of the fourteenth and fifteenth centuries*, Boston and New York, 1916, is partly text, partly translation; W. H. French and G. B. Hale's *Middle English metrical romances*, New York, 1930, texts with introduction, foot-notes, and glossary; Jessie L. Weston's *Romance, vision, and satire*, Boston & New York, 1912, and her *Chief Middle English poets*, Boston & New York, 1914, translations. For more intensive study consult the annual bibliography of the Medieval Academy of America entitled *Progress of Medieval Studies in the United States*.

94.1 For the history of the language see G. P. Krapp's *Modern English* or O. Jespersen's *Growth and structure of the English language*.

94.2 *King Horn*, ed. J. R. Lumby, London, 1866 (reedited, G. G. McKnight, 1901); ed. J. Hall, Oxford, 1901; ed. French and Hale (above); translated (prose) by Laura A. Hibbard in *Three Middle English romances* (Horn, Havelok, Beves), London, 1911; by J. L. Weston in *Chief poets* (above).

98. *The lay of Havelok the Dane*, reedited, W. W. Skeat, Oxford, 1902; ed. French and Hale (above). For translations see the preceding note and Weston's *Chief poets*.

106. For the Tristram story see *The Romance of Tristram and Ysolt* by Thomas of Britain, translated from the Old French and Old Norse by R. S. Loomis, New York, 1931 (revised), or Joseph Bédier's modern French version; for the poem *Sir Tristrem* discussed in the text, the volume *Early Scottish poetry*, Glasgow, 1891, in Abbotsford Series of the Scottish Poets, and J. L. Weston's *Chief poets* (above). The latest verse narrative of Tristram is that of Edwin Arlington Robinson, New York, 1927.

107. Ed. Halliwell Phillips, London, 1844 (Camden Society); Campion and Holthausen, Heidelberg & New York, 1913; French and Hale (above); translated by J. L. Weston in *Chief poets* (above). Miss Weston has also translated a much finer poem, the medieval German *Parzival* of Wolfram von Eschenbach, London, 1894.

108. Ed. Kaluza, Leipzig, 1890; translated (prose) by J. L. Weston, *Sir Cleges and Sir Libeaus Desconus*, London, 1902.

109. Ed. E. Kölbing, London, 1885; translated (see note 94.2 above). The hero's name appears as Beves, Beuve, and Bueve.

112. Ed. J. Zupitza, London, 1883–91.

113. Ed. W. W. Skeat, London, 1870–74 (reedited for the Scottish Text Society, Edinburgh, 1894); translated by J. L. Weston, *Chief poets* (above), and in part by G. Eyre-Todd, London, 1907; selections from the text in Neilson and Webster, *Chief British poets* (above).

CHAPTER VI. MIDDLE–ENGLISH ARTHURIAN ROMANCES

To the head-note of Chapter V (above) add W. L. Jones, *King Arthur in history and legend* (Cambridge University Manuals); and H. Maynadier, *The Arthur of the English poets*, Boston & New York, 1907. For deeper study of the medieval transmission of Arthurian stories see R. S. Loomis, *Celtic myth and Arthurian romance*, New York, 1927 (Columbia University Press). Among modern Arthurian verse romances the best known are Tennyson's *Idylls of the King*. The *Lancelot* (1920) and the *Merlin* (1917) of Edwin Arlington Robinson are distinguished in both conception and composition.

118. Reedited by Bruce, London, 1903; reprinted, with an introduction, by Lucy A. Paton, *Morte Arthur: two early English romances* (Everyman Library).

NOTES 257

The most useful and convenient edition is S. B. Hemingway's, Boston & New York, 1912 (Riverside Literature Series).

121. *Arthurian chronicles represented by Wace and Layamon*, translated by Eugene Mason (Everyman Library); selections from Layamon in J. L. Weston, *Chief poets* (head-note to Chapter V above); text ed. J. Hall, *Layamon's Brut, selections*, Oxford, 1924 (introduction, notes, glossary); selections in French and Hale (above).

122.1 *Joseph of Arimathie*, ed. W. W. Skeat, London, 1871. For the legend see J. A. Robinson, *Two Glastonbury legends*, Cambridge University Press, 1926.

122.2 *Morte Arthure*, an alliterative poem of the 14th century from the Lincoln MS. written by Robert of Thornton, ed. Mary M. Banks, London, 1900; prose translation by A. Boyle in the Everyman volume cited in note 118 above.

127. *Sir Gawain and the Green Knight*, ed. J. R. R. Tolkien and E. V. Gordon, Oxford, 1925; translations: J. L. Weston (prose), London, 1900, and (verse) in her *Romance, vision, and satire*, Boston & New York, 1912; Neilson and Webster (prose) in their *Chief British poets* (above); T. H. Banks (verse), New York, 1929; S. O. Andrew (in the original rhythms), New York, 1929; origins and other critical study, G. L. Kittredge, *Gawain and the Green Knight*, Harvard University Press, 1916, and the *Manual* of Wells. The unknown author is often referred to as "the *Pearl* poet", partly because both poems are found in the same manuscript, partly because of certain similarities of language and style, perhaps mainly because outside of the work of Chaucer the two poems are the most distinguished of their time. Their differences, however, appear to some critics more striking than their likenesses. Two other poems in the same manuscript, *Clannesse* (Purity) and *Patience*, have also been ascribed to the same author. All four, indeed, are alliterative and abundantly descriptive; but the descriptions of these latter two have neither the delicacy nor the brilliance of those in *Gawain* and *Pearl*. The verse shows a less practised hand. In composition there is no likeness at all, *Clannesse* and *Patience* being simple homilies carried out by examples from the Bible. Since the most distinctive beauty of either *Gawain* or *Pearl* is its composition, we may tentatively set aside the other poems and await more definite support for the common authorship of these two. *Clannesse* and *Patience* are edited, with *Pearl*, by R. Morris, London, 1864, 1896; translated by J. L. Weston in her *Romance, vision, and satire* (verse), Boston & New York, 1912. Editions and translations of *Pearl* are given below.

129. The translation here and on the following pages keeps the rhythm and alliteration of the original.

133. Malory's immediate sources are indicated briefly and partially at page xxxvii of W. E. Mead's *Selections from Sir Thomas Malory's Morte Darthur*, Boston, 1897; extensively in H. O. Sommer's introduction to his *Le Morte Darthur by Syr Thomas Malory*, London, 1889–90, which is a complete and careful reprint of the original Caxton. The Globe edition, London, 1889, modernizes the spelling, but not the syntax. Everyman Library also has a reprint. C. G. Child has edited for the Riverside Literature Series the Book of Merlin and the Book of Sir Balin. For discussion see Vida D. Scudder's *Le Morte Darthur of Sir Thomas Malory and its sources*, New York & London, 1917, and E. Vinaver's *Malory*, Oxford, 1929; for biography, E. Hicks, *Sir Thomas Malory*, Harvard University Press, 1928. Laura Hibbard Loomis contributes a significant study of Malory's method to *Medieval studies in* *memory of Gertrude Schoepperle Loomis*, New York, 1927 (Columbia University Press).

138. For a different view of Malory's composition see Scudder (above).

CHAPTER VII. MEDIEVAL LYRIC

143. The Rev. Matthew Britt, O. S. B., *The hymns of the Breviary and Missal*, New York, 1922 (text, translation, notes). *The English Hymnal*, Oxford, 1906, contains many Latin hymns in translation with indication of the original by first line and of the author and date where these are known. J. S. Phillimore has selected *The hundred best Latin hymns*, London & Glasgow, 1926. Hymns are included, of course, in the anthologies; *e.g.*, Harrington's *Medieval Latin* and Gaselee's *Oxford Book of medieval Latin verse*. As general guide use C. S. Baldwin's *Medieval rhetoric and poetic*, New York, 1928, chapters IV, V B, VII C. Eveline W. Brainerd's *Great hymns of the middle ages*, New York, 1909, collects thirty-six translations.

144. *Carmina Burana*, the name of the most important collection, thirteenth century, has become a generic name for such poems. They are also called goliardic. (See in books of reference *goliard*.) J. A. Schmeller's German edition of the Benediktbeuern manuscript, several times reprinted, has been superseded by that of Alfons Hilka, Heidelberg, 1930. Meantime M. Manitius has edited the Latin text to accompany the German translation of R. Ulich, *Vagantenlieder*, Jena, 1927. Another and smaller collection, the *Cambridge Songs*, has been edited by K. Breul, Cambridge University Press, 1915, and by K. Strecker, Berlin, 1926. T. Wright edited a miscellaneous collection, mainly satirical, under the title *Latin poems commonly attributed to Walter Mapes*, London,

1841 (Camden Society). The attribution to Walter Map is no longer taken seriously. K. P. Harrington's *Medieval Latin* has selections from all three collections. Many of the poems are translated by J. A. Symonds in *Wine, women, and song* (now in the Oxford Medieval Library), and incidentally by Helen Waddell in her *Wandering scholars*, London, 1927. See also her translations entitled *Medieval Latin lyrics*, London, 1929.

147. Lyric is well represented in Cook's *Literary Middle English Reader*. See also E. K. Chambers and F. Sidgwick, *Early English lyrics*, London, 1907, and Carleton Brown's *Religious lyrics of the fourteenth century*, Oxford, 1924 (a thirteenth-century volume forthcoming). F. A. Patterson discusses the *Middle English penitential lyric*, New York, 1911 (Columbia University Press).

151. See *Eight troubadour poets* translated by Barbara Smythe in the Oxford Medieval Library.

152. See Helen L. Cohen, *The Ballade*, New York, 1915 (Columbia University Press). Eustache Deschamp's *balade* to Chaucer is reprinted, with emendation and interpretation, by J. M. Manly in his edition of the Canterbury Tales, New York, 1928. Rossetti's translation of Villon's *balade* is reprinted in Helen L. Cohen's *Lyric forms from France* (New York, 1922, page 493), which exhibits the modern revival of medieval courtly lyric forms. Froissart uses the refrain in a different rime scheme to celebrate the fashionable marguerite, or daisy cult echoed in the prologue to Chaucer's *Legend of good women*.

> Sus toutes flours tient on la rose à belle,
> Et en après, je croi, la violette;
> La flour de lys est belle, et la perselle;
> La flour de glay est plaisans et parfette;

Et li plusiour aiment moult l'anquelie,
Le pyone, le muget, la soussie.
Cascune flour a par li son merite;
Mès je vous di, tant que pour ma partie,
Sus toutes flours j'aime la margherite.

Car en tous temps, plueve, gresille ou gelle,
Soit la saisons ou fresque, ou laide, ou nette,
Ceste flour est gracieuse et nouvelle,
Douce, plaisans, blanchete et vermillette;
Close est à point, ouverte et espanie;
Ja n'y sera morte ne apalie;
Toute bonté est dedens li escripte;
Et pour un tant, quant bien y estudie,
Sus toutes flours j'aime la margherite.

Et le douc temps ore se renouvelle
Et esclarcist ceste douce flourette;
Et si voi ci seoir dessus l'asprelle
Deus coeurs navrés d'une plaisant sajette,
A qui le dieu d'Amours soit en aie,
Avec euls est Plaisance et Courtoisie
Et Douls Regars qui petit les respite.
Don c'est raison qu'au chapel faire die:
Sus toutes flours j'aime la margherite.

(From *Paradys d'amours*, in Oeuvres, ed. A. Scheler,
I. 49)

CHAPTER VIII. MEDIEVAL SYMBOLISM

157.1 There are two "debates" in Martha H. Shackford's *Legends and satires*, Boston & New York, 1913. *A good short debate between winner and waster*, an alliterative poem of 1352, is edited with modern rendering by Sir Israel Gollancz, Oxford University Press.

157.2 *The owl and the nightingale*, J. E. Wells, Boston,1909. There is a selection in Cook's *Literary Middle English Reader*.

157.3 The *Roman de la rose* is discussed in all the manuals, French and English. It is translated into modern English verse by F. S. Ellis in Temple Classics.

159. The following quotations from the A text in this section are rendered in slightly modernized form, keeping the alliteration and the rhythm of the original.

Piers Plowman, ed. W. W. Skeat in three parallel texts, Oxford, 1886, and in a single small volume (B text) with notes and glossary, Oxford, 4th ed., 1886; selections in Cook and in Sisam; translations: Kate M. Warren (prose), London, 1913; J. L. Weston (verse) in her *Romance, vision, and satire* (A text and B text); Neilson and Webster (verse) in *Chief British poets;* Skeat (verse) in Oxford Medieval Library. J. J. Jusserand's *L'épopée mystique de William Langland*, Paris, 1893, was translated, with the author's revision and enlargement, by M. E. R. as *Piers Plowman, a contribution to the history of English mysticism*, New York & London, 1894. J. M. Manly's *Piers the Plowman and its sequence*, in the Cambridge History of English Literature, II. 1, was separately reprinted by the Early English Text Society. Jusserand replied in Modern Philology, 6 : 271, 7 : 289. H. W. Wells's *Construction of Piers Plowman*, in Pub. of the Mod. Lang. Assoc. 44 : 123–140 (March, 1929), is an excellent guide to the thought of the poem.

168. The interpretation of Wells in the article above.

170. *Pearl*, ed. C. G. Osgood, Boston, 1906; Sir Israel Gollancz, with translation (Oxford Medieval Library); translated : G. G. Coulton (verse), London, 1907; Sophie Jewett (verse), New York, 1908;

Weir Mitchell (verse), New York, 1906; J. L. Weston (verse), in *Romance, vision, and satire;* C. G. Osgood (prose), Princeton, 1907; Neilson and Webster (prose), in *Chief British Poets.* The most extensive interpretation is Sister M. Madaleva's *Pearl, a study in spiritual dryness,* New York, 1925. See further the *Manual* of Wells. For authorship see note 127 above.

173.1 Lizette A. Fisher, *The mystic vision in the Grail legend and in the Divine Comedy,* New York, 1917; J. B. Fletcher, *The symbolism of the Divine Comedy,* New York, 1921; Gratia E. Baldwin, *The new Beatrice, or the virtue that counsels,* New York, 1928 (all three in Columbia University Press); Helen F. Dunbar, *Symbolism in medieval thought and its consummation in the Divine Comedy,* New Haven, 1929 (Yale University Press).

173.2 C. S. Baldwin, *Medieval rhetoric and poetic,* 124–5, 203–5, 239–44. E. G. Gardner in *The Cell of self-knowledge* (Oxford Medieval Library) has edited seven English mystical treatises of the fourteenth century.

174. O bush unbrent, brenninge in Moyses sighte.
     Chaucer's Tale of the Prioress, 16.

CHAPTER IX. MIDDLE-ENGLISH POPULAR COMPOSITION

177. The authoritative collection, including all significant versions of all known English ballads, with exhaustive notes for study, is F. J. Child's *English and Scottish popular ballads,* Boston, 1882–98, 5 volumes. At least one version of each of these is included in Helen Child Sargent and G. L. Kittredge's one-volume collection with the same title, Boston &

New York, 1904. Professor Kittredge's introduction is an admirable exposition of the ballad form. Among the many other collections are: *The Oxford book of ballads*, the Everyman Library *Book of British ballads* selected by R. B. Johnson, and *English and Scottish popular ballads* selected and edited by R. Adelaide Witham for the Riverside Literature Series. Ballads are included in several of the anthologies listed above; and *American ballads and songs* are collected by Louise Pound, New York, 1922. For Gummere's theory of communal composition see his *Popular ballad*, Boston & New York, 1907; for further discussion, W. M. Hart's *Ballad and epic*, a study in the development of the narrative art, Harvard Studies and Notes in Philology and Literature, XI.

179. It is known as The Loathly Lady, and is the subject of Chaucer's Tale of the Wife of Bath.
185. Gray to Mason, *Works*, ed. Gosse, ii. 316; cited by Gummere, *Popular ballad*, 182.
187. "Percy's Reliques" are reprinted in the Everyman Library (2 vols.).
188. *English miracle plays, moralities, and interludes*, ed. A. W. Pollard, Oxford, 8th ed., 1927; *English Nativity plays*, ed. S. B. Hemingway, New York, 1909 (Yale Studies in English); *The second shepherds' play, Everyman*, etc., ed. and translated, C. G. Child (Riverside Literature Series, 1910); *Everyman and eight miracle plays* in the Everyman Library. For further information and discussion: E. K. Chambers, *The medieval stage;* C. M. Gayley, *Plays of our forefathers*, New York, 1907; and the *Manual* of Wells. A new view is urged by Oscar Cargill, *Drama and liturgy*, New York, 1930 (Columbia University Press).
200. "Mandeville" is reprinted in the Everyman Library, which has also the travels of Marco Polo. Selec-

tions in Cook and in Sisam (above). For editions and discussions see the *Manual* of Wells.

201.1 *Richard Rolle of Hampole*, ed. C. Horstman, London, 1895 (2 vols.); Frances M. M. Comper, *The Fire of love or melody of love and the Mending of life or rule of living*, translated by Richard Misyn from the *Incendium amoris* and *De emendatione vitae* of Richard Rolle . . . ed. and done into modern English, London, 1920 (2nd ed.); M. Deanesly, the *Incendium amoris*, ed. Manchester, 1915; Dom M. Noetinger, *Le feu de l'amour, le Modèle de la vie parfait, le Pater* (modern French translation), Paris & Tours, 1928; selections in Cook and in Sisam (above). For biography and discussion: Frances M. M. Comper, *The Life of Richard Rolle* (with his English lyrics), London & New York, 1929; Hope E. Allen, *The writings ascribed to Richard Rolle . . . and materials for his biography*, New York, 1927 (published for the Modern Language Association). Her edition of the English writings is forthcoming from the Oxford University Press.

201.2 For the *cursus* in medieval Latin prose see C. S. Baldwin, *Medieval rhetoric and poetic*, 216–218, 223–227.

202. Pecock's *Donet* and *Folewer* have been edited by Elsie V. Hitchcock, London, 1921, 1924; his *Reule of Crysten religioun*, by W. C. Greet, London, 1927. Sir Thomas Elyot's *Governour* is reprinted in the Everyman Library. For further study consult G. P. Krapp, *The rise of English literary prose*, New York, 1915.

CHAPTER X. CHAUCER

The mass of Chaucer studies is indexed in the *Manual* of Wells and its supplements. Eleanor P. Hammond's *Chaucer, a bibliographical manual*, New York, 1908, is in process of revision. See also her *English verse between Chaucer and Surrey*, Durham, N. C. (Duke University Press), 1927, 11–13. An important guide for the history of criticism is Caroline F. E. Spurgeon's *Five hundred years of Chaucer criticism and allusion*, Cambridge University Press, 1925. Additions to her record are made by Bond, Bowyer, Millican, and Smith in "A collection of Chaucer allusions", Studies in Philology 28 : 481–512 (July, 1931). The generally accepted complete text is W. W. Skeat's, Oxford, 1894–1897 (7 vols.). This is reprinted without the notes, but with a glossary, in one volume (Oxford). Another one-volume complete text, ed. Pollard, Heath, Liddell, and McCormick, 1903, is in Macmillan's Globe series. Among the many volumes of selections one of the best is edited by W. A. Neilson and H. R. Patch, New York, 1921. The only Chaucer text established by critical comparison of all the manuscripts is R. K. Root's *Troilus and Criseyde*, Princeton University Press, 1926. Root's *Poetry of Chaucer*, Boston & New York, 1922 (revised), is a concise and comprehensive guide. For Chaucer's language see the Appendix preceding this section of notes.

203. The most recent and exhaustive investigation of the facts of Chaucer's life, J. M. Manly's, is embodied conveniently in the introduction to his edition of the Canterbury Tales, New York, 1928, which is used in this section. See further his *Some new light on Chaucer*, New York, 1926, and W. C. Curry's *Chaucer and the medieval sciences*, Oxford, 1926. For the Trivium see the index to C. S. Baldwin's *Medieval rhetoric and poetic*.

210. D. S. Fansler, *Chaucer and the Roman de la Rose*, New York, 1914 (Columbia University Press).

211. Chaucer's source, Alain de Lille's *Complaint of Nature*, is translated by D. M. Moffat, New York, 1908 (Yale Studies in English). For Alain see the index to C. S. Baldwin's *Medieval rhetoric and poetic*.

215. The best text of *Troilus and Criseyde* is Root's (head-note above).

217.1 G. L. Hamilton, *Chaucer's indebtedness to Guido delle Colonne*, New York, 1903 (Columbia University Press).

217.2 N. E. Griffin and A. B. Myrick, *The Filostrato* . . . a translation with parallel text, Philadelphia, 1929, University of Pennsylvania Press; M. M. Cummings (verse translation), Princeton University Press.

220. Gower (1335?–1408), a friend of Chaucer, who calls him "moral Gower", wrote: (1) in French stanzas, *Speculum meditantis* (*Mirour de l'omme*, 30,000 lines, about 1378), "rightly to teach the way by which the sinner who has trespassed ought to return to the knowledge of his Creator", and two collections of *balades;* (2) in Latin, besides the *Cronica tripertita* and several short pieces, *Vox clamantis* (10,000 elegiac lines, about 1382) on "the various misfortunes which happened in England in the time of King Richard II", especially the insurrection of the peasants; and (3) in English, besides the *Confessio amantis* (1390), a poem *In praise of peace*. G. C. Macaulay has edited his *Complete Works*, Oxford, 1899–1902, and *Selections from the Confessio amantis*, Oxford, 1903. Selections in Cook and in Sisam (above).

222. Killis Campbell's *The seven sages of Rome*, Boston & New York, 1907, an ample and suggestive study of manuscripts, sources, and analogues, is of general value as an exposition of medieval literary transmission. See also French and Hale's *Middle English metrical romances* for selections and notes.

INDEX

ADAM OF ST. VICTOR, 9, 143
adventure, 55-58, 71, 128
Aelfric, 49
Æsop, 90
Alcuin, 42
Alexander, 16, 70, 114, 134, 252
Alfred, 49
Alison, 148
allegory, 157-176
alliteration, 31, 121-122, 132, 147, 150, 159, 171
Ambrose, St., 143-144
amour courtois, 54-55, 83, 89, 136, 151, 157, 211, 216, 217, 251
Andreas, 46, 250
Anglo-Saxon, 7, 18-49
Anne, Saint, 253
Aquinas, St. Thomas, 5, 143
Arabs, 13
architecture, 4, 6, 39
Aristotle, 10, 13
Arthurian, 64-72, 118-140, 252, 256
Aucassin et Nicolete, 75, 82, 251, 252

BALADE, 151-156, 205, 260, 267
ballads, 120, 177-188, 263-264
Barbour, John, 113-117, 150, 181, 256
beast-tale, 89-91, 207, 211, 254
Bede, 32-45, 66, 143, 249
Benedict Biscop, 39, 40
Benoît de Sainte-More, 217

Beowulf, 18-32, 58, 61, 101, 284
Bernard of Cluny, 145
Bernard of Ventadour, 55
Bevis of Hampton, 109-112, 255, 256
Bisclavret, 251
Boccaccio, 205, 208, 214-218, 221-222, 224, 267
Boethius, 12, 13, 143, 144, 202, 204, 247
Bok of the Duchesse, 210
Bourges, 5
Bozon, Nicolas, 89
Brome plays, 191-193, 264
Bruce, 113-117, 181, 256
Brunanburh, 48, 250
Byron, 208

CADENCE, 200-202
Cædmonic poems, 42-46, 250
Cambridge Songs, 259
Canterbury Tales, 219-225, 266
Carmina Burana, 259
cathedrals, 6, 11, 38
Caxton, 133-135, 247, 254
Celtic, 17, 30, 33, 62-63, 66-69, 77, 83-84, 136, 256
chansons de geste, 14, 17, 117, 125, 247
characterization, 56, 71, 76, 83, 85-86, 88, 98, 110, 112, 114, 118, 124, 132, 160-166, 189, 193-195, 208, 215, 216-219
Charlemagne, 16, 42, 65, 134, 248
Chastelaine de Vergi, 82-83, 253

INDEX

Chaucer, 8, 9, 10, 13, 14, 75, 77, 80, 89, 91, 132–133, 152, 154–155, 157, 180, 202, 203–225, 260, 263, 265–267, 109, 114, 123–126, 128–132, 157, 162–165, 169, 170–172, 182, 184, 210, 225
Chevalier au lion, 85–88, 253
Chevy chase, 183
Child Waters, 179
chivalry, 58–60, 113, 128, 131, 133–137, 158
Chrétien de Troyes, 9, 75, 83–88, 253
Church, 5, 6, 14, 32–47, 59, 143, 160, 161, 168, 189, 259
Cicero, 12
Clannesse, 257–258
Claudian, 12
classicism, 3, 215
Clerk, tale of the, 207
Coleridge, 187
Comestor, Petrus, 11
common law, 4
compends, 11, 12
concrete detail, 20, 29, 30, 84, 87, 132, 169, 170–172
Confessio amantis, 220–223, 267
conflictus (see debate)
courtesy, 59, 113, 128
courtly love, 54–55, 83, 89, 136, 151, 157, 211, 216, 217, 251
Crusades, 62–3
Cursor mundi, 11, 246
cursus, 265
cycles of romance, 69–71, 138
Cynewulf, 46–48, 250

DAISY POEMS, 260
Dante, 9, 10, 72, 76, 173, 176, 205, 252, 263
Dares, 13
debate (débat), 157, 211, 261
Decameron, 205, 214, 221–223
Deschamps, 205, 260
description, 20, 29, 30, 33, 48, 83, 84, 99, 101–105, 107, 109, 114, 123–126, 128–132, 157, 162–165, 169, 170–172, 182, 184, 210, 225
dialogue, 87, 91, 119, 132, 185, 188–189, 191–193, 211–212, 216, 225
dictamen, 247
Dictys, 13
drama, 16, 188–195, 211, 218, 224, 264
Dryden, 208
Dürer, 166

ELEANOR OF POITOU, 55
epic, 17–47, 54–56, 58, 61, 98–99, 103–104, 114–117, 123–124, 137, 247, 248
Erec, 83–84, 86, 253
exemplum, 78–80, 207, 221, 223, 253
exile and return, 97, 99, 110
Exodus, 45

FABLE, 89–90, 207, 254
fabliau, 91, 207, 214, 215, 222, 254
Faery Queene, 173
Fair Annie, 179
fair unknown, 108–109, 256
fairy mistress, 51
fairy story, 51, 55, 62, 71, 128, 179
feudalism, 4, 14, 93, 136
Filostrato, 205, 217–218, 267
Finn, 25, 248, 249
Firumbras, 114
Flamenca, 251
Flee fro the prees, 154
Florus, 11
folk lore, 51, 62, 70, 128, 179, 181–182, 188
Fortescue, 202
Fortunatus, 145–146
Franklin, tale of the, 207, 208, 214–215

INDEX 271

Friar, tale of the, 207
Froissart, 139, 206, 260

Gawain and the Green Knight,
  76, 106, 127–133, 138, 166,
  169, 170, 176, 257
Genesis, 46
Geoffrey of Monmouth, 66–69,
  251–252
Geoffrey of Vinsauf, 204
Geraint, 83–85
Gesta romanorum, 80, 253
gesture, 87–88, 212, 217, 225
Gingelein, 108
glass, decorative, 5, 14, 38–39,
  175
gleeman, 28
Golden Legend, 253
goliard, 259
gothic, 4
Gower, 220–221, 224, 267
grail, 72–75, 122–123, 173, 252,
  263
grammatica, 204
Gray, 185, 264
Greek, 13, 30, 42, 62, 188
Gregory, St., 33, 144
Griselda, 180, 207
Guest, Lady Charlotte, 83–84,
  254
Guido delle Colonne, 217, 267
guilds, 14, 190
Guillaume de Palerne, 251
Guillaume de Lorris, 157–158,
  210
Guy of Warwick, 112–113, 136,
  256

HARRIS, JOEL CHANDLER, 90
Havelok the Dane, 98–106, 107,
  255
Henno, story of, 51–53, 61, 180
Herebert, William, 149
Herrmann of Reichenau, 143
Higden, Ralph, 11, 246

Historia scholastica, 11
history, 63, 66, 113
Homer, 13, 17, 24–29, 101, 123
Hora novissima, 145
Horn, Hind, 185–186
Horn, King, 94–98, 179, 185,
  255
Hugh, Sir, 180
Hugh of Tabarie, 251
hymns, 7, 8, 41, 143–147, 259

IDEALIZING, 55–56, 58, 73, 89–
  90
illumination, 6, 11, 14, 38
inflections, 93, Appendix
international vogue, of ballads,
  180; of romances, 61–62, 64,
  109
Ipomedon, 70
Irish, 14, 96, 128
isopet, 90, 254
Italian, 204, 205

Jardin de plaisance, 154
Jean de Meun, 158
Jesse windows, 175
John of Salisbury, 14, 15
Joseph, 62, 111
Joseph of Arimathea, 72, 122,
  257
Jusserand, J. J., 168, 262

Kemp Owyne, 177–180, 182,
  184
Kipling, Rudyard, 58, 90, 251
Knight, tale of the, 207–208,
  215

Lady of the Fountain, 85
Lancelot, 70, 252
Langland, William, 159
Latin, 6, 7, 31, 33, 42, 49, 60–
  61, 143–145, 195–199, 201,
  203–204
lay, 77, 98, 253

INDEX

Layamon, 121, 257
Legend of good women, 152, 207–208, 260
Lenten is come, 147
letters, 15
Libeaus desconus, 108–109, 256
liturgy, 143, 174, 189–190
love, romantic, 54–55, 91, 105, 107, 111, 126, 128, 136
Lucan, 12
lyric, 7, 41, 142–156, 207, 259–261

Mabinogion, 83, 254
Machaut, Guillaume, 152
Macrobius, 12
Magdalen, St. Mary, 81, 174, 189
Maldon, 48, 250
Malory, 57, 69, 70, 76, 109, 133–140, 202, 258–259
Mandeville, 200, 264
manuscripts, 6, 11, 13–14, 38–40
Map, Walter, 8, 9, 51, 63–64, 78–80, 82–83, 182, 251, 260
Marguerite poems, 260
Marie de France, 77, 82, 179, 182, 253, 254
Mary Hamilton, 187
matière de Bretagne, 66
matière de France, 66, 114
Maximian, 204
metric (see verse)
Middle English, 7, 8, 209, Appendix
Minot, Laurence, 150–151
miracle plays, 14, 81, 188–195, 264
monasteries, 6, 11, 12, 32, 36–45
Morte d'Arthur, alliterative, 122–127, 257; stanzaic, 118–121, 257 (see Malory)
music, 40, 203

mysteries (mystères), 190
mystical, 173–176, 262–263
myth, 179, 248

NARRATIVE, medieval art of, 4, 9, 16, 18, 28, 71, 75–91, 119, 127–132, 137–139, 168, 177–188, 203–225
Nibelungs, 17, 247, 248
Norman Conquest, 17, 50, 60, 94
Norse, 14, 17, 33, 49–50, 98
Notker, 143
novella, 214, 221
Now welcom, somer, 154
Nun's Priest, tale of the, 204, 207, 211, 215, 224

ORAL, 28, 42, 92, 169, 177, 180–181, 209, 212, 225
Orfeo, Sir, 77, 253
oriental tales, 62, 64, 111, 222
Orosius, 11
Otterburn, 183
Otto of Freising, 247
Ovid, 12, 54, 77, 207, 209–210, 220
Owl and nightingale, 157, 173, 211, 262

PAINTING, 6, 38, 40
Pardoner, tale of the, 204, 207, 208, 212–213, 215
Parlement of foules, 157, 211–212
Patience, 258
Parzival, 256 (see Percival)
Pearl, 120, 166, 170–173, 176, 257–258, 262–263
Pecock, Reginald, 202, 265
Percival, 61, 73–74, 107–109, 120, 122, 255
Percy's Reliques, 187, 264
Petrarch, 156, 205
Philobiblon, 10–11, 246

Piers plowman, 122, 132, 158–169, 173, 174, 176, 201, 262
pilgrimage, 14, 145, 159, 224
Pilgrim's Progress, 73, 159, 166, 167, 169
Polychronicon, 11, 246
popular composition, 94–108, 119–120, 144, 169, 177–202, 255–256, 259, 263–264
preaching, 16, 78, 169, 173, 248
Prioress, tale of the, 180, 203, 207, 263
prose, 49, 60, 139, 195–202, 265
Provençal, 54, 151, 251, 260
Prudentius, 143

QUEST, 57, 72–73

Raoul de Cambrai, 248
Refrain, 120, 148–151, 170–171, 182
Renaissance, 1, 6, 133, 142–143, 205, 215
Reynard, 90, 254
rhythm, prose, 201–202, 265
Richard de Bury, 10–11, 246
rime, 121, 133, 144, 147, 170–171
Robert de Boron, 252
Robin Hood, 183
Robinson, E. A., 255, 256
Roland, 16, 50, 61, 65, 114, 248
Rolle, Richard, 201, 265
Roman de la rose, 157–159, 166, 173, 204, 210–211, 221, 262, 266
Roman law, 4
rondel, 154
Rostand, Edmond, 90, 207

SAGA, 17, 29, 98, 248
saint's legend, 80–81, 207, 253
satire, 88–91, 158
Scaliger, Julius Cæsar, 246
scholasticism, 5

schools, 6, 7, 38–39, 42, 144
Scott, Sir Walter, 58, 63, 89
scribes, 11, 13, 37–40
sculpture, 5, 14, 174–175
Secunda pastorum, 194–195, 264
sentences, 32, 49, 92–94, 139, 169, 199–202
Seven sages, 222–223, 267
Shipman, tale of the, 207, 219–220
short story, 81–83, 91, 128, 185, 222
Sidonius, 12
Sigmund, 27–28
Speculum maius, 12
Speculum meditantis, 267
Spens, Sir Patrick, 183–185, 187
Spenser, 173, 209
Squire, tale of the, 207, 210
Statius, 12, 117
statute law, 4
staves, 31, 169, 201
Sumer is icumen in, 147
Summa theologica, 5
symbolism, 5, 157–175, 261–263

TENNYSON, 64, 69, 74, 83, 109, 256
Teseide, 205
Thomas of Celano, 9, 143
Thopas, tale of Sir, 208, 224
three days' tournament, 70
Tombeor de Notre Dame, 81
Towneley plays, 195
Tristram, 16, 54, 70, 77, 106–107, 255
trivium, 204, 266
Troilus and Criseyde, 205, 208, 209, 214, 215–219, 267
troubadours, 54–55, 151, 251, 260
Troy, 16, 69–70, 134, 215, 217

INDEX

Ubi Sunt (form of balade), 152–153
universities, 6, 12

Vagantenlieder, 259
Vergil, 10, 12, 16–17, 54
verse, 31–32, 42–44, 46, 48, 94, 101, 106, 117, 118, 132–133, 143–149, 151–155, 169–171, 208–209
Vézelay, 174
Villon, 153, 260
Vincent of Beauvais, 12, 247
Volsungs, 17, 248
Voiage and travaile, 200
Vox clamantis, 267
Vulgate, 196–199

Wace, 121, 257
Wagner, 54, 65, 74
Welsh, 63, 83–85, 98, 251
werewolf, 62
Wiclifite Bible, 195–199
Wife of Bath, tale of the, 207–208, 215, 224, 264
William of Palerne, 251
Winner and waster, 261
Wolfram von Eschenbach, 75, 256
Wordsworth, 250

York plays, 193, 264
Yvain, 85–88, 253
Ywain and Gawain, 85–88, 254